HOLIDAY COOKIES

more than 100 very merry recipes

BRIAN HART HOFFMAN

PRESS®

HOLIDAY COOKIES

more than 100 very merry recipes

83 Press
2323 2nd Avenue North
Birmingham, AL 35203
83press.com

ISBN: 978-0-9794090-4-2
Printed in China

contents

· · · · ·

Introducing the definitive holiday cookie collection.

• • • • •

Six years ago we published the first *Holiday Cookies* special issue. I wanted to spotlight the best baking talent and fulfill my craving for the simple yet sweet tradition of baking holiday cookies. And like presents waiting under the tree, these issues have far surpassed my expectations. I've had the pleasure to work with and—more importantly—become friends with some truly fabulous bakers. Each relationship yielded some of the sweetest cookie creations we could have hoped for. Our collaboration with these talented bakers is part of what the holidays are all about: coming together to share sweet traditions.

This cookbook starts with a solid cookie crash course. From tips on what tools to have on hand to our tried-and-true guide to shipping your cookies to faraway loved ones, any cookie question you may have will be satisfactorily answered. Then, I divided up our best of the best recipes into mouthwatering categories. The first chapter explores the decadent world of chocolate. For the perfect cocoa experience, go for Edd Kimber's Chocolate Peppermint Crinkle Cookies, Spencer Lawson's peppermint-frosted chocolate cookies, or Sarah Kieffer's peppermint and chocolate take on her pan-banging cookies. For a touch of peanut butter and chocolate bliss, reach for Annalise Sandberg's Peanut Butter Thumbprints with Chocolate Ganache. Next up is "Holiday Hits," a loving ode to cut-and-iced cookies and standalone classics that deserve to be baked on repeat every holiday season. Here you can learn frosting tips from decorating masters like Tessa Huff, Emily Hutchinson, Josh Lehenbauer, and Jenn Davis. Then we jump into our "Boozy & Bright," an adult-friendly collection of cookies from Marcella DiLonardo, Michele Song, Elisabeth Farris, Kimberlee Ho, and Connie Chong, that packs plenty of rum, bourbon, brandy, and eggnog per cookie. For those looking for a global perspective to the cookie plate look to "Around the World." Highlights include Joshua Weissman's Danish Butter Cookies, Sarah Brunella's Milanesini, and Erin Clarkson's delightful Pinky Bar Cookies.

If spice is your go-to flavor hit, check out "Spice is Nice." Featuring sweet heat-packed cookies like Laura Kasavan's Snickerdoodle Biscotti, Rebecca Firth's Five-Spice Cranberry Jam Thumbprints, and Becky Sue Wilberding's Vanilla Chai Pinwheels, this collection celebrates the best of your spice rack. Up next is "Big on Bars," where Mike Johnson's Peppermint Patty Brownies share space with Emma Duckworth's Tiramisù Cheesecake Bars. The following chapter digs into the stuffed and filled favorite: the sandwich cookie. Offering both updated classics, like Lori Sepp's oatmeal-and-caramel cream pies, and gorgeous innovations, like Amisha Gurbani's chocolate, halvah, and cardamom cookies, this chapter is for those who like twice the cookies and frosting. For those looking for crunch, find our final chapter, "Cookies That Snap." Featuring Lauren Newsome's Muscovado Toffee Crunch Cookies, Allie Roomberg's Iced Lemon Ginger Thins, and Cheryl Norris's snowflake-shaped sablés, this is the chapter for the texture lover.

You'll also find plenty of *Bake from Scratch* cookies interspersed in the pages, curated by a wish list of my favorite flavors for the holiday cookie plate. I was dreaming of marzipan-stuffed gingerbread cookies, White Russian-inspired bars, and a marbled red velvet cookie that would enchant the eyes and the taste buds. Trust me when I say, this cookbook is my holiday dream come true. Don't miss the Speculaas Rum Balls, a nostalgic classic that brings a taste of my bygone days as a flight attendant serving the most delicious in-flight snack around. And if I can convince you to bake one particularly life-changing recipe, please give the Gingerbread Cookie Cheesecake Bars a try. It's my epic holiday hybrid: creamy cookie bars that combine cheesecake and one of my favorite wintry treats, gingerbread.

Without further ado, I invite you to join me on this festive and cheer-filled cookie odyssey. Let's celebrate the merriest season the best way we know how: baking in the kitchen.

Brian

Brian Hart Hoffman
Editor-in-Chief

THE BIG 10

USE OUR EXPERT TIPS AND METHODS TO MASTER EVERY ASPECT OF BAKING COOKIES, FROM HANDLING THE DOUGH TO PROPERLY STORING THE FINAL PRODUCT

1. DON'T OVERMIX YOUR DOUGH.

When creaming your butter and sugar, you'll want to spend 2 to 3 minutes beating it into fluffy, airy goodness. But as soon as you add in the flour, you should keep the mixing to a minimum. Every extra second spent beating your cookie dough at this point will activate more gluten, creating denser cookies. So, keep this mixing step short and sweet and stir in your mix-ins by hand so that you don't overwork the dough.

2. INVEST IN A SPRING-LOADED SCOOP AND A FRENCH ROLLING PIN.

Why buy a spring-loaded scoop? Uniform cookies bake evenly; it's as simple as that. Use a spring-loaded scoop to roll and drop dough balls with ease and precision. Tender doughs—from shortbread to piecrust—require a lighter touch than, say, pizza or bread dough. So, opt for the slim, easy-to-maneuver French pin, which applies delicate pressure to your buttery cookie dough.

3. REFRIGERATE/FREEZE ROLLED OUT DOUGH BEFORE CUTTING OUT SHAPES.

We often say in our recipes to chill the dough for at least 30 minutes before rolling it out in order to improve the flavor. This tip is also meant to help you transition from chilling to rolling out to cutting. So that your dough is easy to cut but not too soft, roll out your dough to the desired thickness and then refrigerate for 15 to 30 minutes before cutting into shapes.

4. ...AND REFRIGERATE/FREEZE DOUGH AFTER CUTTING OUT SHAPES.

The dough will soften if left out while you cut shapes, causing it to spread more during baking. Crisp, well-defined cookie shapes come from a final shock of cold, optimally 15 to 30 minutes in the freezer or refrigerator. Keep your dough scraps chilling in rolled-out disks between cutting as well. Even for molasses, crinkle, or chocolate chip cookies, a final rest in the fridge before popping into the oven will create perfectly puffy, chewy cookies.

OUR TOP Cookie Practices

5. LINE YOUR BAKING PAN WITH PARCHMENT PAPER.

Using parchment paper as your baking sheet liner offers two cookie-baking benefits: One, you'll help your cookies bake and release beautifully, and two, you're cutting your cleanup time in half.

6. GIVE YOUR BUTTERY COOKIES AMPLE SPACE TO SPREAD OUT.

Unless you're looking to bake a sheet cake rather than a sheet full of cookies, leave at least 2 inches of space between each dough ball. This will give them space to crisp up, bake evenly, and keep a nice uniform shape. You can be a little more liberal with shortbread and gingerbread, which will spread less, but always leave enough room for half an inch of space.

Have more cookie-baking questions? Contact us at *bakefromscratch@hoffmanmedia.com*. Expert advice is only an email away.

7. BAKE ONE COOKIE BATCH AT A TIME.

If you're not in a rush or running late to a cookie swap party, take the extra time to bake one sheet of cookies at a time. Baking multiple batches of cookies on alternating oven racks often leads to unevenly baked cookies. For flawless, uniform cookies, bake one sheet at a time on the center rack, rotating halfway through the bake time.

8. COOL YOUR COOKIES COMPLETELY ON A WIRE RACK BEFORE STORING.

Let cookies rest on the cookie sheet for 2 to 3 minutes before transferring to a wire rack. Don't leave your finished cookies on the still-hot sheet for more than 5 minutes; you'll risk burning the bottoms of your cookies. Wire racks allow air to circulate on all sides of the cookies, achieving a tender but not gummy texture. When cookies are cooled on a plate, condensation gets trapped under the bottoms, making them soggy.

9. STORE SOFT COOKIES SEPARATE FROM CRISP COOKIES.

When storing your cookies (tins and airtight containers are your best bet), make sure to keep your crunchy cookies in a separate container from your chewy cookies or the moisture from the chewy cookies will soften up the crisp ones.

10. BE A MAKE-AHEAD PRO BY FREEZING YOUR DOUGH NOW AND BAKING LATER.

Most cookie doughs, from sugar cookies to gingerbread, will keep in the freezer for up to 3 months. That means you could start prepping for your holiday cookie swap party as early as October! On the flip side, avoid stashing wetter doughs, like madeleine or pizzelle doughs, in the freezer.

OUR TOP 10

WITH THESE TRUSTY TOOLS IN YOUR ROTATION, YOU'LL FIND COOKIE PERFECTION COMES EASY

1. STURDY SILICONE SPATULA OR WOODEN SPOON

After adding flour, every extra second spent beating your dough activates more gluten, which means tougher cookies. The key to not overmixing your cookie dough? Use a silicone spatula or wooden spoon to stir in your mix-ins (like chocolate chips, nuts, or sprinkles) by hand so you don't overwork the dough.

2. SIFTER

Use a sifter to lightly dust flour onto your surface before rolling out dough. Sifting the flour instead of throwing it onto the surface ensures that you don't add too much. Excess flour on the surface will stick to your dough and lead to tough, dry cookies. In addition, you can use your sifter to dust your bars and cookies with a snowy layer of confectioners' sugar—instant elegance!

3. SPRING-LOADED SCOOP

This handy tool allows you to scoop and drop consistently sized dough balls with ease and precision. Uniform cookies bake evenly—it's as simple as that.

4. FRENCH ROLLING PIN

Opt for a sleek, wooden French pin to roll your tender cookie doughs efficiently. They're easier to maneuver than marble pins, and they apply just the right pressure. Remember to rub it down with flour before using on particularly buttery dough to prevent sticking. Its tapered design also makes for easy cleaning.

5. RULER

This math class essential can help you measure the thickness of cookie dough when you're rolling it out so you always have evenly sized cookies. It'll also help you properly divide up your dough when rolling out, slicing, or splitting it up into triangles (like the way you would cut rugelach dough).

6. METAL COOKIE CUTTERS

Whether round, square, scalloped, or snowflake-shaped, a good cookie cutter should be made of a sturdy material like metal so it punches cleanly through your dough without catching or getting dented with the constant force of pressing.

ESSENTIAL
Cookie Tools

7. LIGHT-COLORED BAKING SHEETS

You'll want to invest in light-colored baking sheets to ensure even cooking. (We like Williams Sonoma Goldtouch Nonstick Cookie Sheets.) And why multiple sets? For one, you need to let your baking sheet cool completely before placing a new batch of cookies on it. Placing cookies on a hot baking sheet can cause them to spread more as they bake because the heat melts the butter faster than the cookies bake. Having numerous baking sheets waiting in the wings means you don't have to constantly wait for one to cool down. Plus, if your cookies are browning too much on the bottom, you can double up on the baking sheets, stacking a second one under the first to create a protective barrier.

8. PARCHMENT PAPER

Using parchment paper as your baking sheet liner offers easy cleanup and helps keep your cookies from sticking to the pan. Note: stay away from wax paper. While excellent for candy-making and storing in the freezer because it's moisture-resistant, wax paper is not heat-resistant and could melt into your cookies or even catch fire in the oven.

9. OVEN THERMOMETER

If you haven't recently calibrated your oven or have noticed that bake times are significantly off for your home-baked recipes, it might be time to invest in an oven thermometer and hang it on the center rack. No matter what your oven tells you, the oven thermometer will give you a true reading of how hot the oven is. This way, you'll always know whether your oven has been properly preheated or needs to have the temperature dropped or lowered for precision.

10. WIRE RACKS

Wire racks allow air to circulate on all sides of the cookies once they're out of the oven so they achieve a tender texture all around. When cookies are cooled on a plate, condensation gets trapped under the bottoms, making them soggy. Stick with wire racks with a tight grid pattern for proper support; ones with open slats will cause soft cookies to dip in the middle while cooling.

THE
Decoration
DEEP DIVE

YOUR COOKIES ARE DELICIOUS. NOW LET'S MAKE THEM DAZZLE.

Confectioners' Sugar Dusting

PICK A STENCIL, SIFT YOUR SUGAR, AND VOILÀ!
A DELICATELY DETAILED DESIGN IS BORN.

THE PATTERNS

Plain Dusting: When in doubt, no pattern
or stencil is required. A simple dusting of
confectioners' sugar on a cookie is always
embraced as a snowy wonder.

Doily/Lace Pattern: Use the edge of a paper
doily or a lace tablecloth to give your cookies
an intricate design. The fine confectioners'
sugar will sift directly into the eyelet holes
to resemble a lace pattern.

Paper Stencil Pattern: Trace stars,
snowflakes, and trees onto paper and then
cut them out, or use a stencil puncher
(like the kinds found at craft stores such as
Michaels) to create quick, exact designs.

THE METHOD

Lay the desired pattern over the cookie.
With a sifter, cascade confectioners' sugar
onto cookie until completely coated. Gently
remove the stencil or pattern, ensuring you
don't knock any excess sugar onto cookie.

The Sugar Roll

ROLL YOUR SLICE-AND-BAKE AND DROP COOKIES IN THE
FOLLOWING SUGARS TO GIVE THEM SOME HOLIDAY FLARE

THE SUGARS

Sparkling Sugar: For drop cookies that sparkle—
literally—roll them in sparkling sugar. This glistening
coating works best on mild, buttery recipes, like sugar
cookies, or along the edges of slice-and-bake cookies.

Turbinado and Demerara Sugars: Offering plenty of
shine and crunch like sparkling sugar, turbinado sugar
and demerara sugar are large, raw sugar crystals that will
give a slight caramel tinge and flavor to your cookies.
We recommend using them with your more strongly
flavored dough, like spiced or chocolate cookies.

Flavored Sugars: Imparting a hint of extra flavor, try
coating your cookies in a scented sugar, like vanilla sugar
or a homemade citrus sugar flavored with orange zest.

THE METHOD

Drop Cookies: Place about ¼ cup (50 grams) desired
sugar in a small bowl. Roll your cookie dough into balls,
and roll balls in sugar to coat. Add more sugar to bowl as
necessary.

Slice-and-Bake Cookies: Place parchment paper on a
cutting board, and sprinkle about ½ cup (100 grams)
desired sugar onto parchment. After shaping cookie
dough into a log, roll dough log on sugar-covered
parchment, firmly pressing so sugar adheres to surface.
Add more sugar to surface if necessary.

Royal Icing 101

LEARN TO NAVIGATE THE WORLD OF ROYAL ICING, FROM BORDER
TO FLOOD CONSISTENCIES, AND OUR PRO PIPING TIPS

1. BORDER ICING

USES: Think of border icing as the stiff upper lip of royal icing. It provides two key functions for decorating your cookies. First, it acts as a rigid border and dam for the looser flood icing used to fill the majority of the cookie. Second, it offers 3D decoration, creating raised dots, lines, and patterns across your cookie without sinking and losing its shape.

CONSISTENCY: When a spoon or spatula is lifted out of the icing, it should keep a soft peak. Too thick, and it will require too much pressure to pipe and won't come out of the piping tip smoothly. For this problem, add more water, 1 teaspoon (5 grams) at a time, until desired consistency is reached. If it's too thin, your borders and decoration won't keep their shape when piped. Add confectioners' sugar, 1 teaspoon (2 grams) at a time, until desired consistency is reached. Keep in mind that you may have to adjust consistency after adding your gel food coloring.

2. FLOOD ICING

USES: Flood icing is the shapeshifter of royal icing, filling the nooks and crannies of your detailed cookie with ease. Its loose structure helps fill a cookie faster and more smoothly than border icing can. While it is most commonly used to create a matte canvas, it can also be used to make an elaborate marbling design, like for our Ornament Cookies.

CONSISTENCY: Flood icing consistency should resemble the velvet texture of runny honey, with icing that falls from the spoon in smooth ribbons that sit and then slowly settle back into uniformity. It is also occasionally called 10-second icing because if you run your whisk through the icing, it should settle back down after 10 seconds. If your icing is too thick, it won't fill the cookie properly and will have a lot of air bubbles. Add water, 1 teaspoon (5 grams) at a time, until desired consistency is reached. Too thin, and your icing will flow over the border icing and right over the edge of the cookie. Add confectioners' sugar, 1 teaspoon (2 grams) at a time, until desired consistency is reached. Keep in mind that you may have to adjust consistency after adding your gel food coloring.

MAKE YOUR COOKIE CANVAS

Before we begin piping ornate decorations on top of our cookies, we need to create a smooth royal icing base, a mixture of firm border icing and runny flood icing

THE BORDER: Place your border icing in a pastry bag fitted with a Wilton No. 1 piping tip. Pick a starting point. Touch tip to cookie surface and then start applying pressure. Once icing begins to come out, lift the tip off the cookie and continue to apply even pressure. An icing string should form between the cookie surface and your piping tip. Keep applying even pressure, and let the icing fall into place, guiding it with your hand. Your tip should not touch the cookie, only the icing thread. When you reach the end, stop applying pressure, and touch back down to break the thread. Don't rush the process, or it will break or start to curl. Keep piping tips clean and covered with a damp paper towel when not being used.

THE FLOOD: Place your flood icing in a squeeze bottle with a small opening or in a pastry bag fitted with a Wilton No. 3 piping tip. Squeeze out a puddle of icing, allowing it to pool from the center out. Don't squeeze out too much at once, or you'll overwhelm the border. Use a wooden pick to gently shift the icing to fill in the gaps. Then use your pick to spread the icing in other directions. Once filled, you can pop any air bubbles with the pick to create a smooth surface. Let dry for 2 to 3 hours. Keep in mind that humidity affects the drying time, so if it's a wet day, place your cookies near a fan to help speed up the process.

Freeze WITH EASE

LOOKING TO HAVE COOKIES ON DEMAND? YOU'RE ONLY ONE SHORT THAW AWAY WITH OUR COOL GUIDE TO FREEZING DOUGH, BAKED COOKIES AND BARS, AND STAPLE COOKIE-BAKING INGREDIENTS

HOW TO FREEZE COOKIE DOUGH

Drop/Shaped Cookies: Space cookie dough balls or shaped cookie dough out on a baking sheet. Freeze until set, about 15 minutes. Seal frozen cookie dough balls or shaped cookie dough in an airtight container or resealable bag. Dough will keep in the freezer for up to 3 months. When ready to bake, space frozen cookie dough out on a baking sheet, and bake as directed, adding 2 to 3 minutes to the bake time.

Slice-and-Bake Cookies: Roll dough into tight logs with a diameter equaling the size of cookie you want. Wrap dough logs in plastic wrap and then in foil. Dough will keep in the freezer for up to 3 months. When ready to bake, let thaw slightly, until sliceable. Slice and bake as directed.

HOW TO FREEZE BAKED COOKIES

After baking, let cool completely. Do not freeze filled or frosted sandwich cookies. Wrap each cookie individually in plastic wrap, and store in a resealable bag. Cookies can keep in the freezer for up to 3 months. Let thaw, wrapped, at room temperature for about 1 hour; unwrap and serve.

HOW TO FREEZE BAKED BARS

After baking, let cool completely, but do not slice into individual pieces. For bars baked in a 13x9-inch pan, slice the batch in half before wrapping so each half fits nicely in a gallon-size resealable plastic bag. Double-wrap in plastic wrap, and store in a resealable bag. Baked bars can keep in the freezer for up to 3 months. Let thaw, wrapped, at room temperature for a few hours; unwrap and slice.

HOW TO FREEZE STAPLE COOKIE INGREDIENTS

Grated Fresh Ginger: Freeze freshly grated ginger in an ice cube tray. Once solid, you can pop the cubes into a resealable plastic bag and have them on hand for up to 3 months.

Nuts: Fatty nuts have a notoriously short shelf life. Extend that time by toasting, cooling, and placing your nuts in a resealable plastic bag. They'll keep for up to 2 months. Untoasted nuts can keep for up to 6 months.

Almond Meal: Like its whole counterpart, almond meal can go rancid quickly. Store your almond meal in a resealable plastic bag in the freezer for up to 3 months.

Cranberries: Many holiday cookie recipes call for cranberries, and if you can't get ahold of the fresh stuff, frozen will always work in a pinch. Just be sure to thaw and pat dry before using in your recipe. Frozen cranberries will keep for up to 12 months.

Citrus Zest: Juicing some lemons or oranges but have no immediate use for the zest? Zest the citrus, and allow to have a quick freeze on a flat surface covered with parchment paper. Once frozen, place in a resealable plastic bag, and freeze for up to 6 months.

SIGNED, SEALED, >>> Delivered

DON'T LET DISTANCE KEEP YOU FROM SHARING HOMEMADE TREATS WITH LOVED ONES THIS HOLIDAY SEASON. FOLLOW OUR GUIDE TO MAIL YOUR COOKIES TO ENSURE THEY ARRIVE IN PERFECT FORM.

1. PROTECT THE COOKIES.

If your cookie is covered in sugar, icing, or another adornment, use plastic bags, muffin or cupcake liners, plastic wrap, or foil to wrap cookies individually or in stacks of three or four. This will keep your toppings from falling off or smudging. There is no need to wrap sturdier, unadorned cookies, like gingerbread or biscotti. Simply stack or pack in a tight line once in the cookie tin.

2. PLACE THE COOKIES.

Because it is lightweight yet durable, we like to mail cookies in a tin container. Place a small layer of bubble wrap on the bottom of your tin for insulation. Cover the bubble wrap with a sheet of wax or parchment paper. Pack cookies tightly into the tin, filling any excess space with crumpled wax paper or bubble wrap. You want your cookies to have no room to wiggle around in the tin. Place another layer of parchment paper on top of the cookies, followed by a final sheet of bubble wrap. Cover your tin with the top, and tape it down.

3. PACKAGE THE COOKIES.

Select a box that is slightly larger than your cookie tin, ideally one that can give 2 inches of insulation on all sides around the tin. Use packing peanuts, bubble wrap, or brown packing paper to stuff a nice 2-inch layer in the bottom of your box. Place your cookie tin in the center of the box, and fill up any remaining space with more packing peanuts, bubble wrap, or packing paper. Your tin should fit snugly in the middle of the box with no space to move around. Tightly tape your box shut. Bonus points: Slap a "fragile" sticker onto your package so handlers know your box contains precious cargo.

4. SHIP THE COOKIES.

Choose priority mail or two-day shipping to ensure your loved ones receive the freshest cookies. If you know the cookies will stay relatively fresh for a week, you can go with regular five-day shipping; just double-check with your carrier service to make sure they can get your cookies to the intended recipient in time.

Chocolate
CHEER

· · · · ·

Paired with peppermint, peanut butter, and more,
these cookies are chock-full of chocolaty bliss

CHOCOLATE COOKIES WITH PEPPERMINT CREAM CHEESE FROSTING

Makes about 15 cookies

Recipe by Spencer Lawson

This recipe takes the classic taste of an Oreo and elevates it with a holiday twist. The black cocoa-rich cookies are soft, chewy, and chocolaty. Combine that with a tangy yet minty frosting and the flavor can't be beat.

¾   cup plus 2 tablespoons (198 grams) all-vegetable shortening
1   cup (200 grams) granulated sugar
1   cup (210 grams) firmly packed light brown sugar
⅔   cup (50 grams) black cocoa powder
½   cup (120 grams) hot water (160°F/71°C to 180°F/82°C)
2   teaspoons (8 grams) vanilla extract
1   teaspoon (4 grams) peppermint extract
3   large eggs (150 grams)
2   teaspoons (10 grams) baking soda
1   teaspoon (3 grams) kosher salt
4½ cups (563 grams) all-purpose flour
Peppermint Cream Cheese Frosting (recipe follows)
Garnish: crushed hard peppermint candies

1. Preheat oven to 350°F (180°C). Line baking sheets with parchment paper.
2. In the bowl of a stand mixer fitted with the paddle attachment, beat shortening and sugars at medium-high speed until light and fluffy, 5 to 7 minutes, stopping to scrape sides of bowl. Add black cocoa, and beat until combined. Add ½ cup (120 grams) hot water and extracts, and beat until combined. With mixer on low speed, add eggs, one at a time, beating until combined after each addition. Beat in baking soda and salt. Add flour; pulse mixer between "off" and lowest setting until combined. Increase mixer speed to medium-high, and beat until well combined, 1 to 1½ minutes.

Using a 3-ounce spring-loaded scoop, scoop dough, and place 2½ inches apart on prepared pans. Freeze for 10 minutes.
3. Bake until centers are puffed and edges are dry, 14 to 16 minutes, rotating pans halfway through baking. Let cool on pans until firm, about 10 minutes. Remove from pans, and let cool completely on wire racks.
4. Place Peppermint Cream Cheese Frosting in a pastry bag fitted with a large round piping tip. Starting in center, pipe frosting on top of cooled cookies. Garnish with candies, if desired. Refrigerate in an airtight container for up to 3 days.

PRO TIP
A 4-inch round cutter can be used to form still-warm cookies into a more circular shape, if desired. Place cutter around 1 cookie; gently move cutter in a circular, counterclockwise motion while making contact with edges of cookie until desired shape is reached. Repeat as needed.

PEPPERMINT CREAM CHEESE FROSTING
Makes 3 cups

8   ounces (226 grams) cream cheese, softened
½   cup (113 grams) unsalted butter, softened
3   cups (360 grams) confectioners' sugar, sifted
1   teaspoon (3 grams) kosher salt
1   teaspoon (4 grams) vanilla extract
½   teaspoon (2 grams) peppermint extract

1. In the bowl of a stand mixer fitted with the paddle attachment, beat cream cheese and butter at medium-high speed until light and fluffy, about 5 minutes. Add half of confectioners' sugar, and beat at medium-low speed for 1 minute; scrape sides of bowl. Add salt, extracts, and remaining confectioners' sugar, and beat for 1 minute. Use immediately.

CHOCOLATE HAZELNUT SNOWBALLS

Makes 38 cookies

Recipe by Lauren Newsome

These Chocolate Hazelnut Snowballs are a play on the famous Mexican wedding cookies. These cookies forgo the traditional use of pecans and get an extra boost of flavor with the addition of rich cocoa and hazelnuts. Hazelnut liqueur, cinnamon, and vanilla combine to add an extra depth of flavor to the irresistibly tender dough, making these cookies a new holiday classic.

1   cup (227 grams) unsalted butter, softened
2½ cups (300 grams) confectioners' sugar, divided
1   tablespoon (15 grams) hazelnut liqueur*
½   teaspoon (2 grams) vanilla extract
1¾ cups (219 grams) all-purpose flour
¼   cup (32 grams) cornstarch
¼   cup (21 grams) natural cocoa powder, sifted
½   teaspoon (1 gram) ground cinnamon
¼   teaspoon kosher salt
1   cup (113 grams) finely ground toasted hazelnuts (see PRO TIP)

1. In the bowl of a stand mixer fitted with the paddle attachment, beat butter and 1 cup (120 grams) confectioners' sugar at medium speed until light and creamy, 2 to 3 minutes, stopping to scrape sides of bowl. Add liqueur and vanilla, and beat for 1 minute.
2. In a medium bowl, whisk together flour, cornstarch, cocoa, cinnamon, and salt. With mixer on low speed, add flour mixture to butter mixture in two additions, beating just until combined after each addition. Stir in hazelnuts. Cover with plastic wrap, and refrigerate for 1 hour.
3. Preheat oven to 350°F (180°C). Line baking sheets with parchment paper.
4. Using a 1-tablespoon spring-loaded scoop, scoop dough (about 20 grams each), and roll into balls. Place 1 inch apart on prepared pans.
5. Bake until firm to the touch and tops are dry, 11 to 14 minutes. Let cool on pans for 5 minutes.
6. In a small bowl, place remaining 1½ cups (180 grams) confectioners' sugar. Roll warm cookies in confectioners' sugar to coat. Place on wire racks, and let cool for 10 minutes. Roll in confectioners' sugar again to coat. Let cool completely on wire racks. Store in an airtight container for up to 5 days.

*I used Frangelico.

Photo by Lauren Newsome

PRO TIP
To toast hazelnuts: Preheat oven to 350°F (180°C). Arrange hazelnuts in a single layer on a parchment paper-lined baking sheet. Bake until browned and fragrant, 10 to 12 minutes, stirring halfway through baking. Wrap hazelnuts in a kitchen towel, and let stand for 1 minute to steam. Rub hazelnuts in the towel to remove skin. Return to pan, and let cool completely. Transfer cooled toasted hazelnuts to the work bowl of a food processor, and process until finely ground.

CHOCOLATE THUMBPRINT COOKIES WITH A PEPPERMINT TWIST

Makes 24 cookies

Recipe by Kimberlee Ho

These rich chocolate cookies are a fun holiday twist on the classic thumbprint cookie. They're rolled in seasonally colored sanding sugar and filled with a Peppermint Schnapps filling, perfect for office holiday parties, neighborhood gatherings, or adults-only cookie exchanges!

½   cup (113 grams) unsalted butter, softened
1¼ cups (250 grams) granulated sugar
2   tablespoons (42 grams) light corn syrup
2   large eggs (100 grams), room temperature
2   teaspoons (8 grams) vanilla extract
2   ounces (57 grams) 100% cacao unsweetened chocolate, melted and cooled
1¾ cups (219 grams) all-purpose flour
½   cup (43 grams) unsweetened cocoa powder
1   teaspoon (5 grams) baking soda
½   teaspoon (2.5 grams) baking powder
½   teaspoon (1.5 grams) kosher salt
Red, green, and white sanding sugars
Peppermint Filling (recipe follows)

1. In the bowl of a stand mixer fitted with the paddle attachment, beat butter, granulated sugar, and corn syrup at medium speed until fluffy and light in color, 2 to 3 minutes, stopping to scrape sides of bowl. Add eggs and vanilla, beating until combined; scrape sides and bottom of bowl. Add melted chocolate, and beat until lighter in color and well combined, stopping to scrape sides and bottom of bowl.
2. In a medium bowl, whisk together flour, cocoa, baking soda, baking powder, and salt. With mixer on low speed, gradually add flour mixture to butter mixture, beating just until combined after each addition and stopping to scrape sides of bowl. Loosely cover with plastic wrap, and refrigerate for 1 hour.

3. Preheat oven to 350°F (180°C). Line 2 baking sheets with parchment paper.
4. In separate small bowls, place sanding sugars.
5. Using a 1½-tablespoon spring-loaded scoop, scoop dough, and roll into 1-inch balls. Roll in desired sanding sugar. Place 2 inches apart on prepared pans.
6. Bake until tops are slightly cracked, 8 to 10 minutes. Let cool on pans for 2 to 3 minutes. Using your thumb or the back of a teaspoon, gently make an indentation in center of cookies. Remove from pans, and let cool completely on wire racks.
7. Place Peppermint Filling in a pastry bag fitted with a medium round piping tip. (Alternatively, place Peppermint Filling in a resealable plastic bag, and cut a ¼-inch opening in corner of bag.) Pipe filling into center of each cooled cookie. Filled cookies can be prepared several hours in advance. Store unfilled cookies in an airtight container for up to 4 days.

PEPPERMINT FILLING
Makes 1½ cups

3½ cups (420 grams) confectioners' sugar
⅓   cup (113 grams) light corn syrup
¼   cup (57 grams) unsalted butter, softened
1   tablespoon (15 grams) Peppermint Schnapps
½   teaspoon (2 grams) peppermint extract

1. In the bowl of a stand mixer fitted with the paddle attachment, beat all ingredients at low speed until mixture starts to come together; gradually increase mixer speed to medium, and beat until smooth, 1 to 2 minutes. Store in an airtight container until ready to use. (If not using right away, refrigerate in an airtight container for up to 1 week. Let come to room temperature before using.)

Photo by Kimberlee Ho

GELT COOKIE BUTTER BLOSSOM COOKIES

Makes 48 to 50 cookies

Traditionally given to children during Hanukkah, gelt are gold foil-wrapped chocolate coins, often adorned with a menorah. In this playful twist on peanut butter blossoms, the chocolate kiss is replaced with gelt and speculaas cookie butter is added to the dough. For a final touch of sparkle, the dough is rolled in blue and white sparkling sugars, two colors commonly associated with Hanukkah.

1   cup (227 grams) unsalted butter, softened
1   cup (200 grams) granulated sugar
1   cup (220 grams) firmly packed light brown sugar
1   cup (240 grams) speculaas cookie butter
2   large eggs (100 grams), room temperature
1   tablespoon (15 grams) whole milk, room temperature
2   teaspoons (8 grams) vanilla extract
3½ cups (438 grams) all-purpose flour
1   teaspoon (5 grams) baking soda
1   teaspoon (5 grams) baking powder
White and blue sparkling sugars
48 to 50 Hanukkah gelt milk chocolate coins, unwrapped

1. Preheat oven to 375°F (190°C). Line baking sheets with parchment paper.
2. In the bowl of a stand mixer fitted with the paddle attachment, beat butter, granulated sugar, and brown sugar at medium speed until fluffy, 2 to 3 minutes, stopping to scrape sides of bowl. Beat in cookie butter. Add eggs, one at a time, beating well after each addition. Beat in milk and vanilla.
3. In a medium bowl, whisk together flour, baking soda, and baking powder. With mixer on low speed, gradually add flour mixture to butter mixture, beating just until combined and stopping to scrape sides of bowl.
4. In separate small bowls, place sparkling sugars.
5. Using a 1½-tablespoon spring-loaded scoop, scoop dough (28 to 30 grams each), and roll into smooth 1½-inch balls. Roll in desired sparkling sugar until well coated. Place 2 to 2½ inches apart on prepared pans.
6. Bake, one batch at a time, until bottom edges are lightly golden brown, 8 to 10 minutes, rotating pan halfway through baking. Immediately press 1 gelt into center of each cookie. Let cool on pan for 5 minutes. Remove from pan, and let cool completely on wire racks.

PEANUT BUTTER THUMBPRINTS WITH CHOCOLATE GANACHE

Makes 30 cookies

Recipe by Annalise Sandberg

Soft peanut butter cookies with a little mound of Chocolate Ganache in the middle are the from-scratch version of a nostalgic classic we all need.

½   cup (113 grams) unsalted butter, softened
¾   cup (192 grams) creamy peanut butter
⅔   cup (147 grams) firmly packed light brown sugar
⅔   cup (134 grams) granulated sugar, divided
2   large eggs (100 grams)
1   teaspoon (4 grams) vanilla extract
2¼   cups (281 grams) all-purpose flour
1   teaspoon (5 grams) baking soda
½   teaspoon (1.5 grams) kosher salt
Chocolate Ganache (recipe follows)

1. Preheat oven to 375°F (190°C). Line 3 baking sheets with parchment paper.
2. In the bowl of a stand mixer fitted with the paddle attachment, beat butter, peanut butter, brown sugar, and ⅓ cup (67 grams) granulated sugar at medium-high speed until pale and fluffy, 3 to 4 minutes, stopping to scrape sides of bowl. Add eggs, one at a time, beating well after each addition. Beat in vanilla.
3. In a medium bowl, whisk together flour, baking soda, and salt. Add flour mixture to butter mixture, and beat at low speed until combined.
4. In a small bowl, place remaining ⅓ cup (67 grams) granulated sugar.

5. Using a 1½-tablespoon spring-loaded scoop, scoop dough, and roll into balls. Roll in granulated sugar. Place 2 inches apart on prepared pans. Using your thumb or the end of a wooden spoon, gently make an indentation in center of each ball.
6. Bake, one batch at a time, until puffed and just starting to crack, 9 to 10 minutes. Let cool on pan for 5 minutes. Remove from pan, and let cool completely on wire racks.
7. Place Chocolate Ganache in a pastry bag fitted with a small round piping tip. Pipe ganache into indentations of cooled cookies. (Alternatively, spoon Chocolate Ganache into indentations of cooled cookies.) Let stand until ganache is set, about 15 minutes. Store in an airtight container for up to 5 days.

CHOCOLATE GANACHE
Makes 1 cup

4   ounces (113 grams) 60% cacao semisweet chocolate, chopped
½   cup (120 grams) heavy whipping cream
1   tablespoon (20 grams) light corn syrup

1. In a small heatproof bowl, place chocolate.
2. In a small microwave-safe bowl, heat cream on high until steaming, 30 seconds to 1 minute. Pour over chocolate, and let stand for 5 minutes; stir until smooth. (If any lumps of chocolate remain, heat on high in 30-second intervals, stirring between each, until chocolate is melted and mixture is smooth.) Stir in corn syrup until combined. Let cool until ganache starts to hold its shape but is still soft enough to stir with a spoon, about 20 minutes, stirring frequently.

Photo by Annalise Sandberg

CHOCOLATE-COVERED PEANUT BUTTER COOKIES

Makes about 24 cookies

Recipe by Mike Johnson

This easy recipe starts with a sweet, buttery peanut butter slice-and-bake cookie, which is then covered in peanut butter and completely dipped in chocolate.

½ cup (113 grams) unsalted butter, softened
½ cup (110 grams) firmly packed dark brown sugar
1 teaspoon (6 grams) vanilla bean paste
1¾ cups (448 grams) creamy peanut butter, divided
2 cups (250 grams) all-purpose flour
1 tablespoon (15 grams) water, plus more if needed
½ teaspoon (1.5 grams) kosher salt
16 ounces (454 grams) milk chocolate, melted
1 tablespoon (15 grams) canola oil
2 ounces (57 grams) 60% cacao semisweet chocolate, melted

1. In the bowl of a stand mixer fitted with the paddle attachment, beat butter, brown sugar, and vanilla bean paste until light and fluffy, about 3 minutes. Beat in ¾ cup (192 grams) peanut butter until combined. Add flour, 1 tablespoon (15 grams) water, and salt, and beat until combined and dough forms a ball. (If dough seems too crumbly, add water, 1 teaspoon [5 grams] at a time, until it comes together. Dough should not be overly sticky.)

2. Divide dough in half. Place each half on a large piece of plastic wrap. Using your hands, shape each half into a 6x2-inch rectangle. Wrap in plastic wrap, and refrigerate for at least 3 hours or up to overnight. (Alternatively, shape each dough half into a 6-inch log, about 2 inches thick, to make round cookies.)

3. Preheat oven to 350°F (180°C). Line 2 baking sheets with parchment paper.

4. Cut dough rectangle crosswise into ½-inch-thick slices. (Alternatively, cut dough log into ½-inch-thick slices.) Place 1 inch apart on prepared pans.

5. Bake until edges are golden brown, 13 to 15 minutes. Let cool on pans for 10 minutes. Remove from pans, and let cool completely on wire racks.

6. Spread remaining 1 cup (256 grams) peanut butter on top of cooled cookies (about a heaping ½ tablespoon [8 grams] each), and place on a parchment paper-lined baking sheet. Freeze until set, about 20 minutes. (This makes coating in chocolate easier.)

7. In a small bowl, stir together melted milk chocolate and oil. Place each cookie in chocolate mixture; using a fork, lift cookies out of chocolate, and gently tap on side of bowl to remove excess. Return to pan. Refrigerate until chocolate is set, about 15 minutes. Drizzle with melted semisweet chocolate. Refrigerate until chocolate is set, about 15 minutes. Store in an airtight container for up to 5 days.

Photo by Mike Johnson

CHOCOLATE-PEPPERMINT PAN-BANGING COOKIES

Makes 12 cookies

Recipe by Sarah Kieffer

Chocolate and peppermint is a classic holiday combination, bringing to mind so many good memories: peppermint hot chocolate, peppermint mochas, cakes, and ice cream.

1   cup (227 grams) unsalted butter, softened
1½ cups (300 grams) granulated sugar
¼   cup (55 grams) firmly packed light brown sugar
1   large egg (50 grams), room temperature
2   tablespoons (30 grams) water
1   teaspoon (4 grams) vanilla extract
1   teaspoon (4 grams) peppermint extract
2   cups (250 grams) all-purpose flour
⅓   cup plus 1 tablespoon plus 1 teaspoon (32 grams) Dutch process cocoa powder
¾   teaspoon (2.25 grams) kosher salt
½   teaspoon (2.5 grams) baking soda
4   ounces (113 grams) 60% cacao bittersweet chocolate, roughly chopped
2   ounces (57 grams) 60% cacao bittersweet chocolate, melted
10 peppermint candies (60 grams), crushed

1. Position oven rack in center of oven. Preheat oven to 350°F (180°C). Line 3 baking sheets with foil, dull side up.
2. In the bowl of a stand mixer fitted with the paddle attachment, beat butter at medium speed until creamy, about 1 minute. Add sugars, and beat at medium speed until light and fluffy, 2 to 3 minutes. Add egg, 2 tablespoons (30 grams) water, and extracts, and beat at low speed until combined.
3. In a medium bowl, whisk together flour, cocoa, salt, and baking soda. Add flour mixture to butter mixture, and beat at low speed until combined. Beat in chopped chocolate. Using a ¼-cup spring-loaded scoop, scoop dough (about 85 grams each), and roll into balls. Place 4 dough balls on each prepared pan.
4. Bake, one batch at a time, until dough balls are spread flat but centers are puffed slightly, about 9 minutes; lift one side of pan about 4 inches, and gently let it drop against oven rack so edges of cookies set and centers fall back down. Bake until centers are puffed, about 2 minutes more; lift one side of pan about 4 inches, and gently let it drop against oven rack. Bake for 2 minutes more, and repeat lifting and dropping of pan to create ridges around edges of cookies. Bake until cookies have spread out and edges are set and rippled but centers are still soft, 2 to 3 minutes more. Let cool on pans on wire racks for 10 minutes. Remove from pans, and let cool completely on wire racks.
5. Drizzle melted chocolate onto cooled cookies; sprinkle candies onto melted chocolate. Let stand until chocolate is set, about 30 minutes. Store in an airtight container for up to 2 days, or refrigerate in an airtight container for up to 3 days.

Photo by Sarah Kieffer

PEPPERMINT CUSTARD-STUFFED CHOCOLATE COOKIES

Makes about 27 cookies

Cookies get all kinds of delicious fillings these days, but these peppermint custard-filled cookies take it to the next level. These peppermint candy-topped chocolate cookies hide a wintry pastry cream flavored with both peppermint extract and soft peppermint candies. To streamline this process, feel free to make both the pastry cream and the cookie dough a day before baking.

1½ cups (340 grams) unsalted butter, softened
2¼ cups (450 grams) granulated sugar
3   large eggs (150 grams), room temperature
1½ teaspoons (6 grams) peppermint extract
4   cups (500 grams) all-purpose flour
1   cup (85 grams) Dutch process cocoa powder, sifted
4½ teaspoons (22.5 grams) baking powder
1   teaspoon (3 grams) kosher salt
Peppermint Pastry Cream (recipe follows)
2   tablespoons (30 grams) water
1½ cups (270 grams) crushed soft peppermint candies

1. In the bowl of a stand mixer fitted with the paddle attachment, beat butter and sugar at medium speed until fluffy, 3 to 4 minutes, stopping to scrape sides of bowl. Add eggs, one at a time, beating well after each addition. Beat in peppermint extract.
2. In a medium bowl, whisk together flour, cocoa, baking powder, and salt. With mixer on low speed, gradually add flour mixture to butter mixture, beating just until combined and stopping to scrape sides of bowl. Cover and refrigerate until dough doesn't stick to your fingers when pinched, 30 to 45 minutes.
3. Preheat oven to 350°F (180°C). Line 4 rimmed baking sheets with parchment paper.
4. Using a 1½-tablespoon spring-loaded scoop, scoop dough (about 26 grams each), and roll into balls. Press balls into 2½-inch disks. Place 2 teaspoons (12 grams) Peppermint Pastry Cream in center of half of disks; cover with remaining disks, and crimp edges closed.

Gently shape into balls, and place on prepared pans; gently press into 2¼-inch disks, pressing together any cracks in edges, if necessary. Brush tops of cookies with 2 tablespoons (30 grams) water; top with candies.
5. Bake until edges are set and tops look dry, 12 to 14 minutes. (See Note.) Carefully top with any remaining candies. Let cool completely on pans.

Note: *If you need to bake the cookies in batches, refrigerate any disks that are waiting to be baked.*

PEPPERMINT PASTRY CREAM
Makes about 1¾ cups

1½ cups (360 grams) whole milk
6   tablespoons (72 grams) granulated sugar, divided
3   large egg yolks (56 grams)
3½ tablespoons (28 grams) cornstarch
¼   teaspoon kosher salt
2   tablespoons (16 grams) finely crushed soft peppermint candies
1   tablespoon (14 grams) unsalted butter, softened
½   teaspoon (2 grams) vanilla extract
¼   teaspoon (1 gram) peppermint extract

1. In a medium saucepan, heat milk and 3 tablespoons (36 grams) sugar over medium heat, stirring occasionally, until steaming. (Do not boil.)
2. In a medium bowl, whisk together egg yolks, cornstarch, salt, and remaining 3 tablespoons (36 grams) sugar. Whisk hot milk mixture into egg yolk mixture. Return mixture to saucepan, and bring to a boil, whisking constantly. Cook, whisking constantly, until cornstarch flavor has cooked out, 2 to 3 minutes. (Mixture will be thick.)
3. Strain mixture through a fine-mesh sieve into a medium heatproof bowl. Stir in candies, butter, and extracts until completely combined. Cover with plastic wrap, pressing wrap directly onto surface of pastry cream to prevent a skin from forming. Refrigerate until completely cooled, 2 to 3 hours or up to overnight. Whisk smooth before using.

PEPPERMINT BARK COOKIES

Makes 24 cookies

Recipe by Marcella DiLonardo

A holiday twist on a classic chocolate chunk cookie inspired by peppermint bark. No rolling or cookie-cutting required—just a simple drop and bake featuring dark chocolate, white chocolate, and peppermint candy canes. This dough freezes well, so you can have cookie dough on hand at all times in case an unexpected guest arrives. Be sure to use quality chopped chocolate! The chunks make for the best gooey chocolate cookie.

1½ cups (330 grams) firmly packed light brown sugar
1   cup (227 grams) unsalted butter, melted
½   cup (100 grams) granulated sugar
2   large eggs (100 grams), room temperature
1   teaspoon (4 grams) vanilla extract
1   teaspoon (4 grams) peppermint extract
3½ cups (438 grams) all-purpose flour
1   teaspoon (5 grams) baking soda
1   teaspoon (3 grams) fine sea salt
4   ounces (115 grams) white chocolate, roughly chopped
4   ounces (115 grams) 70% cacao dark chocolate, roughly chopped
4   medium peppermint candy canes (48 grams), crushed

1. Preheat oven to 350°F (180°C). Line 2 baking sheets with parchment paper.
2. In the bowl of a stand mixer fitted with the paddle attachment, beat brown sugar, melted butter, and granulated sugar at low speed until combined, about 1 minute. Add eggs, one at a time, beating well after each addition. Beat in extracts.
3. In a medium bowl, sift together flour, baking soda, and sea salt. With mixer on low speed, gradually add flour mixture to butter mixture, beating until dough comes together. Fold in white chocolate, dark chocolate, and candy canes. Wrap dough in plastic wrap, and refrigerate for 15 minutes.
4. Using a 3-tablespoon spring-loaded scoop, scoop 24 dough balls, and place on prepared pans.
5. Bake until edges are golden brown, 10 to 12 minutes. Let cool completely on wire racks. Cover and refrigerate for up to 2 days, or freeze for up to 2 weeks.

Photo by Marcella DiLonardo

CHOCOLATE CARDAMOM SUGAR COOKIES

Makes 24 cookies

Recipe by Erin Clarkson

Adding cream cheese to the dough keeps these cookies soft and imparts a slight tang that works so well with the cardamom and chocolate. For a touch of decoration, finish them off with a generous dusting of confectioners' sugar using a snowflake stencil.

1	cup (227 grams) unsalted butter, softened
½	cup plus 2 tablespoons (140 grams) full-fat cream cheese, softened
¾	cup (150 grams) granulated sugar
¼	cup (55 grams) firmly packed dark brown sugar
1	large egg (50 grams), room temperature
1	large egg yolk (19 grams), room temperature
1	teaspoon (4 grams) vanilla extract
3	cups plus 1 tablespoon (383 grams) all-purpose flour, sifted
1	cup (85 grams) Dutch process cocoa powder
1¼	teaspoons (2.5 grams) ground cardamom
¾	teaspoon (2.25 grams) kosher salt

Garnish: confectioners' sugar

1. In the bowl of a stand mixer fitted with the paddle attachment, beat butter and cream cheese at medium speed until combined, 1 to 2 minutes. Add granulated sugar and brown sugar; increase mixer speed to high, and beat until light and creamy, 2 to 3 minutes. Reduce mixer speed to low. Add egg, egg yolk, and vanilla, beating until combined.

2. In a medium bowl, sift together flour, cocoa, cardamom, and salt. Add flour mixture to butter mixture, and beat at low speed just until combined. Using a rubber spatula, briefly stir to ensure everything is combined. (Dough will be sticky.) Transfer dough to a large piece of plastic wrap, and press into a rough rectangle. Wrap tightly in plastic wrap, and refrigerate until firm, 3 to 4 hours or up to overnight.

3. Preheat oven to 350°F (180°C). Line 2 baking sheets with parchment paper.

4. Divide dough in half; return half of dough to refrigerator. On a lightly floured sheet of parchment paper, roll remaining dough to ⅓-inch thickness. (You may need to give dough a few bangs with the rolling pin to help flatten it a little before you start rolling. This dough is on the stickier side, so rolling it out on a sheet of parchment paper means you can easily transfer it back to the refrigerator to chill a little if needed.) Using a 3-inch round cutter, cut dough, rerolling scraps as necessary. Place on prepared pans. (If at any time dough becomes too warm and hard to work with, return to refrigerator to chill briefly.) Refrigerate for 10 to 15 minutes.

5. Bake in batches for 9 to 10 minutes. (Cookies will still look very soft when they come out of the oven but will firm up as they cool.) Let cool completely on pans. Place a stencil* on top of cooled cookies, and garnish with confectioners' sugar, if desired. Store in an airtight container for up to 3 days.

Make your own stencil with a snowflake paper punch, available online or in local craft stores. A piece of lace draped on top of the cookies also works well.

> **PRO TIP**
> To help keep them moist, these cookies don't have any leaven in them, so the thickness that you roll the dough out to will be the thickness of your finished cookie.

Photo by Erin Clarkson

EVERYTHING CHOCOLATE THUMBPRINT COOKIES

Makes 56 cookies

Dear chocolate lovers, you're welcome. With cocoa powder in the dough, a pool of melty ganache in the center, and chocolate shavings and a light chocolate drizzle on top, this will be the most indulgent cookie you bake this season.

1   cup (227 grams) unsalted butter, softened
¾   cup (165 grams) firmly packed dark brown sugar
2   large egg yolks (37 grams)
1½   teaspoons (6 grams) vanilla extract
2   cups (250 grams) all-purpose flour
⅓   cup (40 grams) unsweetened cocoa powder*
½   teaspoon (1.5 grams) kosher salt
¼   teaspoon (1.25 grams) baking powder
Ganache (recipe follows)
Garnish: melted bittersweet chocolate, flaked sea salt, bittersweet chocolate shavings (see Note)

1. Preheat oven to 350°F (180°C). Line several baking sheets with parchment paper.
2. In the bowl of a stand mixer fitted with the paddle attachment, beat butter and brown sugar at medium speed until creamy, about 2 minutes, stopping to scrape sides of bowl. Beat in egg yolks and vanilla.
3. In a medium bowl, whisk together flour, cocoa, kosher salt, and baking powder. With mixer on low speed, gradually add flour mixture to butter mixture, beating until combined. Shape dough into 1-inch balls (about 13 grams each), and place 2 inches apart on prepared pans. Using a ¼-teaspoon measuring spoon, gently make an indentation in center of each ball.

4. Bake for 9 to 11 minutes. Remove from oven, and press down centers again. Let cool on pans for 10 minutes. Remove from pans, and let cool completely on wire racks.
5. Spoon 1 teaspoon Ganache into center of each cookie. Garnish with melted chocolate, sea salt, and chocolate shavings, if desired.

*We used Guittard Cocoa Rouge Unsweetened Cocoa Powder.

Note: *Using a vegetable peeler, scrape blade lengthwise across room temperature chocolate to create shavings.*

GANACHE
Makes ¾ cup

⅔   cup (113 grams) chopped bittersweet chocolate*
½   cup (120 grams) heavy whipping cream

1. In a large heatproof bowl, place chocolate.
2. In a small saucepan, bring cream just to a boil over medium heat. Pour hot cream over chocolate. Let stand for 1 minute; whisk until smooth. Refrigerate, stirring occasionally, until slightly thickened, about 30 minutes.

*We used Guittard Eureka Works 150th Anniversary Limited Edition 62% Cacao Bar, but Guittard Semisweet Chocolate Baking Bar 64% Cacao will work, too.

CHOCOLATE PEPPERMINT CRINKLE COOKIES

Makes 20 cookies

Recipe by Edd Kimber

If you like your cookies soft, fudgy, and packed with peppermint, these are for you.

7	ounces (200 grams) 70% cacao dark chocolate, roughly chopped
½	cup plus 1 tablespoon (127 grams) unsalted butter, cubed
1	teaspoon (4 grams) peppermint extract*
1	cup (200 grams) castor sugar
¼	cup (55 grams) firmly packed light brown sugar
2	large eggs (100 grams)
1	cup (125 grams) all-purpose flour
3	tablespoons (15 grams) black cocoa powder
1	teaspoon (5 grams) baking powder
¼	teaspoon kosher salt
½	cup (60 grams) confectioners' sugar

1. In the top of a double boiler, combine chocolate and butter. Cook over simmering water, stirring occasionally, until melted and smooth. Remove from heat; add peppermint extract, stirring until combined. Let cool completely, about 30 minutes.
2. In the bowl of a stand mixer fitted with the whisk attachment, beat castor sugar, brown sugar, and eggs at high speed until sugars dissolve, about 1 minute. Add chocolate mixture, beating just until combined.
3. In a medium bowl, whisk together flour, black cocoa, baking powder, and salt. Fold flour mixture into sugar mixture just until combined. Cover with plastic wrap, and refrigerate for 1 hour.
4. Preheat oven to 350°F (180°C). Line 2 (18x13-inch) baking sheets with parchment paper.
5. Using a 3-tablespoon spring-loaded scoop, scoop dough, and roll into balls. Roll balls in confectioners' sugar. (When rolling, you will want to compact the sugar onto the outside of the cookie because some of the sugar will absorb into the dough as it bakes. If you don't add enough, you will lose the decorative look of the sugar. With only a thin layer of sugar, the beautiful cracking will be less pronounced.) Place on prepared pans.
6. Bake until lightly puffed and just slightly set around edges, 11 to 12 minutes. Let cool completely on pans. Store in an airtight container for up to 4 days.

We used Nielsen-Massey Pure Peppermint Extract.

Photo by Edd Kimber

Holiday
HITS

· · · · ·

Highlight the season's most festive flavors with
this collection of classics that are sure to impress

PRESSED MARZIPAN
THUMBPRINT COOKIES

Makes about 20 cookies

These thumbprints are light and bright like the fresh fallen snow of winter and ornate enough to rival even the loveliest snowflake. The buttery, shortbread-like cookies get a spike of homemade almondy Marzipan, and a dollop of white chocolate filling adds the perfect hint of sweetness to round out their flavor.

⅔ cup (150 grams) unsalted butter, softened
¼ cup (50 grams) granulated sugar
⅓ cup (100 grams) Marzipan (recipe follows), room
    temperature
1 large egg yolk (19 grams), room temperature
½ teaspoon (3 grams) vanilla bean paste
2 cups (250 grams) all-purpose flour
¼ teaspoon kosher salt
White Chocolate Ganache (recipe follows)
Garnish: holiday sprinkles

1. In the bowl of a stand mixer fitted with the paddle attachment, beat butter and sugar at medium speed until creamy, 3 to 4 minutes, stopping to scrape sides of bowl. Add Marzipan, and beat until well combined. Beat in egg yolk and vanilla bean paste.
2. In a medium bowl, sift together flour and salt. With mixer on low speed, add flour mixture to butter mixture in two additions, beating until combined after each addition.
3. Turn out dough, and shape into a disk. Wrap in plastic wrap, and refrigerate for 30 minutes or up to overnight. (If refrigerating overnight, let dough stand at room temperature for about 15 minutes before rolling.)
4. Preheat oven to 325°F (170°C). Line baking sheets with parchment paper.
5. Between 2 sheets of parchment paper, roll dough to ¼-inch thickness. Using a 2¼-inch thumbprint cookie stamp* dipped in flour, cut dough, rerolling scraps as necessary. Place 1 inch apart on prepared pans. Freeze until firm, about 15 minutes.
6. Bake until bottoms are lightly golden, 12 to 15 minutes. Let cool slightly on pans, about 5 minutes. Remove from pans, and let cool completely on wire racks. Fill centers with White Chocolate Ganache. Garnish with sprinkles, if desired.

*We used Williams Sonoma Thumbprint Cookie Stamps.

> **PRO TIP**
> No cookie stamp? No problem! Using a 2-inch fluted round cookie cutter, cut dough. Using a ¼-teaspoon measuring spoon dipped in flour, gently make an indentation in the center of each cookie to create the perfect spot for your ganache.

MARZIPAN
Makes 1¾ cups

2¼ cups (216 grams) blanched almond flour
1½ cups (180 grams) confectioners' sugar
1 large egg white (30 grams)
2 teaspoons (8 grams) vanilla extract
2 teaspoons (8 grams) almond extract

1. In the work bowl of a food processor, place flour and confectioners' sugar; pulse until combined. Add egg white and extracts; process until mixture holds together when pressed between two fingers. If mixture is too dry, add water, 1 teaspoon (5 grams) at a time, until desired consistency is reached. Wrap tightly in plastic wrap, and refrigerate for up to 1 month.

WHITE CHOCOLATE GANACHE
Makes about 1 cup

8 ounces (226 grams) white chocolate, chopped
⅓ cup (80 grams) heavy whipping cream

1. In a medium heatproof bowl, place white chocolate.
2. In a small saucepan, heat cream over medium heat just until steaming and bubbles form around edges of pan. (Do not boil.) Pour hot cream over white chocolate. Let stand for 3 to 5 minutes; whisk until smooth. Use immediately.

RED-AND-WHITE COOKIES

Makes 8 cookies

Recipe by Josh Lehenbauer

A holiday twist on the classic New York black-and-whites! These fluffy, almost cake-like cookies are topped with both a peppermint and a vanilla glaze.

6   tablespoons (84 grams) unsalted butter, room temperature
½   cup (100 grams) granulated sugar
1   large egg (50 grams)
1½ cups (188 grams) all-purpose flour
½   teaspoon (2.5 grams) baking soda
½   teaspoon (3 grams) salt
½   cup (120 grams) well-shaken whole buttermilk
1   teaspoon (4 grams) vanilla extract
½   teaspoon (2 grams) almond extract
Cookie Glaze (recipe follows)

1. Position oven rack in center of oven. Preheat oven to 350°F (180°C). Line 2 large baking sheets with parchment paper.
2. In the bowl of a stand mixer fitted with the paddle attachment, beat butter and sugar at medium speed until fluffy, about 1 minute, stopping to scrape sides of bowl. Beat in egg until well combined, about 30 seconds. Scrape sides and bottom of bowl.
3. In a medium bowl, whisk together flour, baking soda, and salt. In a small bowl, stir together buttermilk and extracts. With mixer on low speed, gradually add flour mixture to butter mixture alternately with buttermilk mixture, beginning and ending with flour mixture, beating until smooth after each addition. (This whole process should take about 2 minutes; your dough will look and feel like a pancake mixture.) Using a 3-ounce spring-loaded scoop, scoop dough (about 60 grams each), 2 to 3 inches apart on prepared pans.

4. Bake, one batch at a time, until edges and bottoms are golden and cookies spring back a little when touched, 14 to 16 minutes. Remove from pan, and place, upside down, on wire racks. Let cool completely.
5. Place a bench scraper or offset spatula in center of 1 cooled cookie (as if you're going to cut the cookie in half). Spoon white Cookie Glaze over half of cookie, using the back of your spoon to guide it toward edge without it dripping over. Carefully lift and drag bench scraper or offset spatula toward white Cookie Glaze so you have a clean, straight line. Place bench scraper or offset spatula right up against white glaze. Spoon red Cookie Glaze onto other half of cookie. Carefully lift and drag bench scraper or offset spatula toward red glaze. (There may be a small gap between the two. If so, just use the tip of your spoon to nudge red glaze toward white glaze so they meet.) Repeat with remaining cookies and remaining Cookie Glaze. Let stand until glaze is set, about 15 minutes. Store in an airtight container for up to 3 days.

COOKIE GLAZE
Makes about ¾ cup

2   cups (240 grams) confectioners' sugar, sifted
2   tablespoons (42 grams) light corn syrup
1   teaspoon (4 grams) vanilla extract
2 to 3 tablespoons (30 to 45 grams) whole milk
5 to 7 drops red gel food coloring
⅛   teaspoon peppermint extract

1. In a medium bowl, whisk together confectioners' sugar, corn syrup, and vanilla until smooth. Add milk, 1 tablespoon (15 grams) at a time, until mixture is smooth and slightly thick but can still be drizzled in a fluid stream off a whisk. Transfer half of mixture to a small bowl; add food coloring and peppermint extract, whisking until combined.

Photo by Josh Lehenbauer

PEANUT BUTTER EGGNOG SNOWFLAKE COOKIES

Makes 24 cookies

Recipe by Jenn Davis

These soft peanut butter cookies decorated with piped Eggnog Buttercream deliver melt-in-your-mouth goodness that screams winter is here. Use a little buttercream, or frost the whole cookie. Either way, the combo is just what a snow-loving sweet tooth craving needs.

1 cup (227 grams) unsalted butter, softened
1 cup (200 grams) granulated sugar
1 cup (220 grams) firmly packed light brown sugar
1 cup (256 grams) creamy peanut butter
1 teaspoon (4 grams) vanilla extract
3 large eggs (150 grams)
3 cups (375 grams) all-purpose flour
1 teaspoon (5 grams) baking powder
1 teaspoon (2 grams) ground cinnamon
1 teaspoon (2 grams) ground nutmeg
½ teaspoon (2.5 grams) baking soda
½ teaspoon (1.5 grams) kosher salt
Eggnog Buttercream (recipe follows)
Garnish: sparkling sugar

1. In the bowl of a stand mixer fitted with the paddle attachment, beat butter, granulated sugar, and brown sugar at medium speed until fluffy, 3 to 4 minutes, stopping to scrape sides of bowl. Add peanut butter, beating until smooth. Beat in vanilla. Add eggs, one at a time, beating well after each addition.
2. In a medium bowl, whisk together flour, baking powder, cinnamon, nutmeg, baking soda, and salt. With mixer on low speed, gradually add flour mixture to butter mixture, beating until a dough forms. Divide dough in half, and shape into disks; wrap each in plastic wrap. Refrigerate for 2 hours.
3. Preheat oven to 350°F (180°C). Line 2 baking sheets with parchment paper.
4. Place half of dough on a large sheet of parchment paper. Cover with another large sheet of parchment paper, and roll to ¼-inch thickness. Remove top sheet of parchment.

Using a 3- to 5-inch snowflake cutter dipped in flour, cut dough, re-flouring cutter every 3 to 4 cookies to prevent sticking. Using a small offset spatula lightly coated in flour, transfer cut dough to prepared pans. Refrigerate until firm, about 15 minutes.
5. Bake until edges start to lightly brown, 10 to 12 minutes. Let cool on pans for 3 to 4 minutes. Remove from pans, and let cool completely on wire racks. Repeat with remaining dough.
6. Place Eggnog Buttercream in a pastry bag fitted with a closed star piping tip (Wilton No. 18 or No. 31). Pipe stars onto cooled cookies by gently squeezing from top of bag and then lifting while releasing pressure. Sprinkle with sparkling sugar, if desired. Store in an airtight container, separated by parchment or wax paper, for up to 3 weeks, or freeze cookies, individually wrapped in plastic wrap, in an airtight freezer-safe container for up to 4 months.

> **PRO TIP**
> Cookie dough can be made the day before and stored wrapped in plastic wrap in the refrigerator. Let dough warm slightly at room temperature to roll out but maintain a cold cookie dough.

EGGNOG BUTTERCREAM
Makes about 3 cups

1 cup (227 grams) unsalted butter, softened
¼ cup (60 grams) prepared eggnog
1 tablespoon (13 grams) vanilla extract
½ teaspoon (1.5 grams) kosher salt
4 to 5 cups (480 to 600 grams) confectioners' sugar

1. In the bowl of stand mixer fitted with the whisk attachment, beat butter, eggnog, vanilla, and salt at medium-low speed until combined. Gradually add confectioners' sugar, beating until desired thickness is reached. Use immediately.

Photo by Jenn Davis

MIMOSA CUTOUT COOKIES

Makes 35 cookies

I paired orange zest-packed dough with bright Sparkling Wine Royal Icing to create a mimosa-flavored holiday cookie. This elegant showstopper is surprisingly simple to make thanks to an easy icing method. These cookies are dipped in royal icing, rather than piped and flooded, before getting finished off with a mix of white sprinkles for an easy yet sophisticated look.

1   cup (227 grams) unsalted butter, softened
2   cups (240 grams) confectioners' sugar
1   tablespoon (8 grams) tightly packed orange zest
1   large egg (50 grams), room temperature
1   teaspoon (6 grams) vanilla bean paste
3¼ cups (406 grams) all-purpose flour
2   teaspoons (10 grams) baking powder
1   teaspoon (3 grams) kosher salt
Sparkling Wine Royal Icing (recipe follows)
Garnish: assorted white sprinkles

1. Preheat oven to 350°F (180°C). Line 3 baking sheets with parchment paper.
2. In the bowl of a stand mixer fitted with the paddle attachment, beat butter, confectioners' sugar, and orange zest at low speed just until combined. Increase mixer speed to medium-low, and beat until fluffy, 2 to 3 minutes, stopping to scrape sides of bowl. Add egg and vanilla bean paste, beating until combined.
3. In a medium bowl, whisk together flour, baking powder, and salt. With mixer on low speed, gradually add flour mixture to butter mixture, beating until a dough forms. Divide dough in half; shape each half into a 7-inch disk. Wrap each disk in plastic wrap, and refrigerate for 30 minutes.
4. On a lightly floured surface, roll half of dough to ¼-inch thickness. Using desired cutters dipped in flour, cut dough; using a large offset spatula dipped in flour, place cut dough ¾ to 1 inch apart on prepared pans. Reroll and cut scraps as needed. Repeat with remaining dough. (See Note.)
5. Bake, one batch at a time, until edges are lightly golden, 8 to 10 minutes. Let cool on pan for 1 minute. Remove from pan, and let cool completely on wire racks.
6. Dip tops of cooled cookies in Sparkling Wine Royal Icing; pull straight out, and lightly shake back and forth, letting excess drip off as much as possible. Quickly turn cookies icing side up; using a wooden pick, spread icing into an even layer, popping and filling any air bubbles, if necessary. Garnish with sprinkles, if desired. Let stand until dry, at least 4 hours.

Note: *If dough is refrigerated for a longer period of time, let stand at room temperature until slightly softened, 10 to 20 minutes.*

SPARKLING WINE ROYAL ICING
Makes 2½ cups

1   (1-pound) package (454 grams) confectioners' sugar
6   tablespoons (90 grams) warm water (90°F/32°C to 110°F/43°C)
2½ tablespoons (25.5 grams) meringue powder
2½ to 3½ tablespoons (37.5 to 52.5 grams) sparkling wine, room temperature (70°F/21°C)

1. In the bowl of a stand mixer fitted with the paddle attachment, beat confectioners' sugar, 6 tablespoons (90 grams) warm water, and meringue powder at low speed until well combined, stopping to scrape sides of bowl. Increase mixer speed to medium; beat until mixture is the consistency of toothpaste, 3 to 5 minutes. Add sparkling wine, ½ to 1 teaspoon (2.5 to 5 grams) at a time, until icing reaches "10-second" consistency. (A ribbon of icing drizzled on surface should take 10 seconds to sink back into icing.)
2. Transfer icing to a large shallow bowl; cover with a damp paper towel, and let stand for 20 minutes. Using a wooden pick, pop and fill as many air bubbles that rise to the surface as possible before using.

> **PRO TIP**
> Feel free to flavor your royal icing with your favorite extract to taste. Thin to 10-second consistency using room temperature water (70°F/21°C).
>
> For a little stronger sparkling wine flavor, place 1½ cups (360 grams) sparkling wine in a small saucepan. Bring to a boil over medium-high heat; cook until reduced to ¼ cup (60 grams). Transfer mixture to a small bowl, and let cool to room temperature (70°F/21°C). Use reduced sparkling wine as directed to thin royal icing to 10-second consistency.

CLASSIC SUGAR COOKIES

Makes about 24 cookies (depending on size of cutters used and thickness of dough)

Recipe by Emily Hutchinson

You can't have the holidays without a delicious, soft sugar cookie. Perfected over years and years of baking, Emily Hutchinson considers this recipe to be the best sugar cookie recipe! Remember to read the recipe directions, Notes, and PRO TIPS before starting.

1   cup (227 grams) unsalted butter, softened
¾   cup (150 grams) granulated sugar
½   cup (60 grams) confectioners' sugar
¾   teaspoon (2.25 grams) kosher salt
1   large egg (50 grams)
1½   teaspoons (6 grams) vanilla extract
3   cups (375 grams) all-purpose flour
1½   teaspoons (7.5 grams) baking powder
American Crusting Buttercream (recipe on page 62)

1. In the bowl of a stand mixer fitted with the paddle attachment, beat butter at medium speed for 30 seconds. Add sugars and salt, and beat at medium speed for 1 minute. With mixer on low speed, add egg and vanilla; beat for about 30 seconds.
2. In a medium bowl, whisk together flour and baking powder. Add flour mixture to butter mixture, and beat at low speed until dough comes together and starts to pull away from sides of bowl, 1 to 2 minutes. (Mixture may seem dry at first, but it will come together.)
3. Turn out dough onto a sheet of plastic wrap, and shape into a disk. Wrap in plastic wrap, and refrigerate for at least 1 hour.
4. Preheat oven to 375°F (190°C). Line baking sheets with parchment paper.

5. On a lightly floured surface, roll one-third of dough to ⅓- to ¼-inch thickness. (Keep remaining dough in refrigerator until ready to roll.) Using desired holiday cutters, cut dough, and place 2 inches apart on prepared pans. (See Notes.) Using a pastry brush, brush off any excess flour. Reroll and cut scraps as needed, refrigerating dough if it becomes too soft.
6. Bake until puffed and center is matte, 6 to 8 minutes. Using a small offset spatula, quickly press edges of cookies back into shape, if necessary. Let cool on pans for 1 minute. Remove from pans, and let cool completely on wire racks.
7. Pipe or spread American Crusting Buttercream onto cooled cookies as desired. (Alternatively, freeze cooled cookies in an airtight container for 2 hours or overnight; let thaw at room temperature for 1 hour, and pipe or spread American Crusting Buttercream onto cookies as desired. [See Notes.])

Notes: *To help the flour stick to your work surface, gently press your dough on the clean surface before dusting the surface with flour. To roll your dough to an even thickness, roll slowly up and down and then to the sides. If you run your hand across the top of your rolled dough, you can feel any bumps or slightly raised areas.*

The dough can be refrigerated for 10 minutes after the cookies are cut out and placed on a baking sheet.

This recipe is meant to be frosted with American Crusting Buttercream (recipe on page 62). If you are looking for a sweeter cookie that you can just add sprinkles to, add extra vanilla or almond extract to sweeten the dough.

I prefer to freeze the baked cookies overnight. It gives them added moisture to keep them soft.

PRO TIP

Adding the salt in with the sugars helps the salt dissolve through the dough better in this recipe. Regular table salt can be used, but make sure to reduce it to ½ teaspoon (3 grams). If you can find salted sweet cream butter, use that and omitting salt completely because salted sweet cream butter has the perfect amount of salt for these cookies.

You can add ¼ teaspoon (1 gram) almond extract to the Classic Sugar Cookies recipe to give the cookies a holiday flavor.

Nice and thick cookies balance out the sweetness of the buttercream, so don't roll out the dough thinner than ¼ inch.

Aluminum-free baking powder should be double-acting, which means it's activated in mixing stage and baking stage. Best to keep aluminum out if we can, so get aluminum-free.

Frosted cookies can be frozen for up to 2 weeks. To freeze them, be gentle and treat them like frosted cupcakes until they crust over. When you pull them out of the freezer, be sure to allow the buttercream to crust back over.

If you cream your butter and sugars together too much, it can lead to slight cracks in the baked cookie; cream as instructed.

GINGERBREAD CUTOUT COOKIES

Makes about 24 cookies (depending on size of cutters used and thickness of dough)

Recipe by Emily Hutchinson

Is there anything better than the smell of gingerbread baking in the oven? These cookies are nice and thick and keep their shape very well. They are perfectly chewy, spiced and brown sugared to holiday deliciousness. The buttercream frosting adds a creamy sweetness you won't want to leave off, but if you're in a pinch, simply add cinnamon hard candies or sprinkles before baking.

1	cup (227 grams) unsalted butter, softened
¾	cup (165 grams) firmly packed dark brown sugar
¼	cup (50 grams) granulated sugar
¾	teaspoon (2.25 grams) kosher salt
1	large egg (50 grams)
1½	teaspoons (6 grams) vanilla extract
¼	cup (85 grams) unsulphured molasses
3	cups (375 grams) all-purpose flour
2	teaspoons (4 grams) ground cinnamon
1½	teaspoons (7.5 grams) baking powder
1	teaspoon (2 grams) ground ginger
¼	teaspoon ground nutmeg
⅛	teaspoon ground cloves

American Crusting Buttercream (recipe on page 62)

1. In the bowl of a stand mixer fitted with the paddle attachment, beat butter at medium speed for 30 seconds. Add sugars and salt, and beat at medium speed for 1 minute. With mixer on low speed, add egg and vanilla; beat for about 30 seconds. Beat in molasses just until combined.
2. In a medium bowl, whisk together flour, cinnamon, baking powder, ginger, nutmeg, and cloves. Add flour mixture to butter mixture, and beat at low speed until combined. (Dough will be slightly sticky.)

3. Turn out dough onto a sheet of plastic wrap, and shape into a disk. Wrap in plastic wrap, and refrigerate for at least 1 hour.
4. Preheat oven to 375°F (190°C). Line baking sheets with parchment paper.
5. On a lightly floured surface, roll one-third of dough to ⅓- to ¼-inch thickness. (Keep remaining dough refrigerated until ready to roll.) Using desired holiday cutters, cut dough, and place 2 inches apart on prepared pans. (See Notes.) Using a pastry brush, brush off any excess flour. Reroll and cut scraps as needed, refrigerating dough if it becomes too soft.
6. Bake until puffed and center is matte, 6 to 8 minutes. Using a small offset spatula, quickly press edges of cookies back into shape, if necessary. Let cool on pans for 1 minute. Remove from pans, and let cool completely on wire racks.
7. Pipe or spread American Crusting Buttercream onto cooled cookies as desired. (Alternatively, freeze cooled cookies in an airtight container for 2 hours or overnight; let thaw at room temperature for 1 hour, and pipe or spread American Crusting Buttercream onto cookies as desired. [See Notes.])

Notes: *To help the flour stick to your work surface, gently press your dough on the clean surface before dusting the surface with flour.*

To roll your dough to an even thickness, roll slowly up and down and then to the sides. If you run your hand across the top of your rolled dough, you can feel any bumps or slightly raised areas.

Alternatively, this dough can be rolled out between sheets of parchment paper.

I prefer to freeze the baked cookies overnight. It gives them added moisture to keep them soft.

AMERICAN CRUSTING BUTTERCREAM

Makes about 5 cups

Recipe by Emily Hutchinson

You can frost cookies with delicious, beautiful buttercream, and it won't get completely smashed when stacking—it's true! For this recipe, the butter is cut with vegetable shortening to form a crust.

1   cup (227 grams) unsalted butter, softened
1   cup (184 grams) vegetable shortening, softened
1   teaspoon (3 grams) kosher salt
2   teaspoons (8 grams) vanilla extract
9   cups (1,080 grams) confectioners' sugar, sifted
5 to 6 tablespoons (75 to 90 grams) 2% reduced-fat milk or heavy whipping cream

1. In the bowl of a stand mixer fitted with the paddle attachment, beat butter, shortening, and salt at medium speed until well combined. Add vanilla, and beat at medium speed for 1 minute. Add confectioners' sugar, and place a kitchen towel over mixer, (bowl of stand mixer will be full); beat at low speed, and gradually increase speed to medium, beating until thick and combined. (Do not overmix.) Add 5 tablespoons (75 grams) milk or cream, and beat at medium-high speed until smooth, about 1 minute; add up to remaining 1 tablespoon (15 grams) milk or cream, 1 teaspoon (5 grams) at a time, if too thick. (Do not overmix.) Refrigerate in an airtight container for up to 1 week, or freeze in an airtight container for up to 3 months.

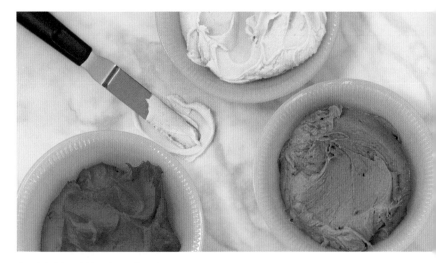

BUTTERCREAM PRO TIPS

Overmixing causes the buttercream to become a bit grainy, with tiny air bubbles. You want a nice and smooth consistency. If you see any air bubbles, beat them out with a rubber spatula by smacking it back and forth against the side of your mixer bowl.

You can still add your food colorings after mixing; it will not ruin the buttercream.

You can use all butter instead of half butter/half shortening and it will still form a crust, but the shortening gives it a smoother texture. If you use a vegetable shortening, use Crisco. Make sure it's fresh and hasn't been sitting in the back of your cupboard.

The weather is a huge factor. When it's hot out, you might need a tablespoon less of milk or cream; when it's cold, you may need an extra tablespoon. The temperature of your house and the humidity where you live will determine how much milk or cream to add. Start out with the minimum and slowly add to find out what works best for you. If you find it's too soft, add in ¼ cup (30 grams) confectioners' sugar to thicken it up.

After piping your buttercream, let cookies stand for 8 to 12 hours to dry the crust before stacking; 24 hours makes the crust stronger. It won't be like royal icing—it can still get smashed.

Store frosted cookies in an airtight container at room temperature. You can freeze frosted cookies for up to 2 weeks, but not longer than that because it will change the texture of the buttercream.

Refrigerate unused buttercream in an airtight container. Let buttercream come to room temperature before using. It will be solid.

One batch of buttercream will frost 24 cookies for the completed set.

COLORING BUTTERCREAM

For red, use Wilton Red No-Taste Icing Color with Wilton Color Right Performance Food Coloring in Crimson/C. You may need ½ to 1 teaspoon Red No-Taste and 10 to 15 drops of the Color Right in Crimson/C per 1 cup buttercream. If you cover the bowl of red buttercream with plastic wrap and let stand overnight, the color will deepen.
For white, use 1 teaspoon Wilton White-White Icing Color per 1 cup buttercream. **For dark green,** use ¼ to ½ teaspoon Wilton Gel Food Coloring in Kelly Green and 3 to 4 drops of AmeriColor Soft Gel Paste Food Color in Forest Green per 1 cup buttercream. **For light green,** use a very small amount of Wilton Gel Food Coloring in Kelly Green, 1 drop per 1 cup buttercream. **For gray,** use 1 drop of black gel food coloring (any brand) per 1 cup buttercream. **For brown,** use ½ teaspoon brown gel food coloring (any brand) per 1 cup buttercream.

TWO-TONED BUTTERCREAM

YOU WILL NEED:
Red American Crusting
    Buttercream (recipe on
    opposite page)
White American Crusting
    Buttercream
3 pastry bags, divided
2 couplers
Clear plastic wrap
Wilton No. 366 piping tip

TWO-TONED BUTTERCREAM PRO TIPS

As you are piping, you will see where the color is going. You can adjust the tip to make it flow from the center or the sides. Give the buttercream a big squeeze before starting in order to make sure the color is flowing right. You will want the thin white strip to come through the center of the tip, where the point of the "beak" is.

Don't overfill your pastry bag with buttercream. It's easier to pipe and guide your hand with less in your bag. Keep refilling for the best results. Fill the bag with ¾ to 1 cup buttercream.

STEP 1: Place red American Crusting Buttercream and white American Crusting Buttercream in separate pastry bags fitted with couplers.

STEP 2: Place an 18-inch-long sheet of plastic wrap horizontally, and without attaching a piping tip to the coupler, pipe several 6-inch-long lines of red American Crusting Buttercream. Continue to layer lines, piping lines on top of each other, so you create about a 2-inch-high mound in the middle. (It will be thick; we are using about 1 cup buttercream total.)

STEP 3: Pipe a 6-inch-long strip (½ inch thick and ⅓ inch high) of white buttercream in the middle of the red buttercream mound.

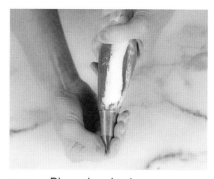

STEP 4: Grab the bottom edge of the plastic wrap, and fold up and over horizontally to the top edge of the plastic wrap. Twist the ends of the plastic wrap. Coil one end so the buttercream doesn't come out of the top when squeezing. Cut the other end about 2 inches from the buttercream.

STEP 5: Place the plastic wrap-encased buttercream, cut end down, in a pastry bag fitted with a Wilton No. 366 piping tip. The piping tip should be perfectly centered over the white icing.

STEP 6: Start squeezing from the top to see where the white will come out. You can gently move the tip to manipulate where the white will come through in the petals. Begin to pipe. Move tip accordingly if needed without removing the plastic wrap-encased buttercream from the pastry bag.

POINSETTIA COOKIES

Recipe by Emily Hutchinson

This cookie is one of Emily's most popular and original designs. You can add this to a cake or cupcakes as well. They are so beautiful and simpler than you'd think. Follow the instructions in Two-Toned Buttercream (page 63) on how to fill the pastry bag. The petals of the poinsettia aren't even the petals. The red, white, and pink/white petals are actually leaves; the flower is the center clusters.

YOU WILL NEED:
Two-Toned Buttercream (instructions on page 63)
6 to 8 (2½- to 3-inch) round cookies
Gold sugar pearls
½ cup green American Crusting Buttercream
     (recipe on page 62)
Pastry bag
1 coupler
Wilton No. 352 piping tip
Wilton No. 366 piping tip

STEP 1: Follow instructions for Two-Toned Buttercream on page 345.

STEP 2: Have the beak (pointed end) of your piping tip facing down. Holding your pastry bag of Two-Toned Buttercream at a 45-degree angle in the center of a cookie, gently squeeze the pastry bag (you will see the buttercream billow out the sides), and slowly move toward the outer edge—but not all the way to the edge, because you want to be able to turn the cookie without accidentally touching the buttercream. Stop squeezing, and pull away to form the petal. (The pressure will get lighter as the petals come to a point.)

STEP 3: Repeat procedure all the way around the cookie, creating a base of 6 petals and leaving a little room for the center petals.

STEP 4: Using the same technique as in step 2, pipe a smaller petal on top of the base petals, making sure not to pipe a small petal directly on top of a base petal.

STEP 5: Repeat procedure all the way around the center, creating 5 center petals.

STEP 6: Place the gold sugar pearls in the center of the petals.

STEP 7: Place green American Crusting Buttercream in a pastry bag fitted with a coupler and Wilton No. 352 piping tip. Using the same technique as in step 2, pipe leaves between base petals.

STEP 8: Turn your cookie as you go. That's why we don't want the petals to be longer than the cookie—they would get smudged.

STEP 9: Repeat procedure all the way around the cookie, creating 6 leaves.

STEP 10: Repeat procedure with remaining cookies.

TWINKLING TREE COOKIES

Recipe by Emily Hutchinson

Emily created this tree for a beautiful pink vintage cookie set and fell in love with this style. The sprinkles really draw your eyes in, making you fall in love with this cookie. The shell piping technique is fairly simple and so versatile.

YOU WILL NEED:
1¼ cups light green American Crusting Buttercream (recipe on page 62)
¼ cup brown American Crusting Buttercream
2 pastry bags
2 couplers
6 (3½-inch-long) tree-shaped cookies
Wilton No. 199 piping tip
Wilton No. 2 piping tip
White confetti sprinkles, colored sugar pearls, and white nonpareils

STEP 1: Place light green and brown American Crusting Buttercream in separate pastry bags fitted with couplers.

STEP 2: Turn a cookie so the top of the tree points toward you. Fit the light green buttercream pastry bag with a Wilton No. 199 piping tip. Holding the bag at a 45-degree angle, with the piping tip about ¼ inch above the cookie, start squeezing the bag hard to allow the buttercream to billow out so it forces the tip up; lower pressure as you pull toward you to create the first shell.

STEP 3: Pipe the very ends and work your way in.

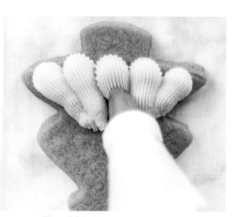

STEP 4: The fifth branch will complete the first layer of branches.

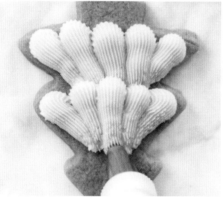

STEP 5: Repeat steps 3 and 4 for the second layer of branches but slightly overlap so no bare cookie shows in between branch layers.

STEP 6: The last layer will be smaller and tight, with 3 shells.

STEP 7: Turn the cookie right side up. Fit the brown buttercream pastry bag with a Wilton No. 2 piping tip. Holding the bag at a slight angle, pipe back and forth horizontally, applying steady pressure.

STEP 8: Place white confetti sprinkles and colored sugar pearls, one at a time, on buttercream. Make sure to place them all around the cookie.

STEP 9: Sprinkle white nonpareils all over cookie.

STEP 10: Repeat procedure with remaining cookies. Change the sugar pearls to fit any theme you're working with.

CHRISTMAS SUGAR COOKIES

Makes about 36 cookies

Our base cookie dough yields tender, buttery sugar cookies prime for our Royal Icing decoration. The best part about these cookies? No chilling or freezing required! Whether you're making ornaments, trees, or snowflakes, simply roll out your dough, cut into desired shapes, and bake.

1   cup (227 grams) unsalted butter, softened
2   cups (240 grams) confectioners' sugar
1   large egg (50 grams), room temperature
2   teaspoons (8 grams) vanilla extract
3¼ cups (406 grams) all-purpose flour
1½ teaspoons (7.5 grams) baking powder
1   teaspoon (3 grams) kosher salt
Royal Icing (recipe follows)

1. Preheat oven to 400°F (200°C). Line 3 baking sheets with parchment paper.
2. In the bowl of a stand mixer fitted with the paddle attachment, beat butter and confectioners' sugar, slowly increasing mixer speed to medium, until fluffy, 3 to 4 minutes, stopping to scrape sides of bowl. Add egg and vanilla, beating until combined.
3. In a medium bowl, whisk together flour, baking powder, and salt. With mixer on low speed, gradually add flour mixture to butter mixture, beating until a dough forms. Scrape sides of bowl, and knead dough 3 to 4 times in bowl to make sure everything is well combined.
4. Divide dough in half; cover one half with plastic wrap. On a heavily floured surface, roll remaining half to ¼-inch thickness. (Lightly flour top of dough if it sticks to rolling pin.) Using desired holiday cutters, cut dough, rerolling scraps as necessary. Using a small offset spatula, place cookies at least 1 inch apart on prepared pans.
5. Bake, one batch at a time, until lightly browned, 7 to 8 minutes. Let cool on pan for 5 minutes. Using a large offset or flat metal spatula, remove from pan, and let cool completely on wire racks. Decorate cooled cookies as desired with Royal Icing.

ROYAL ICING
Makes about 6 cups

Confectioners' sugar, meringue powder, water, and extract are the only ingredients needed to make royal icing, a baker's number one tool for making edible art. For food safety and ease, use meringue powder—a blend of dried pasteurized egg whites, sugar, cornstarch, and citric acid—rather than the traditional raw egg whites. Whipped into a stiff mixture, this icing will appear dense and thick, not light and fluffy like your typical meringue—that's good! The meringue powder isn't needed for creating volume. Instead, it's the secret ingredient to creating a structured, pipable icing that will harden into a resilient edible adornment.

1   (2-pound) package (907 grams) confectioners' sugar
5   tablespoons (50 grams) meringue powder
¾   cup (180 grams) warm water (105°F/41°C to 110°F/43°C)
1   teaspoon (4 grams) almond extract

1. In the bowl of a stand mixer fitted with the paddle attachment, beat confectioners' sugar and meringue powder at low speed until combined. Slowly add ¾ cup (180 grams) warm water and almond extract, beating until fluid, about 1 minute. Increase mixer speed to medium, and beat until stiff, 4 to 5 minutes. Store in an airtight container for up to 3 days.

PRO TIP

It's the nature of this icing to harden and dry out—so if you get busy with other projects in the kitchen, be sure to cover the top of your Royal Icing with a damp paper towel to keep it fluid and fresh for up to 1 hour. For longer periods of time, store in an airtight container.

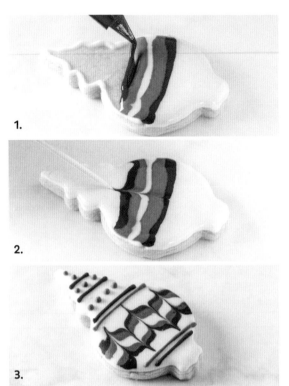

1.

2.

3.

DECORATION DETAILS:

1. Using the white flood icing, fill in the top quarter of the round part of the ornament cookie; pipe a line each of red flood icing, green flood icing, white flood icing, green flood icing, and red flood icing. Keep a steady hand as you pipe your alternating flood icings, as any wiggling will lead to uneven icing bleed. Try to keep the lines an even thickness as well, as one heavier line can overwhelm a thinner line. You don't need to touch the border icing as you pipe; if it doesn't naturally settle into the edges, you can use a wooden pick to gently nudge it to the edge.

2. Using a clean wooden pick, drag a line down through the center of the colored band of icing. Wipe pick clean, and repeat 2 more times, to the left and right of the center, spacing evenly and wiping pick clean after each drag (any residual icing left on the pick will muddy the colors). Then drag up 2 times, between the down drags, wiping pick clean after each drag. Let dry for 2 to 3 hours.

3. Above the marble design, pipe a red line and then a green line. Below design, pipe a green line and then a red line. Pipe 2 more red lines, between each level down the point of the ornament shape on the lower part of the cookie. Pipe a horizontal row of green dots between bottom red lines (4 dots and then 3 dots); pipe a vertical row of 2 green dots on the bottom tip of the ornament. Let dry until hardened, about 30 minutes. Store in an airtight container for up to 1 week.

ORNAMENT COOKIES

Like the vintage ornaments you were never allowed to touch as a kid, these marvelously marbled cookies are extraordinarily ornate and brilliantly colored.

MATERIALS NEEDED:
Royal Icing (recipe on page 68)
Water, as needed
Wilton Gel Food Coloring in Kelly Green, Juniper Green, Christmas Red, Golden Yellow, and Black
3 to 6 pastry bags
3 piping bottles (optional)
3 Wilton No. 1 piping tips
3 Wilton No. 3 piping tips
36 (3½-inch) ornament-shaped Christmas Sugar Cookies (recipe on page 68)
Wooden picks

1. Divide Royal Icing among 3 bowls: 3 cups (540 grams) in the first, 1½ cups (270 grams) in the second, and 1½ cups (270 grams) in the third. Cover bowls with a damp paper towel or kitchen towel to keep icing from drying out.
2. To the first bowl (3 cups [540 grams]), add water, 1 teaspoon (5 grams) at a time, until border consistency is reached. Place 1 cup (180 grams) in a pastry bag fitted with a very small round piping tip (Wilton No. 1). To the remaining 2 cups (360 grams), add water, 1 teaspoon (5 grams) at a time, until flood consistency is reached. Place in a pastry bag or a small piping bottle (if using) fitted with small round piping tip (Wilton No. 3). To the second bowl (1½ cups [270 grams]), slowly add Kelly green food coloring until a bright green is reached; slowly add juniper green until the desired color is reached. Add water, 1 teaspoon (5 grams) at a time, until border consistency is reached. Place ½ cup (90 grams) in a separate bowl, cover airtight, and set aside. To the remaining 1 cup (180 grams), add water, 1 teaspoon (5 grams) at a time, until flood consistency is reached. Place in a pastry bag or a small piping bottle (if using) with small round piping tip (Wilton No. 3).

3. To the third bowl (1½ cups [270 grams]), add Christmas red food coloring until desired color is reached; add golden yellow and a touch of black to keep it from going pink. Add water, 1 teaspoon (5 grams) at a time, until border consistency is reached. Place ½ cup (90 grams) in a separate bowl, cover airtight, and set aside. To the remaining 1 cup (180 grams), add water, 1 teaspoon (5 grams) at a time, until flood consistency is reached. Place in a pastry bag or a small piping bottle fitted with small round piping tip (Wilton No. 3).
4. Using white border icing, pipe an outline along edges of a cookie. Using the white flood icing, fill in the top quarter of the round part of the ornament cookie; pipe a line each of red flood icing, green flood icing, white flood icing, green flood icing, and red flood icing. Fill in the remaining area with white flood icing. Using a wooden pick, remove any air bubbles and make sure there are no gaps in the icing. Using a clean wooden pick, drag down through the center of the colored band of icing, wipe pick clean, and repeat 2 more times, to the left and right of the center, spacing evenly and wiping pick clean after each drag. Then drag up 2 times, between the down drags, wiping pick clean after each drag. Repeat with remaining cookies. Let dry for 2 to 3 hours.
5. Uncover the red and green border icings, and place each in a pastry bag fitted with a very small round piping tip (Wilton No. 1). Above the marble design, pipe a red line and then a green line. Below design, pipe a green line and then a red line. Pipe 2 more red lines, between each level down the point of the ornament shape on the lower part of the cookie. Pipe a horizontal row of green dots between bottom red lines (4 dots and then 3 dots); pipe a vertical row of 2 green dots on the bottom tip of the ornament. Let dry until hardened, about 30 minutes. Store in an airtight container for up to 1 week.

WINTER TREE COOKIES

With a paintbrush and bit of icing, these verdant green trees get a romantic dappling of winter snow.

MATERIALS NEEDED:
Royal Icing (recipe on page 68)
Wilton Gel Food Coloring in Kelly Green, Juniper Green, and Brown
Water, as needed
3 pastry bags
2 Wilton No. 1 piping tips
Squeeze bottle
1 Wilton No. 2 piping tip
36 (3½-inch) tree-shaped Christmas Sugar Cookies (recipe on page 68)
Wooden picks
Paintbrush

1. Divide Royal Icing among 3 bowls: 4 cups (720 grams) in the first, 1¾ cups (315 grams) in the second, and ¼ cup (45 grams) in the third. Cover bowls with a damp paper towel or kitchen towel to keep from drying out.
2. To the first bowl (4 cups [720 grams]), slowly add Kelly green food coloring until a bright green is reached; slowly add juniper green until the desired color is reached. Add water, 1 teaspoon (5 grams) at a time, until border consistency is reached. Place 1 cup (180 grams) in a pastry bag fitted with a very small round tip (Wilton No. 1). To the remaining 3 cups (540 grams), add water, 1 teaspoon (5 grams) at a time, until flood consistency is reached. Place in a large squeeze bottle.

3. To the second bowl (1¾ cups [315 grams]), add water, 1 teaspoon (5 grams) at a time, until border consistency is reached; cover airtight, and set aside.
4. To the third bowl (¼ cup [45 grams]), add brown food coloring until desired color is reached. Add water, 1 teaspoon (5 grams) at a time, until border consistency is reached. Place in a pastry bag fitted with a very small round piping tip (Wilton No. 1).
5. Using green border icing, pipe an outline along edges of tree part of a cookie. Using green flood icing, fill in center. Using a wooden pick, remove any air bubbles and make sure there are no gaps in the icing. Using the brown icing, pipe border of trunk (including next to green icing). Fill in using the same consistency, and use a wooden pick to remove any air bubbles and make sure there are no gaps in the icing. Repeat with remaining cookies. Let dry for 2 to 3 hours.
6. Place white border icing in a pastry bag fitted with small round tip (Wilton No. 2). Place paintbrush in water. Starting at the base of the tree, pipe a row of dots, keeping in mind they will be grouped in 2 or 3. Remove brush from water, and wipe off excess water. Place brush tip in the center of each dot and brush away from you, creating groups of 2 or 3 that meet. (Wipe off any excess icing as needed that the brush picks up.) Place brush back in water and then pipe another row of dots. Remove any excess water from the brush, and repeat procedure until you reach the top of the tree. Repeat with remaining cookies. Let dry until hardened, about 30 minutes. Store in an airtight container for up to 1 week.

DECORATION DETAILS:

1. Once your green and brown base icing has dried, you can begin creating snowy details. Place white border icing in a pastry bag fitted with a small round tip (Wilton No. 2). Place paintbrush in water. Starting at the base of the tree, pipe a row of dots, keeping in mind they will be grouped in 2 or 3. These should be generous dots of icing, not tiny pinpoints, so you can brush them into snowy sweeps.

2. Remove brush from water, and wipe off excess water. Too much water on the brush will dilute your icing and make you lose definition. Place brush tip in the center of each dot and brush away from you, creating groups of 2 or 3 that meet. It should look like dimpled teardrops that join thinly at the top.
3. A fine-tipped paintbrush like the one we used tends to spring into a narrow

cone shape. We want a more fanned-out broom shape, leaving dramatic swept trails in the icing. If you start losing the detailed sweep look, flatten your brush tip between your fingers to fan it out again.
4. Continue to dot and sweep your way to the top of your cookie. Use 2-dot clusters in narrow spaces at the top and edges. Let dry until hardened, about 30 minutes.

1.

2.

3.

4.

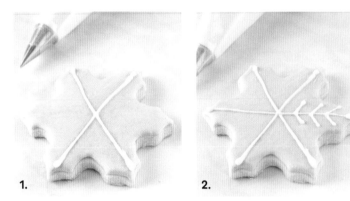

1.   **2.**   **3.**

DECORATION DETAILS: DESIGN #1

1. Starting at one tip of the snowflake, pipe a thin white line to the opposite tip, leaving a rounded end at each tip. Repeat with the remaining tips, making sure each line (there will be 3 total) meets the others in the center. Like when piping a border, you'll make a thread of icing that'll span the expanse of the cookie, only touching down on the cookie with your tip to create the rounded ends.

2. On each line going from the center, pipe 3 "V" shapes with the points going toward the center. Try to keep the "V" shapes tucked to the main line so that as you pipe more "V" shapes on the other lines, they won't overlap and touch.

3. Using the dark blue, pipe a small dot between each line (there will be 6) and 1 larger dot in the center, where the white lines meet. Let dry until hardened, about 30 minutes. Store in an airtight container for up to 1 week.

DESIGN #2

Design 1 is slightly simpler than design 2, but has similar steps. After making the long bisecting lines mentioned in step 1, you'll pipe smaller lines over the center, between the larger lines (3 total). Then you'll pipe 2 "V" shapes at the top of each of the longer lines. A smattering of blue dots fills the empty space, and a pearl sprinkle is placed in the center as a crowning jewel. Use tweezers for exact pearl placement so you keep from accidentally smudging the icing.

SNOWFLAKE COOKIES

Complete with two icy designs, these cookies look like the intricate inner workings of a snowflake. In reality, a simple series of lines, dots, and "V" shapes make up its pattern, offering the gold standard of royal iced cookies: easy execution, dazzling results.

MATERIALS NEEDED:
Royal Icing (recipe on page 68)
Wilton Gel Food Coloring in Cornflower Blue
Water, as needed
3 pastry bags
2 Wilton No. 1 piping tips
Squeeze bottle
36 (3⅛-inch) snowflake-shaped Christmas Sugar
     Cookies (recipe on page 68)
Wooden picks
Wilton No. 2 piping tip
White pearls
Tweezers

1. Divide Royal Icing into 3 bowls: 4 cups (720 grams) in the first, 1½ cups (270 grams) in the second, and ½ cup (90 grams) in the third. Cover bowls with a damp paper towel or kitchen towel to keep from drying out.
2. To the first bowl (4 cups [720 grams]), add cornflower blue food coloring, until a soft blue or desired color is reached. Add water, 1 teaspoon (5 grams) at a time, until border consistency is reached. Place 1 cup (180 grams) in a pastry bag fitted with a very small round tip (Wilton No. 1). To the remaining 3 cups (540 grams), add water, 1 teaspoon (5 grams) at a time, until flood consistency is reached. Place in a large squeeze bottle.
3. To the second bowl (1½ cups [270 grams]), add water, 1 teaspoon (5 grams) at a time, until border consistency is reached; cover airtight, and set aside.
4. To the third bowl (½ cup [90 grams]), add cornflower blue food coloring until dark blue or desired color is reached. Add water, 1 teaspoon

(5 grams) at a time, until border consistency is reached; cover airtight, and set aside.
5. Using the light blue border icing, pipe an outline along edges of a cookie. Using light blue flood icing, fill in center. Using a wooden pick, remove any air bubbles and make sure there are no gaps in the icing. Repeat with remaining cookies. Let dry for 2 to 3 hours.
6. Place white border icing in a pastry bag fitted with very small round tip (Wilton No. 1). Place dark blue border icing in a pastry bag fitted with a small round tip (Wilton No. 2).
7. For design 1: Starting at one tip of snowflake, pipe a thin white line to the opposite tip, leaving a rounded end at each tip. Repeat with the remaining tips, making sure each line (there will be 3 total) meets the others in the center. On each line going from the center, pipe 3 "V" shapes with the points going toward the center. Using the dark blue, pipe a small dot between each line (there will be 6) and 1 larger dot in the center, where the white lines meet.
8. For design 2: Starting at one tip of snowflake, pipe a thin white line to the opposite tip, leaving a rounded end at each tip and making sure to leave space for a dot at each tip. Repeat with the remaining tips, making sure each line (there will be 3 total) meets the others in the center. Pipe smaller lines over the center, between the larger lines (3 total). On each larger line going from the center, pipe 2 "V" shapes with the points going toward the center. Using the dark blue, pipe small dots at each tip of the snowflake; pipe dots between the "V" shapes on each line (1 on each side of the line), and pipe a small dot at the end of the smaller lines coming from the center. Place a white pearl in the center. (Use tweezers for easier placement.) Repeat with remaining cookies. Let dry until hardened, about 30 minutes. Store in an airtight container for up to 1 week.

MITTEN COOKIES

Makes 10 to 12 (3½-inch) cookies

Recipe by Tessa Huff

Swapping honey in for molasses and changing up the spice blend from a typical gingerbread cookie creates a brighter flavor palette in these cookies.

1½	cups (188 grams) all-purpose flour
1½	tablespoons (12 grams) cornstarch
¾	teaspoon (1.5 grams) ground cardamom
½	teaspoon (1.5 grams) kosher salt
½	teaspoon (1 gram) ground cinnamon
¼	teaspoon (1.25 grams) baking powder
⅛	teaspoon grated fresh nutmeg
½	cup (113 grams) unsalted butter, softened
¼	cup (50 grams) granulated sugar
3	tablespoons (63 grams) honey
1	large egg yolk (19 grams)

Lemon Royal Icing (recipe follows)
Gel food coloring (optional)

1. In a medium bowl, stir together flour, cornstarch, cardamom, salt, cinnamon, baking powder, and nutmeg.
2. In the bowl of a stand mixer fitted with the paddle attachment, beat butter at medium speed until creamy, about 1 minute. Add sugar, and beat for 2 minutes, stopping to scrape sides of bowl. Reduce mixer speed to low. Add honey and egg yolk, and beat until combined. With mixer on low speed, gradually add flour mixture, beating until dough comes together.
3. Turn out dough onto a piece of plastic wrap, and shape into a disk. Wrap in plastic wrap, and refrigerate for at least 1 hour.
4. Preheat oven to 350°F (180°C). Line a baking sheet with parchment paper.
5. On a lightly floured surface, roll dough to ¼-inch thickness. Using a 3½-inch mitten cutter, cut dough, rerolling scraps as needed, and place 1 to 2 inches apart on prepared pan. Refrigerate for 15 minutes.
6. Bake until edges begin to brown, 12 to 14 minutes. Let cool completely on pan.

7. Tint Lemon Royal Icing with food coloring (if using). For woven design, thin a portion of Lemon Royal Icing with water until it is the consistency of runny honey to create a glaze. Using an offset spatula, spread a thin coat of glaze around top of cookie, leaving about ⅛-inch border un-iced. (This prevents any cookie from showing through the piped icing.) Place stiff Lemon Royal Icing in a pastry bag fitted with a small petal tip (Wilton No. 101). Pipe interlocking "V" shapes in rows on cookies. Point narrow end of petal tip away from your body and toward top of cookie as you pipe down length of cookie. Turn cookie opposite way to create rows of alternating woven pattern. Alternatively, use the same technique using a small round tip (Wilton No. 5).
8. For spiraled knit design, place Lemon Royal Icing in a pastry bag fitted with a small star piping tip. Starting at top of cookie, pipe tight spirals down length of cookie. Repeat at top to create rows of icing until cookie is completely decorated.
9. For mitten cuff design, thin a portion of Lemon Royal Icing with water until it is the consistency of runny honey to create a glaze. Place glaze in a shallow bowl, and dip top surface of cookie into glaze. Shake off excess, and let dry. Pipe remaining stiff icing onto cuff of mitten using one of the techniques above. Let icing completely dry and harden before carefully storing cookies in an airtight container. Cookies are best served within 2 to 3 days.

LEMON ROYAL ICING
Makes about 1¾ cups

2⅔	cups (320 grams) confectioners' sugar
2	tablespoons (20 grams) meringue powder
3 to 4	tablespoons (45 to 60 grams) water
1	teaspoon (5 grams) fresh lemon juice

1. In the bowl of a stand mixer fitted with the whisk attachment, stir together confectioners' sugar and meringue powder. Add 3 tablespoons (45 grams) water and lemon juice, and beat at medium speed until stiff peaks form, 6 to 7 minutes. Add up to remaining 1 tablespoon (15 grams) water, beating until consistency is slightly thicker than toothpaste and easy to pipe. Use immediately. Cover any icing not being used with a damp cloth.

Photo by Tessa Huff

CREAM CHEESE-STUFFED VANILLA-PEPPERMINT COOKIES

Makes about 14 cookies

These holiday cookies pack a cream cheese surprise. Rolling these cream cheese-stuffed cookie dough balls in crushed soft peppermint candies creates a very merry cookie.

½   cup (113 grams) unsalted butter, softened
¾   cup (150 grams) plus 2 tablespoons (24 grams) granulated sugar, divided
1   large egg (50 grams), room temperature
1½ teaspoons (6 grams) peppermint vanilla extract*
1⅔ cups (208 grams) all-purpose flour
1½ teaspoons (7.5 grams) baking powder
¾   teaspoon (2.25 grams) kosher salt
4   ounces (113 grams) cream cheese, softened
½   cup (64 grams) crushed soft peppermint candies (See Notes)
Garnish: crushed soft peppermint candies

1. In the bowl of a stand mixer fitted with the paddle attachment, beat butter and ¾ cup (150 grams) sugar at medium speed until fluffy, 2 to 3 minutes, stopping to scrape sides of bowl. Beat in egg and peppermint vanilla extract until well combined, stopping to scrape sides of bowl.
2. In a large bowl, whisk together flour, baking powder, and salt. Add flour mixture to butter mixture all at once; beat at low speed just until combined, stopping to scrape sides of bowl.
3. In a small bowl, stir together cream cheese and remaining 2 tablespoons (24 grams) sugar until well combined. Cover cream cheese mixture and dough with plastic wrap; freeze for 25 minutes.
4. Preheat oven to 350°F (180°C). Line 2 rimmed baking sheets with parchment paper.
5. In a small shallow bowl, place candies.
6. Using a 1-tablespoon spring-loaded scoop, scoop dough (about 18 grams each); flatten into 2-inch disks. Place 1½ teaspoons (about 9 grams) cream cheese mixture in center of 1 dough disk; cover with a second disk, and crimp edges to seal. Gently shape into a ball; roll in candies. (See Notes.) Repeat with remaining dough and remaining cream cheese mixture. Place dough balls 1½ inches apart on prepared pans, and gently flatten to ¾-inch thickness, pressing together any cracks in edges, if necessary.
7. Bake, one batch a time, until edges are set and bottoms are golden brown, 12 to 15 minutes. Carefully garnish warm cookies with candies, if desired. Let cool on pans for 3 minutes. Remove from pans, and let cool completely on wire racks.

We used Heilala Peppermint Vanilla Extract.

Notes: *Do not substitute hard peppermint candies.*

If crushed soft peppermint candies aren't sticking well, lightly dampen hands with water as needed before rolling dough into balls and coating in candies.

SUGAR COOKIE WREATHS

Makes about 36 cookies

Is it really the holidays if you don't have festive sugar cookies? These classic cookies are topped with an elegant Royal Icing wreath that's easier to create than you might think.

1   cup (227 grams) unsalted butter, softened
2   cups (240 grams) confectioners' sugar
1   large egg (50 grams), room temperature
1½   teaspoons (6 grams) vanilla extract
½   teaspoon (2 grams) almond extract
3¼   cups (406 grams) all-purpose flour
2   teaspoons (10 grams) baking powder
1   teaspoon (3 grams) kosher salt
Royal Icing (recipe follows)

1. Preheat oven to 400°F (200°C). Line 3 baking sheets with parchment paper.
2. In the bowl of a stand mixer fitted with the paddle attachment, beat butter and confectioners' sugar at medium speed until fluffy, 3 to 4 minutes, stopping to scrape sides of bowl. Add egg and extracts, beating until combined.
3. In a medium bowl, whisk together flour, baking powder, and salt. With mixer on low speed, gradually add flour mixture to butter mixture, beating until a dough forms.
4. Divide dough in half; cover one half with plastic wrap. On a heavily floured surface, roll remaining dough to ¼-inch thickness. (Lightly flour top of dough if it sticks to rolling pin.) Using a 3¼-inch fluted round cutter, cut dough, rerolling scraps as necessary. Using a 1¾-inch fluted round cutter, cut centers from cookies. Repeat with remaining dough. Using a small offset spatula, place cookies at least 1 inch apart on prepared pans.
5. Bake in batches until lightly browned, 7 to 8 minutes. Let cool on pans for 5 minutes. Using a large offset or flat metal spatula, remove from pan, and let cool completely on wire racks.
6. Using pastry bag with plain white Royal Icing, pipe an outline along both edges of each cookie. Let dry for 5 minutes. Fill in center using white Royal Icing in squeeze bottle. Immediately pipe small green dots to left and right of center of ring using small piping bottle. Using a wooden pick,

continuously drag through center of cookie to create leaves. Let dry for 2 to 3 hours.
7. Pipe red Royal Icing berries in groupings around cookie. Let dry until hardened, about 30 minutes. Store in airtight containers for up to 1 week.

ROYAL ICING
Makes about 6 cups

1   (2-pound) package (907 grams) confectioners' sugar
5   tablespoons (50 grams) meringue powder
¾   cup (180 grams) warm water (105°F/41°C to 110°F/43°C)
1   tablespoon (13 grams) vanilla extract
Gel food coloring (juniper green, kelly green, Christmas red, black, yellow)
Water, as needed

1. In the bowl of a stand mixer fitted with the paddle attachment, beat confectioners' sugar and meringue powder at low speed until combined. Slowly add ¾ cup (180 grams) warm water and vanilla, beating until fluid. Increase mixer speed to medium, and beat until stiff, about 5 minutes.
2. Place 1 cup (180 grams) white icing in a pastry bag fitted with a small round piping tip (Wilton No. 3).
3. In a medium bowl, place another 1 cup (180 grams) white icing. Slowly add green food colorings until desired color is reached. Add water, 1 teaspoon (5 grams) at a time, until flood-consistency is reached (about 3 teaspoons [15 grams] total). Place green icing in a small piping bottle fitted with a small round tip (Wilton No. 4).
4. In another medium bowl, place another 1 cup (180 grams) white icing. Slowly add red food coloring until desired color is reached. (Adding a touch of black and yellow will keep it from going pink.) Place in a pastry bag fitted with a small round tip (Wilton No. 2), or trim end of bag to create a small opening.
5. Place remaining white icing in a large bowl. Add water, 1 tablespoon (15 grams) at a time, until fluid (5 to 7 tablespoons [75 to 105 grams] total.) (It should ribbon when a whisk is pulled up out of icing.) Place in squeeze bottle with a small opening.

Boozy
& BRIGHT

· · · · ·

Toast the holidays with these creations that
seamlessly blend cocktail hour with cookies

PRETZEL AND PECAN BOURBON CHOCOLATE CHIP COOKIES

Makes 24 cookies

Recipe by Connie Chong

The spike of bourbon immediately delivers an incredibly soothing aroma of warm vanilla notes. Toasted pecans and salted pretzels give a satisfying crunch and flavor to the soft interior, and pools of melted chocolate make for the ultimate cookie experience.

1   cup (42 grams) mini pretzels
¾   cup (170 grams) unsalted butter, softened
¾   cup (165 grams) firmly packed dark brown
      sugar
½   cup (100 grams) granulated sugar
1   large egg (50 grams)
1   large egg yolk (19 grams)
2   tablespoons (30 grams) bourbon
1   teaspoon (4 grams) vanilla extract
2   cups (250 grams) all-purpose flour
2   teaspoons (6 grams) cornstarch
1   teaspoon (5 grams) baking soda
½   teaspoon (1.5 grams) kosher salt
1½   cups (255 grams) semisweet
      chocolate chips
¾   cup (72 grams) chopped toasted pecans
24   pecan halves

1. Break half of pretzels into smaller pieces. Break remaining pretzels in half.
2. In the bowl of a stand mixer fitted with the paddle attachment, beat butter and sugars at medium speed until light and fluffy, about 2 minutes, stopping to scrape sides of bowl. Add egg and egg yolk, and beat at low speed until well combined. Add bourbon and vanilla, and beat just until combined.
3. In a medium bowl, whisk together flour, cornstarch, baking soda, and salt. With mixer on low speed, gradually add flour mixture to butter mixture, beating until combined. Using a wooden spoon, gently stir in small pretzel pieces, chocolate chips, and chopped pecans. Cover with plastic wrap, and refrigerate for 30 minutes.
4. Line 2 large baking sheets with parchment paper or silicone baking mats.
5. Using a 1½-tablespoon spring-loaded scoop, scoop dough (about 45 grams each), and place at least 2½ inches apart on prepared pans. Insert 1 pecan half and half of a mini pretzel into each dough scoop. Loosely cover with plastic wrap, and refrigerate for 30 minutes.
6. Preheat oven to 375°F (190°C).
7. Bake, one batch at a time, until edges are golden brown, 10 to 12 minutes. Let cool on pan for 5 minutes. Using a thin spatula, remove from pan, and let cool completely on wire racks. Store in an airtight container for up to 5 days.

Photo by Connie Chong

TIRAMISÙ FRANGIPANE THUMBPRINT COOKIES

Makes 22 to 24 cookies

These cookies transform all the rich flavors of tiramisù into a bite-size serving. Dutch process cocoa powder creates an incredibly soft dough that boasts roasted coffee flavors. Hiding beneath creamy Mascarpone Buttercream, you'll find a rum frangipane.

1 cup (227 grams) unsalted butter, softened
¾ cup plus 1 tablespoon (162 grams) granulated sugar
3 tablespoons (18 grams) dark-roast instant coffee granules
1 tablespoon (15 grams) water
2 large egg yolks (37 grams), room temperature
1 teaspoon (6 grams) vanilla bean paste
2 cups (250 grams) all-purpose flour
½ cup (43 grams) Dutch process cocoa powder
¼ teaspoon (1.25 grams) baking powder
½ teaspoon (1.5 grams) kosher salt
Rum Frangipane Filling (recipe follows)
Mascarpone Buttercream (recipe follows)
Garnish: Dutch process cocoa powder

1. Preheat oven to 350°F (180°C). Line 2 baking sheets with parchment paper.
2. In the bowl of a stand mixer fitted with the paddle attachment, beat butter and sugar at medium speed until creamy, about 2 minutes, stopping to scrape sides of bowl.
3. In a small bowl, stir together instant coffee and 1 tablespoon (15 grams) water until granules dissolve. Add coffee mixture, egg yolks, and vanilla bean paste to butter mixture; beat at medium speed just until combined.
4. In a medium bowl, sift together flour, cocoa, and baking powder; whisk in salt. With mixer on low speed, gradually add flour mixture to butter mixture, beating just until combined and stopping to scrape sides of bowl. Scoop dough by 2 tablespoonfuls (about 29 grams each), and roll into balls. Place about 2 inches apart on prepared pans. Using the back of a ½-teaspoon measuring spoon, gently make an indentation in center of each ball.
5. Scoop 1 teaspoon (5 grams) Rum Frangipane Filling, and roll into a ball; place ball in indentation of 1 dough ball, and press into a rounded mound that completely fills indentation. Repeat with remaining Rum Frangipane Filling and remaining dough balls.

6. Bake, one batch at a time, until edges are dry and set, 9 to 12 minutes. Let cool on pan for 5 minutes. Remove from pan, and let cool completely on wire racks.
7. Spoon Mascarpone Buttercream into a pastry bag fitted with a ½-inch round piping tip (Wilton No. 2A). Pipe about 4 teaspoons (about 15 grams) buttercream in center of each cooled cookie; using a small offset spatula, spread and swirl buttercream as desired. Garnish with cocoa, if desired.

Rum Frangipane Filling
Makes about ½ cup

⅔ cup (64 grams) superfine blanched almond flour
2 tablespoons (24 grams) granulated sugar
2 tablespoons (28 grams) unsalted butter, room temperature*
1 large egg yolk (19 grams), room temperature
2 teaspoons (10 grams) dark rum
¼ teaspoon kosher salt
¼ teaspoon (1 gram) almond extract

1. In a small bowl, stir together flour and sugar until well combined. Add butter and all remaining ingredients; stir until well combined, kneading together by hand if necessary.

Unlike softened butter, room temperature butter should provide no resistance when pressed with a finger.

Mascarpone Buttercream
Makes about 2 cups

⅔ cup (150 grams) unsalted butter, softened (see Note)
⅛ teaspoon kosher salt
1⅓ cups (160 grams) confectioners' sugar
1½ teaspoons (7.5 grams) heavy whipping cream
5 ounces (142 grams) mascarpone cheese*, softened (see Note)

1. In the bowl of a stand mixer fitted with the paddle attachment, beat butter and salt at medium speed until creamy, about 1 minute, stopping to scrape sides of bowl. With mixer on low speed, gradually add confectioners' sugar, beating just until combined. Beat in cream.

Increase mixer speed to medium, and beat until fluffy, 3 to 4 minutes, stopping to scrape sides of bowl. Fold in mascarpone by hand just until combined. (Do not overmix; mascarpone will start to break down.) Use immediately.

Note: *For best results, it's important that the butter and mascarpone are both softened and at about the same* temperature. *An instant-read thermometer inserted in the center of each is an easy way to gauge when they're ready to go. Our butter and mascarpone were at about 64°F (18°C). Mascarpone that gets too warm may be more likely to break. Try to handle the buttercream as little as possible; overworking it could cause the mascarpone to start breaking down.*

*We used Vermont Creamery Mascarpone.

CRÈME FRAÎCHE APRICOT COOKIES

Makes about 24 cookies

This decadent cookie fuses warm and golden brandy, jewel-like dried apricots, crunchy pearl sugar, and a dose of silky crème fraîche.

⅔ cup (85 grams) diced dried apricots
½ cup (120 grams) brandy
⅓ cup (76 grams) unsalted butter, softened
¾ cup (150 grams) granulated sugar
2 large egg yolks (37 grams)
1 large egg (50 grams)
½ cup (120 grams) crème fraîche
2½ cups (313 grams) all-purpose flour
½ teaspoon (2.5 grams) baking powder
¼ teaspoon (1.25 grams) baking soda
¼ teaspoon kosher salt
1 cup (200 grams) pearl sugar*

1. In a small saucepan, bring apricots and brandy just to a boil. Reduce heat, and simmer, stirring occasionally, until almost all liquid is evaporated, 8 to 10 minutes. Remove from heat, and let cool completely.
2. In the bowl of a stand mixer fitted with the paddle attachment, beat butter and granulated sugar at medium speed just until combined, 1 to 2 minutes. Beat in egg yolks and egg. Add crème fraîche, beating until combined.
3. In a medium bowl, whisk together flour, baking powder, baking soda, and salt. With mixer on low speed, gradually add flour mixture to butter mixture, beating until combined. Gently stir in cooled apricots. (Dough will be sticky.) Refrigerate for 30 minutes.
4. Preheat oven to 350°F (180°C). Line 3 rimmed baking sheets with parchment paper.
5. Place pearl sugar in a small bowl. Using a 1½-tablespoon scoop, scoop dough, and roll into balls. (If dough is sticky, you can dampen your hands with water to roll into balls.) Roll balls in pearl sugar, and place 2 inches apart on prepared pans. Flatten slightly with the palm of your hand.
6. Bake, one batch at a time, until cookies are set but not browned, 10 to 12 minutes. Let cool on pans for 5 minutes. Remove from pans, and let cool completely on wire racks.

We used Lars Own Swedish Pearl Sugar.

HAZELNUT LINZER COOKIES WITH WINE-INFUSED JAM

Makes 24 cookies

Recipe by Becky Sue Wilberding

Classic Linzer cookies get elevated with a rich hazelnut sandwich cookie base filled with wine-infused jams to toast the spirit of the holiday season.

2   cups (250 grams) plus 2 tablespoons (16 grams) all-purpose flour, divided
1   teaspoon (5 grams) baking powder
1   teaspoon (2 grams) ground cinnamon
½   teaspoon (1.5 grams) kosher salt
½   teaspoon (1 gram) ground ginger
1   cup (142 grams) raw hazelnuts
1   cup (227 grams) unsalted butter, softened
½   cup (100 grams) granulated sugar
1   large egg (50 grams), room temperature
1   teaspoon (4 grams) vanilla extract
½   teaspoon (2 grams) almond extract
¾   cup (240 grams) wine-infused jam*
¼   cup (30 grams) confectioners' sugar

1. Preheat oven to 350°F (180°C).
2. In a medium bowl, whisk together 2 cups (250 grams) flour, baking powder, cinnamon, salt, and ginger. Set aside.
3. Place hazelnuts on a baking sheet, and toast for 8 to 10 minutes. Transfer nuts to a clean towel, and vigorously rub nuts in towel to remove as much of skins as possible. (Don't worry too much about leaving some skin on the nuts—it adds a nice texture and color to the cookies.) Let cool completely.
4. In the work bowl of a food processor, place hazelnuts and remaining 2 tablespoons (16 grams) flour; pulse until nuts are finely ground. (The flour will absorb the oils from the nuts and prevent a nut butter from forming in the food processor.) Add hazelnut mixture to flour mixture, whisking to combine. Set aside.
5. In the bowl of a stand mixer fitted with the paddle attachment, beat butter and granulated sugar at medium speed until creamy, 2 to 3 minutes, stopping to scrape sides of bowl.

Add egg and extracts, beating until combined. With mixer on low speed, gradually add flour mixture, beating until combined. Divide dough in half, and shape each half into a disk. Wrap in plastic wrap, and refrigerate for at least 1 hour or up to overnight.
6. Line 2 baking sheets with parchment paper.
7. On a lightly floured surface, roll half of dough to ¼-inch thickness. Using 2-inch round, fluted round, or fluted square cutters, cut dough, rerolling scraps as necessary. (Refrigerate dough if it becomes too soft to get a clean cut.) Place at least 1 inch apart on prepared pans. Using desired 1-inch or smaller holiday-shaped cutters, cut centers from half of cookies. (Make sure you have the same number of tops to bottoms in each cookie shape.) Reserve some center cutouts for decorative accents. Repeat with remaining dough. Refrigerate for at least 30 minutes or overnight, or freeze until ready to bake.
8. Preheat oven to 350°F (180°C).
9. Bake until edges are golden, 10 to 12 minutes, rotating pans halfway through baking. Let cool completely on wire racks.
10. Spread 1½ teaspoons wine-infused jam on flat side of all solid cookies. Sprinkle cookies with cutouts with confectioners' sugar. Place cookies with cutouts, flat side down, on top of jam. Refrigerate cookies layered between sheets of wax or parchment paper in an airtight container for up to 2 weeks.

*Use various wine-infused jams for variety in taste and color. I used Grapefruit Ginger Rosé Jam, Strawberry & Pinot Noir Jam, and Marionberry Jam with Port from Vintner's Kitchen, available at vintnerskitchen. com. You can also use regular jam.

Note: *You can get creative with sizes and shapes of cookies, but remember to account for the sizes and shapes when baking. If you make varying sizes, be sure to bake the cookies of similar size together as smaller cookies will bake more quickly than larger cookies.*

Photo by Becky Sue Wilberding

BOURBON-SPIKED APPLE CIDER COOKIES

Makes 24 cookies

Recipe by Elisabeth Farris

Filled with real apple cider and chopped apples, these Bourbon-Spiked Apple Cider Cookies are moist and delicious. The Bourbon Glaze takes them to another level and makes them perfect for the holidays.

½   cup (113 grams) unsalted butter, softened
½   cup (100 grams) granulated sugar
¼   cup (55 grams) firmly packed light brown sugar
1   large egg (50 grams)
1   teaspoon (4 grams) vanilla extract
1¼ cups (300 grams) apple cider
1½ cups (188 grams) all-purpose flour
1   teaspoon (2 grams) ground cinnamon
½   teaspoon (1.5 grams) kosher salt
½   teaspoon (2.5 grams) baking soda
1   cup (110 grams) finely chopped Granny Smith apple
2   teaspoons (10 grams) fresh lemon juice
Bourbon Glaze (recipe follows)

1. Preheat oven to 400°F (200°C). Line 2 baking sheets with parchment paper.
2. In the bowl of a stand mixer fitted with the paddle attachment, beat butter and sugars at medium-high speed until light and fluffy, 2 to 3 minutes, stopping to scrape sides of bowl. Add egg and vanilla, beating well.
3. In a medium saucepan, heat cider over medium-high heat until thickened and reduced to 2 tablespoons, 10 to 15 minutes. (An instant-read thermometer should register at least 150°F [65°C].) You can pour the reduced cider into a glass measuring cup to check the volume. (This transfer will also help the foam to subside.) Let cool for 1 to 2 minutes. (It will harden if cooled any longer.) Beat reduced cider into butter mixture.

4. In a medium bowl, whisk together flour, cinnamon, salt, and baking soda. In a small bowl, toss together apple and lemon juice. With mixer on low speed, gradually add flour mixture to butter mixture, beating just until combined. Stir in apple mixture. Using a 1½-tablespoon spring-loaded scoop, scoop dough into balls (about 25 grams each), and place 2 inches apart on prepared pans.
5. Bake until golden brown but still soft, 8 to 10 minutes. Let cool on pans for 5 minutes. Remove from pans, and let cool completely on wire racks. Using a pastry bag or spoon, drizzle Bourbon Glaze onto cooled cookies. Store in an airtight container for up to 3 days.

Note: *The apple cider reduction will harden if not used within a few minutes, so make sure to beat it into the batter while it's still warm.*

BOURBON GLAZE
Makes about ½ cup

1   cup (120 grams) confectioners' sugar
1   tablespoon (15 grams) bourbon
1   tablespoon (15 grams) apple cider

1. In a small bowl, whisk together all ingredients until smooth. Use immediately.

Photo by Elisabeth Farris

HOT BUTTERED RUM RUGELACH

Makes 36 cookies

Recipe by Michele Song

These rum-spiked rugelach are inspired by the classic holiday drink and are sure to be a hit at the adult table. The cream cheese rugelach dough is super buttery and flaky, and the brown sugar filling has chopped spiced pecans with hints of ground cinnamon, nutmeg, and cloves. The glaze is also spiked with rum, so don't be shy with those drizzles!

2   cups (250 grams) all-purpose flour
2   tablespoons (24 grams) granulated sugar
½   teaspoon (1.5 grams) kosher salt
1   cup (227 grams) cold unsalted butter, cubed
8   ounces (226 grams) cold cream cheese, cubed
1   teaspoon (4 grams) vanilla extract
¾   cup (165 grams) firmly packed dark brown sugar
1   tablespoon (21 grams) honey
1   tablespoon (15 grams) dark or spiced rum
2   teaspoons (4 grams) ground cinnamon
¼   teaspoon ground nutmeg
¼   teaspoon ground cloves
Hot Buttered Rum Spiced Pecans (recipe follows), chopped
1   large egg (50 grams)
1   tablespoon (15 grams) water
Turbinado sugar, for sprinkling
Rum Glaze (recipe follows)

1. In the work bowl of a food processor, pulse together flour, granulated sugar, and salt until combined. Add cold butter, cold cream cheese, and vanilla, and pulse 3 to 4 times; process just until dough comes together, about 30 seconds. (Do not overwork dough.) Turn out dough onto a lightly floured surface, and divide into 3 portions. Shape each portion into a disk, and wrap in plastic wrap. Refrigerate for at least 2 hours or up to overnight.
2. In a medium bowl, stir together brown sugar, honey, rum, cinnamon, nutmeg, and cloves. Cover and set aside.
3. Line 2 baking sheets with parchment paper.
4. On a lightly floured surface, roll one-third of dough into a 10-inch circle. Spoon one-third of brown sugar mixture onto dough, and spread using an offset spatula. Sprinkle with one-third of Hot Buttered Rum Spiced Pecans. Gently press pecans into dough to ensure they stick. Using a pizza wheel, cut dough into 12 wedges. Starting at base of each triangle, carefully roll up dough

and filling into a log. Place on prepared pans, tucking ends under. Repeat with remaining dough, remaining brown sugar mixture, and remaining Hot Buttered Rum Spiced Pecans. Refrigerate for 30 minutes.
5. Preheat oven to 350°F (180°C).
6. In a small bowl, whisk together egg and 1 tablespoon (15 grams) water. Brush egg wash onto dough, and sprinkle with turbinado sugar.
7. Bake until golden brown, 20 to 25 minutes, rotating pans halfway through baking. (See Note.) Let cool completely on pans. Drizzle with Rum Glaze. Store in an airtight container for up to 3 days.

Note: *Some of the spiced sugar filling will ooze out during baking. This is normal. Once you've let your rugelach cool completely on the pan, the puddles of spiced sugar filling will detach easily from the cookies and leave them clean and crisp.*

HOT BUTTERED RUM SPICED PECANS
Makes 1 cup

1   cup (100 grams) pecan halves
1   tablespoon (12 grams) granulated sugar
½   teaspoon (1.5 grams) kosher salt
¼   teaspoon ground cinnamon
⅛   teaspoon ground nutmeg
⅛   teaspoon ground cloves
2   tablespoons (30 grams) dark rum
1   tablespoon (14 grams) firmly packed dark brown sugar
1   tablespoon (14 grams) unsalted butter
½   teaspoon (2 grams) vanilla extract

1. Preheat oven to 350°F (180°C). Line a baking sheet with parchment paper.
2. Spread pecans in an even layer on prepared pan.
3. Bake until fragrant, 5 to 7 minutes, rotating pan halfway through baking.
4. In a medium bowl, stir together granulated sugar, salt, cinnamon, nutmeg, and cloves.
5. In a medium saucepan, bring rum, brown sugar, butter, and vanilla to a boil over medium heat, stirring constantly. Add toasted pecans, stirring to coat; cook until glaze is absorbed and pecans are shiny, 1 to 2 minutes. Transfer pecans to sugar mixture, and toss to coat. Return to parchment-lined baking sheet, and let cool. Store in an airtight container.

Rum Glaze
Makes ½ cup

2	tablespoons (28 grams) unsalted butter
1	tablespoon (15 grams) dark or spiced rum
¾	cup (90 grams) confectioners' sugar
1	tablespoon (15 grams) milk
¼	teaspoon ground cinnamon

1. In a small saucepan, heat butter and rum over medium heat until butter is melted and bubbly. Remove from heat; transfer to a small bowl. Add confectioners' sugar, milk, and cinnamon, whisking until smooth. Use immediately.

Photo by Michele Song

EGGNOG THUMBPRINT COOKIES

Makes 18 cookies

Recipe by Marcella DiLonardo

These cookies are like biting into a cup of holiday cheer featuring the three important flavors of eggnog: cinnamon, nutmeg, and rum. A unique treat perfect for endless cookie exchanges!

½   cup (113 grams) unsalted butter, room temperature
⅓   cup (73 grams) firmly packed light brown sugar
1   large egg (50 grams), room temperature
1   tablespoon (15 grams) spiced rum
1   teaspoon (4 grams) vanilla extract
1½ cups (188 grams) all-purpose flour
½   teaspoon (1 gram) ground cinnamon
½   teaspoon (1 gram) ground nutmeg
¼   teaspoon (1.25 grams) baking powder
½   teaspoon fine sea salt
Eggnog Frosting (recipe follows)
Turbinado sugar, for sprinkling

1. Preheat oven to 350°F (180°C). Line 2 baking sheets with parchment paper.
2. In the bowl of a stand mixer fitted with the paddle attachment, beat butter and brown sugar at medium speed until creamy, about 2 minutes. Beat in egg; beat in rum and vanilla.
3. In a medium bowl, sift together flour, cinnamon, nutmeg, baking powder, and sea salt. Gradually add flour mixture to butter mixture, beating until dough comes together. Shape dough into 1½-inch balls (about 23 grams each), and place 2 inches apart on prepared pans. Using your thumb or the back of a spoon, gently make an indentation in center of each ball. Refrigerate for 15 minutes.
4. Bake until edges are slightly golden, 11 to 13 minutes. Let cool completely.
5. Place Eggnog Frosting in a pastry bag fitted with a star tip. Pipe a dollop of frosting into center of each cookie. Sprinkle with turbinado sugar. Cover and refrigerate for up to 2 days, or freeze in an airtight container for up to 2 weeks.

EGGNOG FROSTING
Makes about 1 cup

½   cup (113 grams) unsalted butter, softened
1   teaspoon (4 grams) vanilla extract
¼   teaspoon ground cinnamon
¼   teaspoon ground nutmeg
⅛   teaspoon fine sea salt
1½ cups (180 grams) confectioners' sugar
1   tablespoon (15 grams) prepared eggnog

1. In the bowl of a stand mixer fitted with the paddle attachment, beat butter at medium speed until creamy, about 2 minutes. Reduce mixer speed to medium-low. Beat in vanilla, cinnamon, nutmeg, and sea salt. Gradually beat in confectioners' sugar, ¼ cup (30 grams) at a time, until creamy and smooth. Beat in eggnog until combined. Use immediately.

Photo by Marcella DiLonardo

ICED EGGNOG SHORTBREAD COOKIE TREES

Makes 2 cookie trees (30 cookies)

Stars aren't just for topping the tree. Turns out, the shape is perfect for stacking to create your most eye-catching centerpiece yet. A favorite holiday drink inspired the flavor for the tender, delicately spiced shortbread. You'll love the little kick from the spiced rum.

1   cup (227 grams) unsalted butter, softened
2   cups (240 grams) confectioners' sugar
1   large egg (50 grams), room temperature
1½   teaspoons (7.5 grams) spiced rum
½   teaspoon (2 grams) vanilla extract
3¼   cups (406 grams) all-purpose flour
2   teaspoons (10 grams) baking powder
1   teaspoon (3 grams) kosher salt
1   teaspoon (2 grams) ground cinnamon
1   teaspoon (2 grams) ground nutmeg
Spiked Royal Icing (recipe follows)
2   tablespoons (30 grams) water
Garnish: assorted sprinkles

1. Preheat oven to 375°F (190°C). Line baking sheets with parchment paper.
2. In a large bowl, beat butter and confectioners' sugar with a mixer at medium speed until fluffy, 2 to 3 minutes, stopping to scrape sides of bowl. Add egg, rum, and vanilla, beating until combined.
3. In a medium bowl, whisk together flour, baking powder, salt, cinnamon, and nutmeg. With mixer on low speed, gradually add flour mixture to butter mixture, beating until a dough forms.
4. Divide dough in half; cover one half with plastic wrap. On a lightly floured surface, roll uncovered dough to ¼-inch thickness. Using 5 graduated-size, star-shaped cookie cutters*, cut out 3 cookies for each size, rerolling scraps as necessary. Repeat with remaining dough. (Each tree will have 15 cookies.) Working in batches and using a small offset spatula, place cookies, sorted by size, at least ½ inch apart on prepared pans.
5. Bake until edges are just beginning to brown, 7 to 10 minutes. Let cool on pans for 1 minute. Remove from pans, and let cool completely on wire racks.
6. Transfer about 1 cup (206 grams) Spiked Royal Icing to a small bowl; add 2 tablespoons (30 grams) water, stirring until icing is flood-consistency. (If icing is too thick, add more water, and if it's too thin, add more confectioners' sugar. For reference, flood-consistency icing has the appearance of runny honey.) Dip tops of cooled cookies into flood-consistency Spiked Royal Icing, letting excess drip off. Let stand until dry, at least 4 hours. (Don't rush this process—if you start to move your cookies or ice with new details, you'll risk smudging.)
7. Spoon 1 cup (206 grams) Spiked Royal Icing into a small pastry bag fitted with a small round piping tip (Wilton No. 2) or cut a ⅛-inch opening. Pipe desired decorations onto dipped cookies. Refill pastry bag as needed. Garnish with sprinkles, if desired. Let stand until dry, at least 1 hour.
8. For first set of 15 cookies, start with largest star and stack cookies in order of size, spiraling them so points do not line up; use Spiked Royal Icing as an adhesive, piping a little icing onto the center of each cookie before layering with the next. Stand final cookie upright as a tree topper, securing with Spiked Royal Icing. (To help top cookie stand up, gently grate bottom points until flat and dot with icing before securing to the top of the tree.) Repeat procedure with second set of 15 cookies.

Our largest cookie was 5 inches, and our smallest cookie was 1 inch. We like Williams Sonoma Stainless-Steel Star Biscuit 5-Piece Cookie Cutter Set.

Note: *Any leftover flood-consistency icing can be frozen in an airtight container for up to 3 months.*

MAKE AHEAD
Store cookies in an airtight container for up to 3 days. If icing, let icing dry and harden completely before storing.

SPIKED ROYAL ICING
Makes 2½ cups

3¾   cups (450 grams) confectioners' sugar
2½   tablespoons (22.5 grams) meringue powder*
6   tablespoons (90 grams) warm water (80°F/26°C to 105°F/41°C)
¾   teaspoon (3.75 grams) spiced rum
¾   teaspoon (3 grams) vanilla extract

1. In the bowl of a stand mixer fitted with the paddle attachment, beat confectioners' sugar, meringue powder, 6 tablespoons (90 grams) warm water, rum, and vanilla at low speed until well combined. Increase mixer speed to medium; beat until mixture is the consistency of toothpaste, 3 to 5 minutes. (See Note). Use immediately. (See PRO TIP.)

*Find meringue powder at Michaels or your local craft store.

Note: *Use gel food coloring to tint your Spiked Royal Icing. Gel food coloring won't affect the icing's consistency like liquid food coloring does. For green icing, tint Spiked Royal Icing with 1 to 2 teaspoons Wilton Gel Icing Color in Kelly Green.*

PRO TIP
It's the nature of royal icing to harden and dry out. If you're not using it immediately, cover the top of your icing with a damp paper towel to keep it fluid and fresh, but for no more than 1 hour. You can also put the icing in an airtight container.

SPECULAAS RUM BALLS

Makes 18 balls

A glorious cross between a cookie and a truffle, these rum balls are the buttery speculaas cookie take on a holiday classic. Loaded with rum and coated in white chocolate, this is a delicious no-bake entry to your cookie plate.

1½   cups (250 grams) finely ground speculaas cookies* (about 32 cookies)
¼   cup (56 grams) cream cheese, room temperature
¼   cup (30 grams) confectioners' sugar
2   tablespoons (30 grams) dark rum
1   tablespoon (15 grams) heavy whipping cream, room temperature
¼   teaspoon kosher salt
8   ounces (226 grams) white chocolate, chopped
Garnish: speculaas cookie crumbs, holly sprinkles

1. Line a baking sheet with parchment paper.
2. In the bowl of a stand mixer fitted with the paddle attachment, beat ground cookies, cream cheese, and confectioners' sugar until combined. Add rum, cream, and salt, beating until combined. Using a 1-tablespoon spring-loaded scoop, scoop mixture; roll into balls, and place on prepared pan. Cover and freeze for at least 1 hour or up to overnight.
3. In the top of a double boiler, place white chocolate. Cook over simmering water, stirring frequently, until melted and smooth. Remove from heat.
4. Insert a wooden pick into top of each frozen ball. Working with one at a time, dip into melted white chocolate, gently wiping bottoms on side of bowl. Return to pan, and let stand until chocolate is slightly firm, 3 to 5 minutes. Dip in melted white chocolate again, and return to pan. (If balls become soft, freeze for 10 minutes until firm again). Let stand until chocolate is set, about 10 minutes. Using a twisting motion, remove wooden picks.
5. Pour remaining melted white chocolate into a pastry bag, and cut a ³⁄₁₆-inch opening in tip. Drizzle balls with remaining melted white chocolate. Garnish with cookie crumbs and holly sprinkles, if desired. Refrigerate in airtight containers for up to 1 week.

We used Biscoff Cookies.

EGGNOG BRÛLÉE COOKIES

Makes about 12 cookies

Recipe by Spencer Lawson

This soft sugar cookie creates the perfect Christmas flavor we all know and love. Pair the spicy nutmeg and creamy eggnog with a crunchy brûlée top and have an impressive dessert that is deceptively easy.

1   cup (227 grams) unsalted butter, softened
1   cup (200 grams) granulated sugar
1   cup (220 grams) firmly packed light brown sugar
½   cup (120 grams) prepared eggnog
1   tablespoon (13 grams) dark rum
1   teaspoon (4 grams) vanilla extract
2   large eggs (100 grams)
3   large egg yolks (56 grams)
2   teaspoons (10 grams) baking soda
1   teaspoon (3 grams) kosher salt
1   teaspoon (2 grams) ground cinnamon
½   teaspoon (1 gram) ground nutmeg
5½   cups (688 grams) all-purpose flour
Garnish: granulated sugar

1. Preheat oven to 350°F (180°C). Line 3 baking sheets with parchment paper.
2. In the bowl of a stand mixer fitted with the paddle attachment, beat butter and sugars at medium-high speed until light and fluffy, 5 to 7 minutes, stopping to scrape sides of bowl. Add eggnog, rum, and vanilla. Beat at medium speed until well combined; scrape sides of bowl. With mixer on low speed, add eggs and egg yolks, one at a time, beating until combined after each addition. Beat in baking soda, salt, cinnamon, and nutmeg. Add flour; pulse mixer between "off" and lowest setting until combined. Increase mixer speed to medium-high, and beat until well combined, 1 to 1½ minutes.
3. Using a 3-ounce spring-loaded scoop, scoop dough (about 100 grams each), and roll into balls. Place 2 inches apart on prepared pans, and refrigerate for 10 to 15 minutes.
4. Bake, one batch at a time, until puffed and edges are set, 15 to 18 minutes. Let cool on pans until firm, about 10 minutes. Remove from pans, and let cool completely on wire racks.
5. Garnish cooled cookies with granulated sugar, if desired. Using a handheld kitchen torch, carefully brown sugar. Let cool completely. Store in an airtight container for up to 1 week.

ODE-TO-PANETTONE COOKIES

Makes 25 to 28 cookies

Recipe by Kimberlee Ho

These slice-and-bake spiced cookies are filled with citrus zest and speckled with dried candied fruit and raisins. Before slicing, brush the cookie log with brandy and roll in sugar for crispy edges and a sparkly holiday finish.

1   cup (240 grams) brandy or orange liqueur*
¾   cup (118 grams) raisins
½   cup (79 grams) dried fruit and peel mix*
1   cup plus 2 tablespoons (255 grams) cold unsalted butter, cut into ½-inch cubes
½   cup (100 grams) granulated sugar
¼   cup (55 grams) firmly packed dark brown sugar
2   tablespoons (6 grams) orange zest (about 1 medium navel orange)
1   tablespoon (3 grams) lemon zest (about 1 large lemon)
1   teaspoon (4 grams) almond extract
2¼ cups (281 grams) all-purpose flour
½   teaspoon (1.5 grams) kosher salt
¼   cup (50 grams) turbinado sugar or Demerara sugar
Gold sanding sugar (optional)

1. In a medium bowl, combine brandy or liqueur, raisins, and fruit and peel mix. Cover and let stand overnight.
2. In the bowl of a stand mixer fitted with the paddle attachment, beat butter, granulated sugar, brown sugar, orange zest, lemon zest, and almond extract at medium-high speed until super light and creamy, 3 to 5 minutes, stopping to scrape sides of bowl. Add flour and salt, and beat at low speed just until combined.
3. Drain raisin mixture, reserving soaking liquid. Add raisin mixture to dough, and beat at low speed just until combined. Divide dough in half, and place each half on a large piece of plastic wrap. Shape each half into a smooth 2- to 2¼-inch-wide log. Wrap in plastic wrap, and refrigerate for at least 2 hours.
4. Preheat oven to 325°F (170°C). Line 2 rimmed baking sheets with parchment paper.
5. On a plate, combine turbinado sugar or Demerara sugar and sanding sugar (if using).
6. Using a pastry brush, brush dough logs with reserved soaking liquid. Roll logs in sugar mixture. Cut each log crosswise into ½-inch-thick slices. Place about 1 inch apart on prepared pans.
7. Bake until edges are just beginning to brown, 15 to 18 minutes, rotating pans halfway through baking. Let cool on pans for 5 minutes. (See Note.) Remove from pans, and let cool completely on wire racks. Store in an airtight container for up to 4 days.

We used Grand Marnier and Paradise Holiday Fruit Old English Fruit & Peel Mix.

Note: *A 2½- to 3-inch round cutter can be used to form still-warm cookies into a more circular shape, if desired. Place cutter around 1 cookie; gently move cutter in a circular, counterclockwise motion while making contact with edges of cookie until desired shape is reached. Repeat as needed.*

> **MAKE AHEAD**
> Recipe can be prepared through step 3 and refrigerated for up to 1 week.

Photo by Kimberlee Ho

GLAZED FRUITCAKE COOKIES

Makes about 36 cookies

Studded with candied fruit and spiked with rum, these tender cookies are the from-scratch version of my grandfather's cookies. I finished them off with a Rum Drizzle to make them extra merry. From our family to yours, these cakey cookies are sure to become a part of your own holiday traditions.

1¼ cups (300 grams) spiced rum
½   cup (100 grams) finely chopped candied red cherries
½   cup (100 grams) finely chopped candied green cherries
½   cup (87 grams) finely chopped dried pineapple
½   cup (83 grams) finely chopped crystallized ginger
½   cup (85 grams) finely chopped candied orange
1   cup (227 grams) unsalted butter, softened
1¾ cups (350 grams) granulated sugar, divided
¼   cup (55 grams) firmly packed light brown sugar
2   large eggs (100 grams), room temperature
1   teaspoon (4 grams) rum extract
3½ cups (438 grams) all-purpose flour
1   teaspoon (5 grams) baking soda
1   teaspoon (3 grams) kosher salt
1   teaspoon (2 grams) ground nutmeg
1   teaspoon (2 grams) ground cinnamon
1   teaspoon (2 grams) ground ginger
½   teaspoon (1 gram) ground cloves
1   cup (113 grams) chopped toasted pecans
Rum Drizzle (recipe follows)

1. In a medium microwave-safe bowl, combine rum, cherries, pineapple, crystallized ginger, and orange, and heat on high until hot, 2 to 3 minutes; let stand at room temperature for at least 1 hour, stirring occasionally. Drain fruit mixture. Set aside.
2. Preheat oven to 350°F (180°C). Line 4 baking sheets with parchment paper.
3. In the bowl of a stand mixer fitted with the paddle attachment, beat butter, 1¼ cups (250 grams) granulated sugar, and brown sugar at medium speed until fluffy, 2 to 3 minutes, stopping to scrape sides of bowl. Add eggs, one at a time, beating well after each addition. Beat in rum extract.
4. In a medium bowl, whisk together flour, baking soda, salt, nutmeg, cinnamon, ground ginger, and cloves. Add flour mixture to butter mixture all at once; beat at low speed just until combined, stopping to scrape sides of bowl. Fold in fruit mixture and pecans. (Dough will be sticky.)
5. On a rimmed plate, place remaining ½ cup (100 grams) granulated sugar. Using a 2-tablespoon spring-loaded scoop, scoop dough, and shape into balls (42 grams each). Roll in sugar, and place 1½ to 2 inches apart on prepared pans. Using the palm of your hand, gently flatten balls to 1-inch thickness.
6. Bake until light golden brown and set around edges, about 12 minutes. Let cool on pans for 3 minutes. Remove from pans, and let cool completely on wire racks. Place Rum Drizzle in a pastry bag, and cut a ¼-inch opening in tip. Drizzle onto cooled cookies.

RUM DRIZZLE
Makes about ½ cup

1   cup (120 grams) confectioners' sugar
1½   tablespoons (22.5 grams) heavy whipping cream
1   tablespoon (15 grams) spiced rum
2   teaspoons (10 grams) unsalted butter, melted
¼   teaspoon kosher salt

1. In a medium bowl, stir together all ingredients until smooth. Use immediately.

Brian's grandad with his famous
Fruitcake Cookies

Brian and his grandad

STOLLEN MARZIPAN SHORTBREAD

Makes 24 cookies

Stollen, a classic German Christmas treat, packs booze-saturated fruit, ropes of marzipan, and warm, aromatic spices into a sweetened, yeasted bread loaf. This shortbread is a scaled-down affair, with rich, chewy Marzipan mixed directly into the dough and a buttery drizzle of Rum Glaze topping it off.

⅔ cup (150 grams) unsalted butter, softened
¼ cup (50 grams) granulated sugar
⅓ cup (100 grams) Marzipan (recipe follows)
1 large egg yolk (19 grams)
2 teaspoons (2 grams) orange zest
1 vanilla bean, split lengthwise, seeds scraped and reserved
2 cups (250 grams) all-purpose flour
¼ teaspoon kosher salt
⅛ teaspoon ground nutmeg
⅛ teaspoon ground ginger
Rum-Soaked Fruit (recipe follows)
Rum Glaze (recipe follows)

1. In the bowl of a stand mixer fitted with the paddle attachment, beat butter and sugar at medium speed until creamy, 3 to 4 minutes, stopping to scrape sides of bowl. Add Marzipan, and beat until well combined. Beat in egg yolk. Beat in zest and vanilla bean seeds.
2. In a medium bowl, sift together flour, salt, nutmeg, and ginger. With mixer on low speed, add flour mixture to butter mixture in 2 additions, letting first addition fully incorporate before adding the second. Stir in Rum-Soaked Fruit. Turn out dough, and shape into a 7-inch square. Wrap in plastic wrap, and refrigerate for 30 minutes.
3. Preheat oven to 325°F (170°C). Line a baking sheet with parchment paper.
4. Between 2 sheets of parchment paper, roll dough into a 9-inch square. Freeze for 15 minutes. Using a sharp knife, cut dough into 2¼x1½-inch rectangles. Place 1 inch apart on prepared pan. (If dough starts to soften, place back in freezer until firm again.)

5. Bake until lightly browned, 15 to 17 minutes. Let cool on pans for 3 minutes. Remove from pans, and let cool completely on wire racks. Pipe Rum Glaze over cooled cookies.

MARZIPAN
Makes about 1 cup

2¼ cups (216 grams) blanched almond flour
1½ cups (180 grams) confectioners' sugar
1 large egg white (30 grams)
2 teaspoons (8 grams) vanilla extract
2 teaspoons (8 grams) almond extract

1. In the work bowl of a food processor, place almond flour and confectioners' sugar; pulse until combined. Add egg white and extracts; process until mixture holds together. If mixture is too dry, add water, 1 teaspoon (5 grams) at a time. Wrap tightly in plastic wrap, and refrigerate for up to 1 month.

RUM-SOAKED FRUIT
Makes ¾ cup

¼ cup (32 grams) diced dried apricots
¼ cup (32 grams) dried cherries, halved
3 tablespoons (45 grams) dark spiced rum
2 tablespoons (24 grams) raisins
2 tablespoons (24 grams) golden raisins

1. In a small bowl, toss together all ingredients. Cover and let stand at room temperature overnight.

RUM GLAZE
Makes about ¾ cup

2 cups (240 grams) confectioners' sugar
3 tablespoons (45 grams) whole milk
2 tablespoons (30 grams) dark spiced rum

1. In a small bowl, stir together all ingredients until smooth. Use immediately.

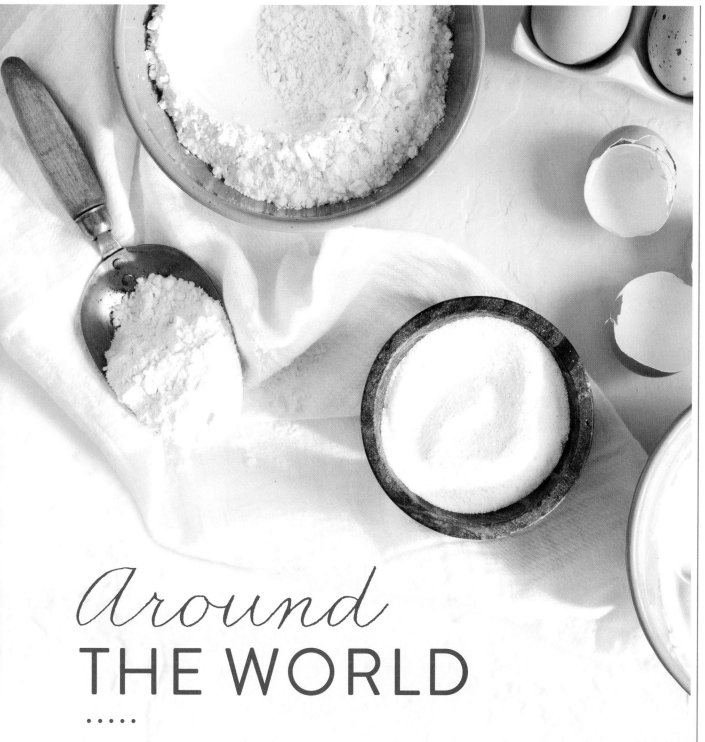

Around THE WORLD

· · · · ·

Take a trip without leaving your kitchen and celebrate
the holidays with flavors from around the world

ITALIAN RAINBOW COOKIES

Makes 32 (3x1-inch) bars

These tender cookies are made of brightly colored almond cakes layered with apricot preserves and topped off with a thin chocolate coating. Resembling the Italian flag, they were actually created in the United States by homesick Italian American bakers to commemorate their native land around the holidays.

5   large eggs (250 grams), separated and room temperature
1   cup (200 grams) granulated sugar, divided
8   ounces (226 grams) almond paste, cut into ¼-inch pieces
1   cup (227 grams) cold unsalted butter, cubed
1   teaspoon (4 grams) vanilla extract
1   teaspoon (4 grams) almond extract
2   cups (250 grams) all-purpose flour
¾   teaspoon (2.25 grams) kosher salt
30 drops (3 grams) red food coloring
20 drops (2 grams) green food coloring
⅔   cup (228 grams) strained apricot preserves
6   ounces (175 grams) 70% cacao bittersweet chocolate baking bars, chopped
1   teaspoon (5 grams) coconut oil
Flaked sea salt, for sprinkling

1. Preheat oven to 350°F (180°C). Line 3 (13x9-inch) baking pans with parchment paper, letting excess extend over sides of pan.
2. In the bowl of a stand mixer fitted with the whisk attachment, beat egg whites at medium-high speed until foamy, about 1 minute. Gradually add ¼ cup (50 grams) sugar, beating until stiff peaks form. Gently transfer to a medium bowl.
3. Clean bowl of stand mixer, and switch to the paddle attachment. Add almond paste to bowl. With mixer on medium-low speed, gradually add remaining ¾ cup (150 grams) sugar, beating until combined. Add cold butter, 1 tablespoon (14 grams) at a time, beating until well combined after each addition. Increase mixer speed to medium, and beat until fluffy, 2 to 3 minutes, stopping to scrape sides of bowl. Add egg yolks, one at a time, beating well after each addition. Beat in extracts.

4. In a medium bowl, whisk together flour and kosher salt. With mixer on low speed, add flour mixture to butter mixture, beating just until combined. (Batter will be thick.) Stir one-fourth of egg white mixture into batter. Gently fold in remaining egg white mixture in three additions until well combined.
5. Divide batter among 3 bowls (about 1½ cups [356 grams] each). Add red food coloring to first bowl; using a silicone spatula, fold until well combined. Add green food coloring to second bowl; using a clean silicone spatula, fold until well combined. Leave third bowl uncolored. Spread each batter separately in prepared pans.
6. Bake until layers begin to pull away from sides of pans, 10 to 12 minutes. Let cool completely in pans on wire racks.
7. To assemble, transfer green layer to a cutting board; spread half of preserves on top in an even layer. Top with uncolored layer; spread remaining preserves on uncolored layer. Top with red layer, and cover red layer with plastic wrap. Place an empty 13x9-inch baking pan on top; weigh down with cans. Refrigerate for 4 hours or up to overnight.
8. In a small microwave-safe bowl, heat chocolate on high in 10-second intervals, stirring between each, until melted and smooth (1 to 1½ minutes total). Stir in coconut oil until well combined.
9. Using a small offset spatula, spread chocolate mixture onto red layer. (It's OK if some chocolate runs down sides.) Gently tap cutting board on counter to smooth chocolate into an even layer. Refrigerate for 15 minutes. Using a warm serrated knife, trim edges. Cut into bars, dipping knife in warm water and wiping clean between each cut. Sprinkle with sea salt.

RED RUGELACH

Makes about 28 cookies

A spin on the classic Jewish baked good, this recipe transforms crescent-shaped rugelach into playful pinwheels. The zesty, fruity filling of these cookies gets a satisfying element of crunch from the addition of toasted walnuts, a burst of sweet from golden raisins, and a citrusy kick from the orange zest, and the enrobing pastry is blissfully crisp, light, and buttery.

2½ cups (313 grams) all-purpose flour
¼   cup (50 grams) granulated sugar
¾   teaspoon (2.25 grams) kosher salt
1   cup (227 grams) cold unsalted butter, cubed
8   ounces (226 grams) cold cream cheese, cubed
1   teaspoon (4 grams) vanilla extract
⅔   cup (75 grams) finely chopped toasted walnuts
½   cup (75 grams) finely chopped golden raisins
1   teaspoon (2 grams) packed orange zest
⅔   cup (213 grams) fruit preserves*

1. In the work bowl of a food processor, place flour, sugar, and salt; pulse until combined. Add cold butter, cold cream cheese, and vanilla; process just until large clumps form, about 20 seconds. (Do not overprocess.) Turn out dough onto a lightly floured surface, and shape into a 9x8-inch rectangle. Wrap in plastic wrap, and refrigerate until firm, about 30 minutes or up to overnight.
2. In a medium bowl, stir together walnuts, raisins, and orange zest until combined.
3. On a lightly floured surface, roll dough into a 15x10-inch rectangle, about ¼ inch thick. Spread fruit spread onto dough, leaving a ½-inch border on all sides. Sprinkle walnut mixture on top of fruit spread. Starting at one long side, tightly roll up dough, jelly roll style; pinch seam to seal. Wrap in plastic wrap, and freeze until firm, about 1 hour.
4. Preheat oven to 375°F (190°C). Line baking sheets with parchment paper.
5. Unwrap dough, and let stand at room temperature for 10 to 15 minutes. Using a serrated knife, trim ends in a sawing motion. Gently cut log crosswise into ½-inch-thick slices. Place at least 1½ inches apart on prepared pans. (If dough gets soft while cutting, freeze for 5 to 10 minutes.)
6. Bake until edges are lightly golden, 15 to 20 minutes. Let cool on pans for 5 minutes. Remove from pans, and let cool completely on wire racks. Store in an airtight container for up to 3 days.

We used St. Dalfour Four Fruits Spread.

CHERRY BELGIAN BISCUITS

Makes about 25 sandwich cookies

Belgian biscuits, also called Belgium biscuits, are thought to have originated in Germany but are most popular in British Commonwealth countries, particularly New Zealand. Traditionally, they consist of two spiced cookies sandwiched together with raspberry jam, topped with pink icing, and sprinkled with sugar. For this spin, a splash of rum extract is added to both the biscuits and the cherry preserves filling, making these biscuits particularly bright and merry.

1 cup (227 grams) unsalted butter, softened
⅔ cup (147 grams) firmly packed dark brown sugar
2 large eggs (100 grams), room temperature
3 teaspoons (12 grams) rum extract, divided
2½ cups (313 grams) all-purpose flour
1 tablespoon (6 grams) ground cinnamon
2 teaspoons (10 grams) baking powder
2 teaspoons (4 grams) ground ginger
¾ teaspoon (2.25 grams) kosher salt
¾ teaspoon (1.5 grams) ground cardamom
¼ teaspoon ground cloves
1¼ cups (150 grams) confectioners' sugar
2 tablespoons (30 grams) tart cherry concentrate*
Pink sparkling sugar (optional)
1 cup (320 grams) cherry preserves

1. In the bowl of a stand mixer fitted with the paddle attachment, beat butter and brown sugar at medium speed until creamy, 2 to 3 minutes, stopping to scrape sides of bowl. Add eggs, one at a time, beating well after each addition. Beat in 2 teaspoons (8 grams) rum extract.
2. In a medium bowl, whisk together flour, cinnamon, baking powder, ginger, salt, cardamom, and cloves. With mixer on low speed, gradually add flour mixture to butter mixture, beating until dough begins to clump together. Turn out dough onto a lightly floured surface, and shape into a disk. Wrap in plastic wrap, and refrigerate until chilled, about 1 hour.
3. Preheat oven to 350°F (180°C). Line baking sheets with parchment paper.
4. On a lightly floured surface, roll dough to ¼-inch thickness. Using a 2½-inch fluted round cutter, cut dough, rerolling scraps as needed, and place 1 inch apart on prepared pans.
5. Bake, one batch at a time, until tops are dry and edges are lightly golden brown, 10 to 12 minutes. Let cool slightly on pan for 5 minutes. Remove from pan, and let cool completely on wire racks.
6. In a small bowl, whisk together confectioners' sugar and cherry concentrate until smooth. Dip tops of half of cookies in glaze. Sprinkle with sparkling sugar (if using). Refrigerate until firm, about 10 minutes.
7. In a small bowl, combine preserves and remaining 1 teaspoon (4 grams) rum extract. Spoon ¾ teaspoon (12 grams) preserves mixture onto flat side of remaining cookies. Place glazed cookies, flat side down, on top of preserves mixture. Refrigerate in an airtight container until ready to serve.

We used Tart Is Smart Tart Cherry Concentrate, found in the fruit juice aisle of the grocery store or online.

DULCE DE LECHE BACI DI DAMA

Makes about 42 sandwich cookies

Recipe by Rebecca Firth

Baci di dama *are petite Italian sandwich cookies made with ground hazelnuts, and the cookie base has cocoa powder added for that perfect hazelnut-chocolate combination that we love so much. These cookies are chocolaty without being too sweet, and they melt and crumble once bitten. The Dulce de Leche Buttercream filling is so decadent, you'll want to eat it by the spoonful.*

1   cup (126 grams) raw hazelnuts, skinned and coarsely chopped
1   cup plus 1½ tablespoons (137 grams) all-purpose flour
⅓   cup (25 grams) Dutch process cocoa powder, sifted
⅓   cup (73 grams) firmly packed light brown sugar
¼   cup (30 grams) confectioners' sugar, sifted
½   teaspoon (1.5 grams) sea salt
¾   cup (170 grams) unsalted butter, cubed and softened
2   tablespoons (30 grams) whole milk
1   teaspoon (4 grams) vanilla extract
Dulce de Leche Buttercream (recipe follows)

1. Preheat oven to 325°F (170°C). Line several baking sheets with parchment paper.
2. In the work bowl of a food processor, pulse hazelnuts until finely chopped and they have the appearance of fine bread crumbs. Add flour, cocoa, sugars, and sea salt, and pulse until completely combined. Scatter butter on top of hazelnut mixture; add milk and vanilla, and pulse for about 30 seconds to combine. Using a spatula, scrape sides and bottom of bowl to make sure everything is combined. Shape dough into 1-teaspoon (6-gram) balls, and place 1 inch apart on prepared pans.
3. Bake for 10 minutes. Let cool on pans for 10 minutes. Remove from pans, and let cool completely on wire racks. Spread Dulce de Leche Buttercream onto flat side of half of cookies. Place remaining cookies, flat side down, on top of buttercream.

DULCE DE LECHE BUTTERCREAM
Makes about 2 cups

1¾   cups (420 grams) whole milk
¾   cup (150 grams) plus ⅔ cup (133 grams) granulated sugar, divided
¼   cup (60 grams) heavy whipping cream
½   vanilla bean, split lengthwise, seeds scraped and reserved
½   teaspoon sea salt, divided
¼   teaspoon (1.25 grams) baking soda
2   large egg whites (60 grams), room temperature
3   tablespoons (63 grams) corn syrup
¾   cup (170 grams) unsalted butter

1. In a large saucepan, whisk together milk, ⅔ cup (133 grams) sugar, cream, vanilla bean and reserved seeds, and ¼ teaspoon sea salt; bring to a boil over medium-high heat. Reduce to a simmer; whisk in baking soda. Cook, stirring occasionally and adjusting temperature to keep it from boiling (see PRO TIP), for 1 hour and 15 minutes to 1 hour and 30 minutes. Strain through a fine-mesh sieve into a heatproof bowl. (You will have about ⅔ cup.) Refrigerate in an airtight container until ready to use. (It will thicken more as it cools.)
2. In the bowl of a stand mixer, combine egg whites, remaining ¾ cup (150 grams) sugar, and remaining ¼ teaspoon sea salt; place bowl over a saucepan of simmering water. Cook, whisking occasionally, until mixture no longer feels gritty when rubbed between two fingers and an instant-read thermometer registers 155°F (68°C) to 160°F (71°C). Return bowl to stand mixer fitted with the whisk attachment, and beat at high speed until bowl feels cool to the touch, 5 to 6 minutes. Add butter, a piece at a time, beating until well combined after each addition. Beat until mixture is smooth, glossy, and voluminous. Beat in ⅓ cup (104 grams) dulce de leche; reserve remaining dulce de leche for another use.

Note: *The cookies come together quickly, but take note of the cook time for the dulce de leche in the buttercream so you can plan accordingly. You can also use store-bought dulce de leche in place of this homemade version.*

Photo by Rebecca Firth

PRO TIP
When preparing the dulce de leche, you just want some bubbles around the edges of the pan. After 30 to 45 minutes, the color will start to deepen and the mixture will begin to thicken a bit. When this happens, it'll be more prone to a heavy boil, which is bad, so continue adjusting the temperature as needed and stirring more frequently. This dulce de leche deepens and thickens faster than usual because of the addition of cream, so keep an eye on it. You want it to have a nice, thick consistency and a bronzed and deep caramel appearance.

LEBKUCHEN

Makes about 32 cookies

Inspired by the centuries-old lebkuchen recipe of Nuremberg, Germany, these large, cakey cookies are packed with a blend of warm spices and spiked with rum.

½   cup (113 grams) unsalted butter, softened
1½   cups (330 grams) firmly packed dark brown
         sugar
½   cup (170 grams) honey
2   large eggs (100 grams)
1   tablespoon (3 grams) lemon zest
1   tablespoon (15 grams) spiced rum
4   cups (500 grams) all-purpose flour
½   cup (48 grams) almond flour
3   tablespoons (15 grams) cocoa powder
1   tablespoon (6 grams) ground cinnamon
2   teaspoons (4 grams) ground ginger
1   teaspoon (3 grams) kosher salt
1   teaspoon (5 grams) baking powder
½   teaspoon (1 gram) ground cloves
½   teaspoon (1 gram) ground allspice
¼   teaspoon (1.25 grams) baking soda
¼   teaspoon ground mace
⅛   teaspoon ground cardamom
1   cup (240 grams) whole milk
128 whole blanched almonds
Rum Sugar Glaze (recipe follows)

1. Preheat oven to 325°F (170°C). Line 4 baking sheets with parchment paper.
2. In the bowl of a stand mixer fitted with the paddle attachment, beat butter and brown sugar at medium speed until fluffy, 3 to 4 minutes, stopping to scrape sides of bowl. Add honey, beating until combined. Add eggs, one at a time, beating well after each addition. Beat in lemon zest and rum.
3. In a medium bowl, whisk together flours, cocoa, cinnamon, ginger, salt, baking powder, cloves, allspice, baking soda, mace, and cardamom. With mixer on low speed, gradually add flour mixture to butter mixture alternately with milk, beginning and ending with flour mixture, beating just until combined after each addition. Using a 3-tablespoon spring-loaded scoop, scoop dough, and place 2 inches apart on prepared pans. Press 4 almonds, touching, into center of each dough ball. (Almonds will move apart as cookies bake.)
4. Bake until a wooden pick inserted in center comes out clean, 16 to 18 minutes. Let cool on pans for 5 minutes. Remove from pans, and place on wire racks. Using a pastry brush, brush tops of cookies with Rum Sugar Glaze. (If glaze gets too thick, heat in the microwave on high for 10 seconds, stir, and continue brushing cookies.) Let dry and cool completely on wire racks before serving.

RUM SUGAR GLAZE
Makes about ¾ cup

½   cup (100 grams) granulated sugar
¼   cup (60 grams) water
2   tablespoons (30 grams) spiced rum
1   cup (120 grams) confectioners' sugar

1. In a small saucepan, whisk together granulated sugar and ¼ cup (60 grams) water. Heat over medium heat, stirring occasionally, until bubbles form around edges of pan. (Do not boil.) Simmer for 3 minutes. Remove from heat, and whisk in rum. Sift confectioners' sugar over mixture, and whisk until smooth. (Clumps will form in your glaze if you do not sift.) Transfer to a microwave-safe bowl.

VIENNESE SANDWICH COOKIES

Makes about 18 sandwich cookies

Inspired by Gemma Stafford's take on the traditional Viennese whirl in her cookbook, Bigger Bolder Baking, *this recipe reimagines the British teatime favorite as holiday-ready sandwich cookies packed with mulling spices for a touch of warmth and filled with sweet, sophisticated Cherry-Port Buttercream.*

2   cups (454 grams) unsalted butter, softened
⅔   cup (80 grams) confectioners' sugar
2   tablespoons (16 grams) tightly packed orange zest
1½   teaspoons (3 grams) ground cinnamon
1½   teaspoons (3 grams) ground ginger
1½   teaspoons (3 grams) ground cloves
1   teaspoon (3 grams) kosher salt
1   teaspoon (2 grams) ground nutmeg
1   teaspoon (2 grams) ground allspice
½   teaspoon (1 gram) ground black pepper
3⅓   cups (417 grams) all-purpose flour
6   tablespoons (48 grams) cornstarch
Cherry-Port Buttercream (recipe follows)

1. Preheat oven to 350°F (180°C). Using a permanent marker, draw 12 (4x1-inch) rectangles on each of 3 sheets of parchment paper (36 rectangles total). Turn parchment over, and place on 3 baking sheets.
2. In the bowl of a stand mixer fitted with the paddle attachment, beat butter, confectioners' sugar, orange zest, cinnamon, ginger, cloves, salt, nutmeg, allspice, and pepper at medium speed until well combined and creamy, 2 to 3 minutes, stopping to scrape sides of bowl.
3. In a medium bowl, sift together flour and cornstarch. With mixer on low speed, gradually add flour mixture to butter mixture, beating until combined.
4. Place about 1 cup (247 grams) dough into a pastry bag fitted with a medium open star tip (Wilton 4B); pipe small dots of batter under

parchment to adhere to pans. Using drawn rectangles as guides, pipe dough in a zigzag pattern. (Dough will take some effort to pipe.) Repeat with remaining dough. Refrigerate for 15 minutes.
5. Bake until lightly golden and firm to the touch, about 14 minutes, rotating pans halfway through baking. Let cool on pans for 5 minutes. Carefully remove from pans, and let cool completely on wire racks.
6. Spoon Cherry-Port Buttercream into a large pastry bag fitted with a medium open star tip (Wilton 4B); pipe about 2 tablespoons (30 grams) buttercream onto flat side of half of cookies. Place remaining cookies, flat side down, on top of buttercream. Serve immediately.

CHERRY-PORT BUTTERCREAM
Makes about 2⅔ cups

¾   cup (170 grams) ruby port wine
¼   cup (80 grams) cherry preserves
1   cup (227 grams) unsalted butter, softened
½   teaspoon (2 grams) vanilla extract
¼   teaspoon kosher salt
4   cups (480 grams) confectioners' sugar

1. In a small saucepan, bring port and preserves to a boil over medium-high heat. Reduce heat to medium; cook, stirring occasionally, until mixture is reduced to ¼ cup, 15 to 20 minutes. Strain mixture through a fine-mesh sieve, pressing out as much liquid as possible; discard solids. Let cool completely.
2. In the bowl of a stand mixer fitted with the paddle attachment, beat butter at medium speed until smooth and creamy, 1 to 2 minutes. Beat in vanilla and salt. With mixer on low speed, gradually add confectioners' sugar until combined. Add 2 tablespoons (about 34 grams) cooled port mixture; beat at medium speed until fluffy and well combined, 1 to 2 minutes, stopping to scrape sides of bowl. Use immediately.

JAM-FILLED KOLACZKI COOKIES

Makes about 22 cookies

Popular throughout central and Eastern Europe around the holidays, these jewel-toned cookies consist of a tender cream cheese dough folded over your favorite thick preserves or jam and dusted with confectioners' sugar. This recipe is true to the original, save for one decadent detail: rather than dusting with confectioners' sugar, the cookies are drizzled with a creamy glaze for a festive touch.

½ cup (113 grams) unsalted butter, softened
4 ounces (113 grams) cream cheese, softened
1 cup (120 grams) confectioners' sugar, divided
2 teaspoons (2 grams) lemon zest (about 2 medium lemons)
¾ teaspoon (3 grams) vanilla extract, divided
1¼ cups (156 grams) all-purpose flour
½ teaspoon (1 gram) ground cardamom
½ teaspoon kosher salt, divided
⅓ cup (100 grams) thick jam or preserves
2 tablespoons (30 grams) heavy whipping cream

1. In the bowl of a stand mixer fitted with the paddle attachment, beat butter and cream cheese at medium speed until smooth and well combined, about 1 minute, stopping to scrape sides of bowl. Add ⅓ cup (40 grams) confectioners' sugar, lemon zest, and ½ teaspoon (2 grams) vanilla; beat at medium speed until well combined, about 1 minute.
2. In a medium bowl, whisk together flour, cardamom, and ¼ teaspoon salt. With mixer on low speed, gradually add flour mixture to butter mixture, beating just until combined. (Dough will be sticky.) Shape dough into a 5½-inch square, about ¾ inch thick, and wrap in plastic wrap. Refrigerate until firm, at least 2 hours or overnight.
3. Preheat oven to 350°F (180°C). Line baking sheets with parchment paper.
4. On a heavily floured surface, roll dough to ⅛-inch thickness, lightly flouring dough and work surface as needed. (If dough is refrigerated overnight, let stand at room temperature until softened, 10 to 15 minutes, if needed). Using a 2½-inch square cutter, cut dough, rerolling scraps as necessary. Using a large offset or flat metal spatula, place on prepared pans.
5. Spread about ¾ teaspoon (4.5 grams) jam on each square, leaving about a ¼-inch border. Fold 2 opposite corners of dough over jam, and press together lightly to seal, using a small amount of water to adhere. Repeat with remaining cookies.
6. Bake until lightly golden, about 12 minutes. Let cool on pans for 2 minutes; remove from pans, and let cool completely on wire racks.
7. In a small bowl, stir together cream, remaining ⅔ cup (80 grams) confectioners' sugar, remaining ¼ teaspoon salt, and remaining ¼ teaspoon (1 gram) vanilla until smooth; spoon into a small piping bag, and cut a ¼-inch opening in tip. Drizzle glaze onto cookies.

CASADINHOS

Makes 35 to 40 sandwich cookies

Derived from the Portuguese word for "married," these sandwich cookies are a staple at Brazilian weddings. Speckled with warm spice and spiked with rum, the tender butter cookies are joined by a sweet-tart guava jam, symbolizing the union of two people through marriage. Commonly filled with guava paste, casadinhos are so beloved in Brazil that they're also baked for any special occasion.

1   cup (227 grams) unsalted butter, softened
⅔   cup (133 grams) granulated sugar
1   large egg (50 grams), room temperature
2   large egg yolks (37 grams), room temperature
2   tablespoons (30 grams) spiced rum
1   tablespoon (13 grams) vanilla extract
2   cups (250 grams) all-purpose flour
1   cup (128 grams) cornstarch (see Note)
1   teaspoon (5 grams) baking powder
¾   teaspoon (2.25 grams) kosher salt
½   teaspoon (1 gram) ground cinnamon
¼   teaspoon ground allspice
1½ (14.1-ounce) packages (600 grams)
    guava paste, cubed
⅓   cup (80 grams) water
2   tablespoons plus 1 teaspoon (35 grams) fresh
    lemon juice
Confectioners' sugar, for dusting

1. In the bowl of a stand mixer fitted with the paddle attachment, beat butter and granulated sugar at medium speed until creamy, about 2 minutes, stopping to scrape sides of bowl. Add egg and egg yolks, one at a time, beating until well combined after each addition. Beat in rum and vanilla.
2. In a medium bowl, whisk together flour, cornstarch, baking powder, salt, cinnamon, and allspice. With mixer on low speed, gradually add flour mixture to butter mixture, beating just until combined. Divide dough in half; shape each half into a disk, and wrap in plastic wrap. Freeze until firm, about 2 hours.
3. Preheat oven to 350°F (180°C). Line baking sheets with parchment paper.
4. Unwrap one half of dough, and let stand at room temperature until slightly softened, 10 to 15 minutes. On a heavily floured surface, roll dough to ⅛-inch thickness; lightly flour dough and work surface as needed. Using a 2-inch fluted round cutter dipped in flour, cut dough, rerolling scraps as necessary, and place 1 inch apart on prepared pans. Repeat with remaining half of dough.
5. Bake, in batches if needed, until edges are lightly golden, 10 to 13 minutes, rotating pans halfway through baking. Let cool on pans for 2 minutes. Remove from pans, and let cool completely on wire racks.
6. In a small saucepan, combine guava paste, ⅓ cup (80 grams) water, and lemon juice; cook over medium heat, stirring occasionally, until melted and smooth. Remove from heat; let stand at room temperature or refrigerate until an instant-read thermometer registers 85°F (29°C).
7. Dust half of cookies with confectioners' sugar. Transfer guava mixture to a pastry bag fitted with a ¼-inch round piping tip (Wilton No. 10). Pipe about 1½ to 2 teaspoons (about 12 grams) filling onto flat side of remaining cookies. Place sugar-dusted cookies, flat side down, on top of filling.

Note: *Don't be alarmed by using a whole cup of cornstarch in your cookie dough. This ingredient helps create that signature melt-in-your-mouth casadinhos texture.*

"FOOD FOR THE GODS" BARS

Makes 24 bars

During the holiday season in the Philippines, these walnut- and date-studded bars are baked and given to loved ones as individually wrapped treats. The grand name (pagkain para sa mga diyos in Filipino) is thought to go back to the days of Spanish rule over the archipelago, when dates and walnuts were delicacies not many could afford, making them fit only for divine consumption. While we can't vouch for the accuracy of that story, we can confirm these bars are pure buttery bliss.

1½ cups (334 grams) bourbon
1½ cups (270 grams) packed whole Medjool dates
2 cups (440 grams) firmly packed dark brown sugar
1½ cups (340 grams) unsalted butter, melted
¼ cup (50 grams) granulated sugar
3 large eggs (150 grams), room temperature
1 teaspoon (4 grams) vanilla extract
1½ cups (187 grams) all-purpose flour, divided
1½ teaspoons (7.5 grams) baking powder
¾ teaspoon (2.25 grams) kosher salt
¾ cup (85 grams) roughly chopped toasted pecans
¾ cup (85 grams) roughly chopped toasted walnuts

1. Line a baking sheet with paper towels.
2. In a large microwave-safe bowl, heat bourbon on high until an instant-read thermometer registers 180°F (82°C), about 2 minutes. (Alternatively, in a small heavy-bottomed saucepan, heat bourbon over medium heat until an instant-read thermometer registers 180°F [82°C].) Stir in dates; let stand for 20 minutes, stirring occasionally. Drain dates, reserving liquid for another use, if desired. Spread dates on prepared pan, and pat dry. Remove pits; chop dates into ¼- to ⅓-inch pieces.
3. Preheat oven to 350°F (180°C). Line a 13x9-inch baking pan with parchment paper, letting excess extend over sides of pan.
4. In a large bowl, whisk together brown sugar, melted butter, and granulated sugar until well combined. Beat in eggs and vanilla until well combined.
5. In another large bowl, whisk together 1¼ cups (156 grams) flour, baking powder, and salt. Gradually fold flour mixture into butter mixture just until combined.
6. In a medium bowl, stir together chopped dates, pecans, and walnuts; add remaining ¼ cup (31 grams) flour, stirring until well combined. Fold date mixture into batter. Spoon into prepared pan, smoothing top.
7. Bake for 10 minutes. Reduce heat to 300°F (150°C); bake until a wooden pick inserted in center comes out clean and an instant-read thermometer inserted in center registers 205°F (96°C), about 40 minutes more. Let cool completely in pan. Using excess parchment as handles, remove from pan. Using a serrated knife, cut into bars.

FINNISH PINWHEEL COOKIES (JOULUTORTTU)

Makes about 24 cookies

Walking the fine line between a cookie and a tart, the joulutorttu *is a favorite holiday treat found in bakeries and homes across Finland. The traditional recipe calls for a prune preserve filling, but we opted for a bright, boozy cranberry and ruby port reduction.*

3   cups (375 grams) all-purpose flour
1   cup (227 grams) cold unsalted butter, cubed
1   teaspoon (3 grams) kosher salt
1   cup (225 grams) ricotta cheese
¼   cup (60 grams) whole milk
Cranberry Port Preserves (recipe follows)
Garnish: confectioners' sugar

1. In the work bowl of a food processor, place flour, cold butter, and salt; pulse until mixture is crumbly. Add ricotta and milk, and pulse until dough comes together. Divide dough into 3 equal portions. Shape each portion into a disk, and wrap in plastic wrap. Refrigerate overnight.
2. Preheat oven to 400°F (200°C). Line 3 rimmed baking sheets with parchment paper.
3. Working with one disk of dough at a time, roll dough to ⅛-inch thickness on a lightly floured surface. Using a 3-inch square cutter, cut dough, and place on prepared pans. On each square, make 4 (1-inch) cuts at corners diagonally toward center. Place 1 teaspoon (7 grams) Cranberry Port Preserves in center of each cookie. Fold every other tip over toward center, forming a pinwheel. Dab ends of tips with water to help adhere and prevent separation during baking.
4. Bake until edges are just barely golden brown, 11 to 12 minutes. Let cool completely on pans. Dust with confectioners' sugar, if desired.

CRANBERRY PORT PRESERVES
Makes about 1 cup

2   cups (210 grams) frozen cranberries, thawed
¼   cup (55 grams) firmly packed light brown sugar
¼   cup (60 grams) water
¼   cup (60 grams) ruby port wine

1. In a medium saucepan, bring all ingredients to a boil over medium-high heat. Mash cranberries, and reduce heat to low; simmer for 10 minutes. Pour mixture into a jar with a tight-fitting lid, and let cool completely. Refrigerate any leftover cranberry preserves for up to 2 weeks. (Leftover hot preserves can be transferred to sterilized jars, water bath processed for 10 minutes, and stored for up to 6 months.)

DANISH BUTTER COOKIES

Makes 15 to 20 cookies

Recipe by Joshua Weissman

This is a homemade rendition of the classic Royal Dansk cookies that are ubiquitous during the holidays. The crisp cookies come in all sorts of shapes and textures in a round blue tin. With a snappy crunch and buttery background flavor, this from-scratch version has even better flavor and richness.

¾   cup plus 1 tablespoon (184 grams) unsalted
      butter, softened
¾   cup (150 grams) granulated sugar
2   tablespoons (26 grams) vanilla extract
3   large eggs (150 grams), divided
1¾ cups (219 grams) all-purpose flour*
1   teaspoon (3 grams) kosher salt
Gold sparkling sugar, for sprinkling

1. In the bowl of a stand mixer fitted with the paddle attachment, beat butter, granulated sugar, and vanilla at medium speed until creamy, 2 to 3 minutes, stopping to scrape sides of bowl. Add 2 eggs (100 grams), one at a time, beating well after each addition.
2. With mixer on low speed, gradually add flour and salt, beating until a cohesive dough forms. Turn out dough, and use a bench scraper to divide into thirds. Shape each piece into a disk, and wrap in plastic wrap. Refrigerate until firm, about 2½ hours.
3. Preheat oven to 350°F (180°C). Line baking sheets with parchment paper.
4. Remove one disk of dough from refrigerator, and let stand at room temperature until slightly softened, about 5 minutes. Between 2 sheets of lightly floured parchment paper, roll dough to ¼-inch thickness. Remove top sheet of parchment. Using a 2¾-inch round cutter, cut dough, and place on prepared pans. Using a 1-inch round cutter, cut centers from cookies. Repeat with remaining dough.
5. In a small bowl, lightly whisk remaining 1 egg (50 grams). Brush egg wash onto cookies, and sprinkle with sparkling sugar. Freeze until firm, about 12 minutes.
6. Bake until edges are just beginning to brown, 10 to 15 minutes. Let cool completely on wire racks. Store in an airtight container.

*I used Bob's Red Mill All-Purpose Flour.

Photo by Joshua Weissman

MILANESINI

Makes 50 to 60 cookies

Recipe by Sarah Brunella

Originating at the end of the 18th century, Milanesini are one of the most beloved Christmas cookies in Switzerland, where you can purchase them by the bag in various shapes. The citrusy, crunchy cookies taste even better when made from scratch.

1   cup (227 grams) unsalted butter, softened
1   cup (200 grams) granulated sugar
2   large eggs (100 grams), room temperature
½   teaspoon (1.5 grams) kosher salt
4   cups (500 grams) all-purpose flour
2   teaspoons (2 grams) lemon zest
Lemon Glaze (recipe follows)

1. In the bowl of a stand mixer fitted with the paddle attachment, beat butter, sugar, eggs, and salt at low speed until well combined, about 30 seconds. With mixer on medium-low speed, gradually add flour and zest, beating until a dough starts to form. Turn out dough, and knead for a few seconds. Shape into a ball, and wrap in plastic wrap. Refrigerate until firm, about 1 hour.
2. Preheat oven to 400°F (200°C). Line baking sheets with parchment paper.
3. On a heavily floured surface, roll dough to ⅛-inch thickness. Using various star-shaped cutters, cut dough, and place on prepared pans. Refrigerate for at least 15 minutes.
4. Bake for 10 to 12 minutes. Let cool on pans for 10 minutes. Dip cookies in Lemon Glaze, and let cool completely on wire racks.

LEMON GLAZE
Makes ⅔ cup

1½ cups (180 grams) confectioners' sugar
3   tablespoons (45 grams) fresh lemon juice
Yellow gel paste food coloring

1. In a small bowl, stir together confectioners' sugar and lemon juice with a fork until smooth. Add food coloring, stirring to combine.

Photo by Sarah Brunella

ORANGE-VANILLA JAM RIBBONS

Makes about 36 cookies

Taking a cue from the traditional Finnish raspberry ribbons, this dough is formed into a log that receives a sweet channel of jam; then it's baked and sliced to form crunchy, jam-filled cookies. In a departure from the original recipe, we added orange zest to the dough and have both apricot preserves and raspberry jam represented.

¾ cup (170 grams) unsalted butter, softened
½ cup (100 grams) granulated sugar
¼ cup (30 grams) confectioners' sugar
¼ teaspoon packed orange zest
1 large egg (50 grams), room temperature
1½ teaspoons (9 grams) vanilla bean paste
2 cups (250 grams) all-purpose flour
½ teaspoon (2.5 grams) baking powder
¼ teaspoon kosher salt
4 tablespoons (64 grams) seedless raspberry jam or apricot preserves*
Orange Glaze (recipe follows)

1. Preheat oven to 350°F (180°C).
2. In the bowl of a stand mixer fitted with the paddle attachment, beat butter, sugars, and orange zest at medium speed until creamy, about 2 minutes, stopping to scrape sides of bowl. Beat in egg and vanilla bean paste until combined.
3. In a medium bowl, whisk together flour, baking powder, and salt. Add flour mixture to butter mixture all at once; beat at low speed just until combined.
4. Turn out dough onto a clean surface, and divide into 4 portions (about 148 grams each). Roll each portion into a 10-inch log (about 1 inch thick).

Place logs 1½ to 2 inches apart on a sheet of parchment paper; flatten each log until about 1¼ inches wide. Using a thin rounded spoon handle or a finger, make a ¾-inch-wide, ¼-inch-deep channel lengthwise down center of each log. (Dough logs will now be about 1½ inches wide.) Transfer dough logs, still on parchment, to a baking sheet.
5. In a small bowl, whisk jam or preserves until smooth; spoon into a small pastry bag or resealable plastic bag, and cut a ½-inch opening in tip or corner. Pipe jam or preserves into channels (about 1 tablespoon [16 grams] each), spreading into an even layer as needed.
6. Bake until edges are lightly golden, 10 to 15 minutes. Let cool on pans for 5 minutes. Using a serrated knife, cut logs diagonally crosswise into 1-inch-thick strips, wiping knife clean between cuts. Transfer to a wire rack set over a parchment paper-lined baking sheet; let cool completely.
7. Spoon Orange Glaze into a small pastry bag or resealable plastic bag; cut a ¼-inch opening in tip or corner. Drizzle glaze onto cooled cookies; let stand until set, about 15 minutes.

We used Smucker's Seedless Red Raspberry Jam and Apricot Preserves.

ORANGE GLAZE
Makes about ⅓ cup

1 cup (120 grams) confectioners' sugar
1½ tablespoons (22.5 grams) fresh orange juice

1. In a small bowl, stir together confectioners' sugar and orange juice until smooth and well combined. Use immediately.

PINKY BAR COOKIES

Makes about 16 cookies

Recipe by Erin Clarkson

This is a cookie version of a classic New Zealand candy bar Erin's grandfather always gave her at Christmastime when she was growing up. The Cadbury Pinky bar is made up of a fluffy pink marshmallow, a thin layer of caramel, and a coating of milk chocolate. She added freeze-dried raspberry powder into the marshmallow.

1   cup plus 1½ tablespoons (248 grams) unsalted butter, softened
¾   cup plus 4 teaspoons (98 grams) confectioners' sugar, sifted
½   teaspoon (2 grams) vanilla extract
¼   teaspoon kosher salt
2⅛   cups (265 grams) all-purpose flour
⅔   cup plus 1 tablespoon (55 grams) Dutch process cocoa powder
Salted Caramel Sauce (recipe follows)
Raspberry Marshmallow (recipe follows)

1. In the bowl of a stand mixer fitted with the paddle attachment, beat butter, confectioners' sugar, vanilla, and salt at medium speed until creamy, 2 to 3 minutes, stopping to scrape sides of bowl. With mixer on low speed, add flour and cocoa, beating just until combined.
2. Cut 2 (18x13-inch) sheets of parchment paper. Turn out dough onto 1 sheet of parchment, and flatten into a rough rectangle. Top with second sheet of parchment, smoothing down well. Roll to ¼-inch thickness. (Remove top sheet, and smooth down again if you are getting wrinkles.) Transfer dough between parchment to a half sheet pan. Freeze until completely solid, 20 to 30 minutes.
3. Preheat oven to 350°F (180°C). Line 2 baking sheets with parchment paper.
4. Remove dough from freezer, and remove top sheet of parchment. Using a 2¼-inch round cutter, cut dough, and carefully place on prepared pans, leaving a little room between each. (They do not spread much.) If at any point your dough gets hard to work with or gets too soft, place in freezer again for 5 minutes to firm up. Reroll any scraps, refreeze, and cut out more rounds. Repeat until you have used all dough.
5. Bake, one batch at a time, until set, 11 to 12 minutes. Let cool on pans for 15 minutes. Remove from pans, and let cool completely on wire racks.

6. Generously spread Salted Caramel Sauce onto flat side of half of cookies. Freeze until caramel firms up, about 5 minutes. Place Raspberry Marshmallow in a large pastry bag fitted with a large round tip, such as an Ateco #807. Holding pastry bag straight up and down about 1 inch from cookie, pipe a blob of Raspberry Marshmallow wide enough to cover caramel, bearing in mind that when you sandwich it, it will spread out slightly. Place remaining cookies, flat side down, on top of marshmallow. (Do one to start to test the amount of marshmallow you are piping on to make sure you are happy with it.) Repeat piping process with remaining cookies. Let stand until marshmallow is set, 1 to 2 hours. Refrigerate in an airtight container. These cookies are best eaten on the day they are made.

Note: *Chocolate shortbread dough can be made ahead of time and stored rolled out in freezer until you are ready to use.*

SALTED CARAMEL SAUCE
Makes 1¼ cups

½   cup (120 grams) heavy whipping cream
1   cup (200 grams) granulated sugar
6   tablespoons (84 grams) unsalted butter, cubed and softened
1   teaspoon (3 grams) kosher salt

1. In a small saucepan, heat cream over low heat, watching carefully to ensure it warms but does not burn.
2. In a medium heavy-bottomed saucepan, heat sugar over medium heat, stirring constantly. (Sugar will clump as you heat, but continue to stir, and it will soon smooth out.) Cook until sugar turns amber colored; remove from heat, and immediately add butter. (Use caution as it may bubble.) Whisk vigorously until all butter is incorporated; add hot cream, and whisk until well combined and emulsified. Stir in salt. Transfer to a jar or other container, and let cool to room temperature. Refrigerate until ready to use.

PRO TIP

For Salted Caramel Sauce, have everything ready to go because things move quickly once the sugar is ready. Salted Caramel Sauce needs time to cool, so ensure that you allow enough time for this.

RASPBERRY MARSHMALLOW
Makes about 5 cups

½   cup plus 2 tablespoons (150 grams) cold water, divided

3½   teaspoons (14 grams) unflavored gelatin

2¼   cups plus 1½ tablespoons (468 grams) granulated sugar

¼   cup plus 1 tablespoon (106 grams) light corn syrup

2   tablespoons (18 grams) freeze-dried raspberry powder

1   tablespoon (18 grams) vanilla bean paste or 1 vanilla bean, split lengthwise, seeds scraped and reserved

1   tablespoon (15 grams) liquid red food coloring

1. In the bowl of a stand mixer fitted with the whisk attachment, stir together ¼ cup plus 1 tablespoon (75 grams) cold water and gelatin by hand. Let stand until softened, about 5 minutes.

2. In a medium heavy-bottomed saucepan, heat sugar, corn syrup, raspberry powder, vanilla bean paste, and remaining ¼ cup plus 1 tablespoon (75 grams) cold water over medium heat. Cook, stirring occasionally, until a candy thermometer registers 240°F (116°C). Remove from heat, and let cool to 210°F (99°C).

3. With mixer on medium speed, break up gelatin slightly. Add sugar syrup mixture in a slow, steady stream. Increase mixer speed to high, and beat until marshmallow is doubled in size, holds a small peak, and is fluffy, 5 to 7 minutes, adding food coloring during last 1 minute. Use immediately. Leftovers can be piped into a greased dish and allowed to cure to be used for Raspberry Marshmallows.

Note: *It is especially important to make this marshmallow recipe using grams—with all the sticky ingredients, such as corn syrup, it is much easier to weigh them all directly into the saucepan and mixing bowl.*

Photo by Erin Clarkson

Spice
IS NICE

· · · · ·

It wouldn't be holiday baking without warm winter spices, and these
cookies turn up the heat with chai spice, ginger, five-spice, and more

FIVE-SPICE CRANBERRY JAM THUMBPRINT COOKIES

Makes 21 cookies

Recipe by Rebecca Firth

These little thumbprint cookies are a cinch to throw together and require zero fridge time. The Five-Spice Cranberry Jam is a holiday favorite—consider making extra to serve with your next cocktail hour cheese board!

½   cup (113 grams) unsalted butter, softened and cut into 8 pieces
½   cup (100 grams) granulated sugar
1   large egg yolk (19 grams), room temperature
2   tablespoons (30 grams) whole milk, room temperature
1   teaspoon (4 grams) almond extract
1   cup (125 grams) all-purpose flour
½   cup (64 grams) bread flour
½   teaspoon (2.5 grams) baking powder
½   teaspoon (1.5 grams) sea salt
½   cup (60 grams) confectioners' sugar
Five-Spice Cranberry Jam (recipe follows)

1. Position oven rack in center of oven. Preheat oven to 350°F (180°C). Line several baking sheets with parchment paper.
2. In the bowl of a stand mixer fitted with the paddle attachment, beat butter and granulated sugar at medium speed until light and fluffy, 4 to 5 minutes, stopping to scrape sides of bowl. Add egg yolk, milk, and almond extract, and beat at low speed for 1 minute.
3. In a medium bowl, whisk together flours, baking powder, and salt. Add flour mixture to butter mixture, and beat at low speed until dough comes together, stopping to scrape sides and bottom of bowl. Using a 1-tablespoon spring-loaded scoop, scoop dough, and roll into balls; place 2 inches apart on prepared pans. Using your thumb, press down center of each dough ball. Freeze or refrigerate for 10 minutes.

4. Bake, one batch at a time, until tops are dry to the touch, about 11 minutes. Using the curved end of a wooden spoon, immediately press down centers. Let cool on pan for 5 minutes. Remove from pan, and let cool completely on wire racks.
5. Sift confectioners' sugar over cooled cookies. Spoon 1 teaspoon (7 grams) Five-Spice Cranberry Jam into center of each cookie.

Note: *These are best served the same day they are made. If you want to prepare them ahead of time, wait to sift with confectioners' sugar and fill with the Five-Spice Cranberry Jam until just before serving.*

FIVE-SPICE CRANBERRY JAM
Makes about 1 cup

1½   cups (165 grams) fresh or thawed frozen cranberries
⅓   cup (67 grams) granulated sugar
2   tablespoons (12 grams) packed orange zest
¼   cup (60 grams) fresh orange juice
1   teaspoon (2 grams) Chinese five-spice powder

1. In a medium saucepan, bring cranberries, sugar, and orange zest and juice to a boil over medium-high heat. Reduce heat, and simmer until liquid is reduced, about 15 minutes. Using the edge of a spatula, mash cranberries. Stir in five-spice powder. Transfer to a heatproof bowl, and let cool completely before using. Refrigerate in an airtight container for up to 1 week.

Photo by Rebecca Firth

FRANGIPANE-STUFFED GINGER COOKIES

Makes 18 cookies

Stuffed cookies are just better. In this recipe, an aromatic ginger cookie dough gets a soft and chewy Frangipane Filling, pairing nutty decadence with warm spice.

⅓ cup (76 grams) unsalted butter, softened
⅓ cup (73 grams) firmly packed light brown sugar
¼ cup (50 grams) granulated sugar
¼ cup (85 grams) molasses (not blackstrap)
1 large egg (50 grams), room temperature
1¾ cups (219 grams) all-purpose flour
1 tablespoon (8 grams) cornstarch
1½ teaspoons (3 grams) ground ginger
¾ teaspoon (2.25 grams) kosher salt
½ teaspoon (2.5 grams) baking soda
½ teaspoon (1 gram) ground cinnamon
¼ teaspoon (1.25 grams) baking powder
¼ teaspoon ground cloves
¼ teaspoon ground cardamom
Frangipane Filling (recipe follows)
¾ cup (85 grams) sliced almonds, roughly crushed
½ cup (100 grams) sanding sugar or sparkling sugar

1. In the bowl of a stand mixer fitted with the paddle attachment, beat butter, brown sugar, and granulated sugar at medium speed until fluffy, 2 to 3 minutes, stopping to scrape sides of bowl. Add molasses and egg; beat until well combined, stopping to scrape sides of bowl.
2. In a medium bowl, whisk together flour, cornstarch, ginger, salt, baking soda, cinnamon, baking powder, cloves, and cardamom. Add flour mixture to butter mixture all at once; beat at low speed just until combined. Cover and freeze for 40 minutes.
3. Line a rimmed baking sheet with parchment paper.

4. Divide Frangipane Filling into 18 portions (about 7 grams each), and place on prepared pan. Shape each portion into a 1½-inch disk. Cover and set aside.
5. Preheat oven to 350°F (180°C). Line 2 baking sheets with parchment paper.
6. In a small shallow bowl, place almonds. In another small shallow bowl, place sanding sugar or sparkling sugar.
7. Divide dough into 36 portions (about 15 grams each); flatten portions into 2-inch disks. Place 1 Frangipane Filling disk in center of 1 dough disk; cover with a second dough disk, and crimp edges closed. Gently shape into a ball. Roll in almonds; roll in sanding sugar or sparkling sugar. (See Note.) Repeat with remaining dough and remaining Frangipane Filling. Place dough balls 1½ to 2 inches apart on prepared pans; gently flatten to ¾-inch thickness, pressing together any cracks in edges, if necessary. Sprinkle tops with sanding sugar or sparkling sugar.
8. Bake, one batch at a time, until edges are just set and bottoms are golden brown, 8 to 10 minutes. Let cool on pans for 3 minutes. Remove from pans, and let cool completely on wire racks.

Note: *If sliced almonds and sanding or sparkling sugar aren't sticking as well, lightly dampen hands with water before rolling and coating dough balls.*

FRANGIPANE FILLING
Makes about ½ cup

⅔ cup (64 grams) superfine blanched almond flour
2 tablespoons (24 grams) granulated sugar
2 tablespoons (28 grams) unsalted butter, cubed and softened
1 large egg yolk (19 grams), room temperature
½ teaspoon (2 grams) almond extract

1. In a small bowl, stir together flour and sugar until well combined. Add butter, egg yolk, and almond extract; stir until well combined, kneading together by hand if needed.

PEARL SUGAR GINGER COOKIES

Makes about 24 cookies

Pearl sugar saves the day again with these beautiful, polka-dotted ginger cookies. Acting as gorgeous decoration and a protective crunchy layer, pearl sugar helps make sure the cookies arrive to your far-flung loved ones in serious style. The molasses also helps the cookies stay fresher for longer, as the hygroscopic sugar keeps them moist.

½   cup (113 grams) unsalted butter, softened
¾   cup (150 grams) granulated sugar
¼   cup (55 grams) firmly packed light brown
     sugar
1   teaspoon (3 grams) lemon zest
⅓   cup (113 grams) molasses (not blackstrap)
1   large egg (50 grams), room temperature
2¼ cups (281 grams) all-purpose flour
2   teaspoons (4 grams) ground ginger
1   teaspoon (5 grams) baking soda
1   teaspoon (3 grams) kosher salt
¾   teaspoon (1.5 grams) ground cinnamon
½   teaspoon (1 gram) ground cardamom
½   teaspoon (1 gram) ground cloves
½   cup (104 grams) Swedish pearl sugar

1. Preheat oven to 350°F (180°C). Line 2 rimmed baking sheets with parchment paper.
2. In the bowl of a stand mixer fitted with the paddle attachment, beat butter, granulated sugar, brown sugar, and lemon zest at medium speed until fluffy, 2 to 3 minutes, stopping to scrape sides of bowl. Add molasses and egg; beat until well combined, stopping to scrape sides of bowl.
3. In a medium bowl, whisk together flour, ginger, baking soda, salt, cinnamon, cardamom, and cloves. Add flour mixture to butter mixture all at once; beat at low speed until combined, stopping to scrape sides of bowl.
4. In a small shallow bowl, place pearl sugar.
5. Using a 1½-tablespoon spring-loaded scoop, scoop dough (about 30 grams each), and roll into balls. Roll dough balls in pearl sugar (see Note), and place 1¾ to 2 inches apart on prepared pans.
6. Bake, one batch at a time, until cookies appear cracked and edges are just set but centers look slightly underdone, about 10 minutes. Let cool on pan for 4 minutes. Remove from pan, and let cool completely on wire racks. Store in an airtight container for up to 1 week.

Note: *If the pearl sugar isn't sticking as well, lightly dampen hands with water before rolling dough into balls and coating in sugar.*

GINGERBREAD CHOCOLATE CHIP COOKIES

Makes 22 cookies

Recipe by Edd Kimber

Nothing says the holidays more than spiced bakes, and very few recipes will please the crowd more than a soft gingerbread cookie. Because the cookies have both muscovado sugar and molasses, there is already a hint of bitterness in them, so when choosing your chocolate, you can go a little lower in cacao percentage than you might usually; even a milk chocolate would work wonderfully here.

1   cup (220 grams) firmly packed light
     muscovado sugar
1   cup (227 grams) unsalted butter, softened
½   cup (170 grams) unsulphured molasses
2   large eggs (100 grams)
4   cups plus 3 tablespoons (524 grams)
     all-purpose flour
2   tablespoons (12 grams) grated fresh ginger
2   teaspoons (10 grams) baking soda
2   teaspoons (4 grams) ground cinnamon
1   teaspoon (2 grams) ground ginger
½   teaspoon (1.5 grams) kosher salt
¼   teaspoon grated fresh nutmeg
11 ounces (315 grams) 60% cacao dark chocolate,
     roughly chopped
½   cup (100 grams) demerara sugar

1. In a large saucepan, heat muscovado sugar, butter, and molasses over medium-high heat until butter is melted and sugar is dissolved. Remove from heat; let cool for 30 minutes. Once cool, add eggs, whisking until well combined.
2. In a large bowl, whisk together flour, grated ginger, baking soda, cinnamon, ground ginger, salt, and nutmeg. Add sugar mixture, and stir with a wooden spoon until almost fully combined. Add chocolate, and stir until a uniform dough forms. Wrap in plastic wrap, and refrigerate for 2 hours.
3. Preheat oven to 375°F (190°C). Line 2 baking sheets with parchment paper.
4. Using a ¼-cup spring-loaded scoop, scoop dough, and roll into balls. Coat dough balls in demerara sugar. Place 2 inches apart on prepared pans.
5. Bake until set and lightly browned around edges but still soft in center, 10 to 12 minutes. Let cool on pans for 10 minutes. Remove from pans, and let cool completely on wire racks. Store in an airtight container for up to 3 days.

PRO TIP
For more melty chocolate on top of your cookies, press a few pieces of chopped chocolate onto the exterior of each dough ball right before popping them in the oven.

Photo by Edd Kimber

CHAI SPICE CRESCENT COOKIES

Makes about 23 cookies

Spice up your holidays with these chai spice-packed crescent cookies. This buttery, crumbly dough is flecked with a homemade chai spice blend and rolled in chai spice sugar after baking for an extra dose of warmth.

1   cup (227 grams) unsalted butter, softened
¾   cup (90 grams) confectioners' sugar
1   teaspoon (4 grams) vanilla extract
2½ cups (313 grams) all-purpose flour
2   teaspoons (4 grams) ground cinnamon, divided
1   teaspoon (2 grams) ground ginger, divided
½   teaspoon ground cloves, divided
¼   teaspoon kosher salt
¼   teaspoon ground cardamom, divided
¼   teaspoon ground black pepper, divided
1   cup (200 grams) granulated sugar

1. Preheat oven to 350°F (180°C). Line 2 baking sheets with parchment paper.
2. In the bowl of a stand mixer fitted with the paddle attachment, beat butter and confectioners' sugar at medium speed until creamy, 3 to 4 minutes. Beat in vanilla.
3. In a medium bowl, stir together flour, 1 teaspoon (2 grams) cinnamon, ½ teaspoon (1 gram) ginger, ¼ teaspoon cloves, salt, ⅛ teaspoon cardamom, and ⅛ teaspoon pepper. With mixer on low speed, gradually add flour mixture to butter mixture, beating until a dough forms.
4. Using a 1½-tablespoon spring-loaded scoop, scoop dough into balls (about 25 grams each). Roll each dough ball into a 4¾-inch log with tapered ends, and bend into a crescent shape, flouring work surface as needed. Place about 1 inch apart on prepared pans.
5. In a medium bowl, stir together granulated sugar, remaining 1 teaspoon (2 grams) cinnamon, remaining ½ teaspoon (1 gram) ginger, remaining ¼ teaspoon cloves, remaining ⅛ teaspoon cardamom, and remaining ⅛ teaspoon pepper.
6. Bake in batches until edges are just beginning to turn golden (not browned), 12 to 15 minutes. Sprinkle spiced sugar onto hot cookies. Let cool completely; dust with spiced sugar again. Store in an airtight container for up to 3 weeks.

CINNAMON SWIRL COOKIES WITH MAPLE BUTTER FROSTING

Makes 40 to 45 cookies

Recipe by Tessa Huff

These cinnamon roll-inspired cookies are packed with spice and draped with Maple Butter Frosting. The maple pays tribute to the season and pairs perfectly with the cinnamon.

1   cup (227 grams) unsalted butter, softened
1   cup (200 grams) granulated sugar
1   large egg (50 grams)
1   teaspoon (4 grams) vanilla extract
2⅔ cups (333 grams) plus ¼ cup (31 grams) all-purpose flour, divided
½   teaspoon (1.5 grams) kosher salt
¼   teaspoon (1.25 grams) baking soda
2   tablespoons (12 grams) ground cinnamon
¼   cup (85 grams) maple syrup
Maple Butter Frosting (recipe follows)

1. In the bowl of a stand mixer fitted with the paddle attachment, beat butter at medium speed until creamy, about 1 minute. Add sugar, and beat for 2 to 3 minutes. With mixer on low speed, add egg and vanilla. Increase mixer speed to medium, and beat until combined, about 2 minutes, stopping to scrape sides and bottom of bowl.
2. In a medium bowl, sift together 2⅔ cups (333 grams) flour, salt, and baking soda. With mixer on low speed, add flour mixture to butter mixture in two additions, beating until dough comes together in a loose, shaggy ball.
3. Turn out dough onto 2 sheets of parchment paper or nonstick baking mats. Divide in half, and roll each half into an 11-inch square, about ¼ inch thick. (Lightly dust with flour if dough becomes sticky while rolling.) Place dough on baking sheets, and refrigerate for 8 to 10 minutes (Do not chill the dough for too long, or it may crack when rolled.)
4. In a small bowl, stir together cinnamon and remaining ¼ cup (31 grams) flour. Stir in maple syrup to create a thin paste. Spread maple-cinnamon filling on each half of dough, leaving a ¼-inch border. Tightly roll up each portion of dough into a log. Wrap in parchment paper, and refrigerate until firm enough to slice, at least 2 hours.
5. Preheat oven to 350°F (180°C). Line 2 baking sheets with parchment paper.
6. Using a sharp knife, cut logs into ¼- to ½-inch-thick slices, and place 1 to 2 inches apart on prepared pans.
7. Bake until very lightly browned around edges, 12 to 14 minutes. Let cool completely on pans. Spread Maple Butter Frosting onto cooled cookies. Serve immediately, or store in an airtight container for up to 2 days.

MAPLE BUTTER FROSTING
Makes about ¾ cup

½   cup (113 grams) unsalted butter, softened
1¼ to 1½ cups (150 to 180 grams) confectioners' sugar
⅓   cup (105 grams) maple butter*
2   tablespoons (30 grams) heavy whipping cream
⅛   teaspoon kosher salt

1. In a medium bowl, stir unsalted butter with a small rubber spatula or spoon until smooth. Add 1¼ cups (150 grams) confectioners' sugar, maple butter, cream, and salt, and stir until smooth and creamy. Add remaining ¼ cup (30 grams) confectioners' sugar, if needed, stirring until frosting reaches a spreadable consistency. Use immediately.

*Available in specialty food stores or online.

PRO TIP
If making in advance, store unfrosted cookies in an airtight container for up to 4 days.

Photo by Tessa Huff

CARDAMOM HONEY CUTOUT COOKIES

Makes 36

This recipe is inspired by the holiday honey bread cookies of Croatia known as licitars. Since the 16th century, these brilliant red cookies have been displayed as ornaments and edible gifts during the Christmas season. Our warmly spiced adaptation pairs mellow honey with bold cardamom and swaps the traditional gelatin glaze with an easier-to-maneuver and tastier Vanilla-Almond Royal Icing.

½ cup (113 grams) unsalted butter, softened
⅓ cup (67 grams) granulated sugar
1 large egg yolk (19 grams)
2 tablespoons (42 grams) honey
¾ teaspoon (3 grams) vanilla extract
1½ cups (188 grams) all-purpose flour
¾ teaspoon (1.5 grams) ground cardamom
½ teaspoon (1.5 grams) kosher salt
¼ teaspoon (1.25 grams) baking soda
Vanilla-Almond Royal Icing (recipe follows)
Garnish: nonpareils

1. In the bowl of a stand mixer fitted with the paddle attachment, beat butter and sugar at medium speed until creamy, 3 to 4 minutes, stopping to scrape sides of bowl. Add egg yolk, honey, and vanilla, beating until well combined.
2. In a medium bowl, whisk together flour, cardamom, salt, and baking soda. With mixer on low speed, gradually add flour mixture to butter mixture, beating until combined. Divide dough in half, and shape into disks. Wrap in plastic wrap, and refrigerate for 1 hour.
3. Preheat oven to 350°F (180°C). Line 3 baking sheets with parchment paper.
4. Working with 1 disk at a time, roll dough to ¼-inch thickness on a lightly floured surface. Using desired 2½-inch holiday cutters, cut dough, rerolling scraps as necessary. Place on prepared pans. Freeze for 15 minutes.
5. Bake until lightly golden, 8 to 10 minutes. Let cool on pans for 3 minutes. Remove from pans,

and let cool completely on wire racks. Decorate as desired with Vanilla-Almond Royal Icing. Garnish with nonpareils, if desired. Let dry completely. Store in airtight containers for up to 1 week.

Note: *If decorating with the traditional Licitar colors, let red icing dry completely before adding white icing on top, or colors will bleed.*

VANILLA-ALMOND ROYAL ICING
Makes about 4 cups

4½ cups (540 grams) confectioners' sugar, divided
2 large egg whites (60 grams)
2 teaspoons (8 grams) almond extract
1½ teaspoons (6 grams) clear vanilla extract
¾ teaspoon (2.25 grams) kosher salt
½ teaspoon (1 gram) cream of tartar
3 tablespoons (45 grams) heavy whipping cream
Gel food coloring

1. In the top of a double boiler, stir together 4 cups (480 grams) confectioners' sugar, egg whites, extracts, salt, and cream of tartar. Cook over simmering water, stirring occasionally, until mixture registers 140°F (60°C) on a candy thermometer. Pour mixture into the bowl of a stand mixer fitted with the paddle attachment.
2. With mixer on low speed, add remaining ½ cup (60 grams) confectioners' sugar, beating until well combined and cooled to room temperature. Add cream, 1 tablespoon (15 grams) at a time, beating until desired consistency is reached. To test consistency, dip a spoon in frosting and lift, moving it in a figure-eight pattern over bowl as icing drizzles down. The figure-eight shape should disappear in 8 seconds for a cookie glaze and in 10 seconds for a thicker icing used for detail work. Color as desired with food coloring. Use immediately, or refrigerate with a piece of plastic wrap pressed directly onto surface for up to 2 days. Bring to room temperature, and stir before using.

VANILLA CHAI PINWHEEL COOKIES

Makes 40 cookies

Recipe by Becky Sue Wilberding

Vanilla and chai-spiced cookie doughs are swirled together in a hypnotizing spiral of simple sweetness and aromatic spice with festive sparkling sugar edges.

2¾ cups (344 grams) all-purpose flour, divided
2 teaspoons (4 grams) ground cinnamon
1 teaspoon (2 grams) ground cardamom
¾ teaspoon (1.5 grams) ground ginger
1 teaspoon (5 grams) baking powder, divided
1 teaspoon (3 grams) kosher salt, divided
¼ teaspoon ground allspice
¼ teaspoon ground white pepper
½ cup (113 grams) pecan halves
1 cup (227 grams) unsalted butter, softened and divided
½ cup (110 grams) firmly packed light brown sugar
3 large eggs (150 grams), divided
2½ teaspoons (10 grams) vanilla extract, divided
½ cup (100 grams) granulated sugar
¼ cup (50 grams) sparkling or turbinado sugar

1. Preheat oven to 350°F (180°C).
2. In a medium bowl, whisk together 1¼ cups (156 grams) flour, cinnamon, cardamom, ginger, ½ teaspoon (2.5 grams) baking powder, ½ teaspoon (1.5 grams) salt, allspice, and white pepper. Set aside.
3. Arrange pecans on a baking sheet, and toast until they start to deepen in color, about 8 minutes. Let cool slightly. Transfer to the work bowl of a food processor. Add 2 tablespoons flour mixture, and pulse until pecans are finely ground. (The flour will absorb the oils from the nuts and will prevent a nut butter from forming in the food processor.) Add pecan mixture to remaining flour mixture, whisking to combine.
4. In the bowl of a stand mixer fitted with the paddle attachment, beat ½ cup (113.5 grams) butter and brown sugar at medium speed until creamy, 2 to 3 minutes, stopping to scrape sides of bowl. Add 1 egg (50 grams) and 1 teaspoon (4 grams) vanilla, beating until combined. With mixer on low speed, gradually add flour mixture, beating until combined. Turn out dough onto a lightly floured surface, and shape into a disk. Wrap in plastic wrap, and refrigerate for at least 1 hour.

5. In the bowl of a stand mixer fitted with the paddle attachment, beat granulated sugar and remaining ½ cup (113.5 grams) butter at medium speed until creamy, 2 to 3 minutes, stopping to scrape sides of bowl. Add 1 egg (50 grams) and remaining 1½ teaspoons (6 grams) vanilla, beating until combined.
6. In a medium bowl, whisk together remaining 1½ cups (188 grams) flour, remaining ½ teaspoon (2.5 grams) baking powder, and remaining ½ teaspoon (1.5 grams) salt. With mixer on low speed, gradually add flour mixture to butter mixture, beating until combined. Turn out dough onto a lightly floured surface, and shape into a disk. Wrap in plastic wrap, and refrigerate for at least 1 hour.
7. Let doughs stand at room temperature until slightly softened, about 5 minutes. On a lightly floured sheet of parchment paper, roll vanilla cookie dough into a 16x12-inch rectangle, ⅛ inch thick. Transfer dough on parchment to a baking sheet. Refrigerate for 15 minutes. Repeat procedure with chai cookie dough.
8. Transfer vanilla cookie dough on parchment to a flat surface. Carefully invert chai cookie dough on top of vanilla cookie dough. Between sheets of parchment, gently roll over doughs a few times to press together. Peel away top sheet of parchment.
9. Starting at one long side, roll dough into a log, using bottom sheet of parchment to help lift and roll. (If dough cracks, stop rolling, and let stand for a few minutes until pliable.) Be sure to roll doughs together as tight as possible to avoid gaps. Tightly wrap in parchment paper, twisting ends to seal. Transfer to a baking sheet, seam side down. Refrigerate for at least 2 hours, or freeze until ready to use.
10. Preheat oven to 350°F (180°C). Line 2 baking sheets with parchment paper.
11. In a small bowl, whisk remaining 1 egg (50 grams). Brush log with egg wash, and sprinkle with sparkling or turbinado sugar. Roll back and forth a few times so sugar sticks to log. Using a sharp knife, cut into ¼-inch-thick slices. Place about 1 inch apart on prepared pans.
12. Bake on upper and middle racks of oven until edges are just beginning to turn golden, 12 to 15 minutes, rotating pans halfway through baking. Let cool completely on pans. Store in an airtight container for up to 2 weeks.

Note: *Dough can be refrigerated for up to 3 days or frozen for up to 1 month.*

Photo by Becky Sue Wilberding

BROWNED BUTTER-CHAI SPICE SNICKERDOODLES

Makes 18 cookies

Recipe by Annalise Sandberg

Browned butter adds a nutty depth of flavor to these snickerdoodles, and the addition of cardamom, ginger, cloves, nutmeg, and allspice along with the traditional cinnamon is a warm and cozy surprise.

1   cup (227 grams) unsalted butter
½   cup (100 grams) plus ⅓ cup (67 grams) granulated sugar, divided
½   cup (110 grams) firmly packed light brown sugar
2   large eggs (100 grams)
1   teaspoon (4 grams) vanilla extract
2¾   cups (344 grams) all-purpose flour
2   teaspoons (6 grams) cream of tartar
1   teaspoon (5 grams) baking soda
½   teaspoon (1.5 grams) kosher salt
Chai Spice Mix (recipe follows), divided

1. In a medium saucepan, melt butter over medium heat. Cook, stirring frequently, until butter turns a medium-brown color and has a nutty aroma, about 10 minutes. (Watch carefully so butter solids don't burn.) Pour into a heatproof bowl, and refrigerate until solid, 1 to 2 hours.
2. Let browned butter stand at room temperature until softened, about 30 minutes.
3. Preheat oven to 350°F (180°C). Line 3 baking sheets with parchment paper.
4. In the bowl of a stand mixer fitted with the paddle attachment, beat browned butter, ½ cup (100 grams) granulated sugar, and brown sugar at medium-high speed until pale and creamy, 3 to 4 minutes, stopping to scrape sides of bowl. Add eggs, one at a time, beating well after each addition. Beat in vanilla.

5. In a medium bowl, whisk together flour, cream of tartar, baking soda, salt, and ½ teaspoon (1 gram) Chai Spice Mix. Add flour mixture to butter mixture, and beat at low speed until combined.
6. In a small bowl, stir together remaining ⅓ cup (67 grams) granulated sugar and remaining Chai Spice Mix.
7. Using a 3-tablespoon spring-loaded scoop, scoop dough, and roll into balls. Roll in chai sugar, and place 2 inches apart on prepared pans.
8. Bake, one batch at a time, until slightly cracked and bottoms are starting to turn golden brown, about 13 minutes. Let cool on pan for 5 minutes. Remove from pan, and let cool completely on wire racks. Store in an airtight container for up to 5 days.

PRO TIP
To make smaller cookies, use a 1½-tablespoon spring-loaded scoop, and bake for about 11 minutes.

CHAI SPICE MIX
Makes 2¼ teaspoons

½   teaspoon (1 gram) ground cinnamon
½   teaspoon (1 gram) ground cardamom
½   teaspoon (1 gram) ground ginger
¼   teaspoon ground allspice
¼   teaspoon ground cloves
¼   teaspoon ground nutmeg

1. In a small bowl, whisk together all ingredients.

Photo by Annalise Sandberg

ICED GINGERBREAD CUTOUT COOKIES

Makes about 36 cookies

Is there a more classic holiday cookie than the gingerbread cutout cookie decorated with icing? With the quintessential blend of warm spices and a spritz of lemon zest to brighten the flavor, these cookies might become your new go-to.

1 cup (227 grams) unsalted butter, softened
¾ cup (165 grams) firmly packed dark brown sugar
¼ cup (50 grams) granulated sugar
1 large egg (50 grams), room temperature
1½ teaspoons (6 grams) vanilla extract
¼ cup (85 grams) unsulphured molasses
3 cups (375 grams) all-purpose flour
2 teaspoons (4 grams) ground cinnamon
1½ teaspoons (7.5 grams) baking powder
1 teaspoon (2 grams) ground ginger
¾ teaspoon (2.25 grams) kosher salt
½ teaspoon (1 gram) packed lemon zest
¼ teaspoon ground nutmeg
¼ teaspoon ground cloves
Royal Icing (recipe follows)

1. In the bowl of a stand mixer fitted with the paddle attachment, beat butter and sugars at medium speed until creamy, 3 to 4 minutes, stopping to scrape sides of bowl. Beat in egg and vanilla until combined. Beat in molasses just until combined, stopping to scrape sides of bowl.
2. In a medium bowl, whisk together flour, cinnamon, baking powder, ginger, salt, lemon zest, nutmeg, and cloves. With mixer on low speed, gradually add flour mixture to butter mixture, beating just until combined and stopping to scrape sides of bowl. (Dough will be slightly sticky.) Turn out dough onto a lightly floured surface. Divide dough in half (about 480 grams each), and shape each half into a disk. Wrap in plastic wrap, and refrigerate until firm, about 1 hour.

3. Preheat oven to 375°F (190°C). Line baking sheets with parchment paper.
4. On a lightly floured surface, roll half of dough to ¼-inch thickness. (Keep remaining dough refrigerated until ready to use.) Using desired 3½-inch holiday cutters dipped in flour, cut dough, rerolling scraps as needed, and place 2 inches apart on prepared pans. (Refrigerate dough if it becomes too soft when rerolling.) Repeat with remaining dough.
5. Bake until centers are slightly puffed and dry and edges are slightly golden, 6 to 8 minutes. Let cool on pans for 3 minutes. Remove from pans, and let cool completely on wire racks.
6. Place Royal Icing in pastry bag fitted with a coupler to switch between piping tips* as desired. Decorate cooled cookies with icing as desired. Store in an airtight container for up to 1 week.

We used Wilton No. 1, No. 3, and No. 4 piping tips.

ROYAL ICING
Makes 2½ cups

3¾ cups (450 grams) confectioners' sugar
2½ tablespoons (25 grams) meringue powder
6 tablespoons (90 grams) warm water (105°F/41°C to 110°F/43°C)

1. In the bowl of a stand mixer fitted with the paddle attachment, beat confectioners' sugar and meringue powder at low speed until combined. With mixer on low speed, add 6 tablespoons (90 grams) warm water in a slow, steady stream, beating until fluid, about 1 minute. Increase mixer speed to medium, and beat until stiff, 4 to 5 minutes. Refrigerate in an airtight container for up to 5 days.

CHAI SPICE SNOWBALL COOKIES

Makes about 25 cookies

We remixed the classic snowball cookie recipe by adding a touch of aromatic Chai Spice Mix.

1   cup (227 grams) unsalted butter, softened
1¾ cups (210 grams) confectioners' sugar, divided
1   large egg yolk (19 grams)
1   tablespoon (15 grams) bourbon
½   teaspoon (2 grams) almond extract
2¾ cups (344 grams) all-purpose flour
2   teaspoons (4 grams) Chai Spice Mix (recipe follows)
½   teaspoon (2.5 grams) baking powder
½   teaspoon (1.5 grams) kosher salt

1. Preheat oven to 350°F. Line 2 baking sheets with parchment paper.
2. In the bowl of a stand mixer fitted with a paddle attachment, beat butter at medium speed until smooth and creamy, 2 to 3 minutes, stopping to scrape sides of bowl. Add ¼ cup (30 grams) confectioners' sugar, and beat until well combined, about 1 minute. Beat in egg yolk. Slowly add bourbon and almond extract, beating until combined.
3. In a medium bowl, whisk together flour, Chai Spice Mix, baking powder, and salt. Gradually add flour mixture to butter mixture on low speed, beating until just combined. (Dough should be firm enough to shape, but still soft).
4. Divided dough into 25 portions (25 grams each). Roll into a smooth ball and place on prepared baking pans.

5. Bake until tops are light tan, and bottoms are lightly golden, 15 to 20 minutes. Let cool on pans for 5 minutes.
6. On a piece of parchment on the counter, place ½ cup (60 grams) confectioners' sugar in an even layer. Working in batches, place cookies on confectioners' sugar. Use remaining ½ cup (60 grams) confectioners' sugar to sift on top of cookies as needed. Use a fork to push confectioners' sugar around to cover any bare spots. Lift cookies with the fork, tapping on counter to remove excess sugar. Place on wire rack over parchment paper to cool completely. Reuse excess sugar to sift with as needed. Store in an airtight container.

CHAI SPICE MIX
Makes about ⅓ cup

3   tablespoons (18 grams) ground cinnamon
1½ tablespoons (9 grams) ground ginger
1   tablespoon (6 grams) ground clove
½   tablespoon (3 grams) ground cardamom
½   tablespoon (3 grams) finely ground black pepper

1. In a small bowl, stir together all ingredients. Store in an airtight container for up to 2 months.

SNICKERDOODLE BISCOTTI

Makes 24 to 28 biscotti

Recipe by Laura Kasavan

Golden cinnamon-sugar biscotti dipped in white chocolate make for a delicious spin on classic snickerdoodle cookies! These twice-baked cookies bake up lightly golden and make a scrumptious treat with a cozy latte.

1   cup (200 grams) granulated sugar, divided
½   cup (113 grams) unsalted butter, melted and slightly cooled
¼   cup (52 grams) brandy
3   large eggs (150 grams), room temperature
3   cups (375 grams) all-purpose flour
1½ teaspoons (7.5 grams) baking powder
½   teaspoon (1.5 grams) kosher salt
2   teaspoons (4 grams) ground cinnamon
10 ounces (283 grams) white chocolate, chopped

1. In a large bowl, whisk together ¾ cup (150 grams) sugar, melted butter, and brandy. Add eggs, one at a time, whisking until smooth after each addition. Stir in flour, baking powder, and salt until combined and no streaks of flour remain. Cover with plastic wrap, and refrigerate for 30 minutes.
2. Preheat oven to 350°F (180°C). Line 2 baking sheets with parchment paper.
3. Divide dough in half. Using moistened hands, shape each half into a 10x4-inch rectangle, and place on prepared pans. (Dough will be sticky; shaping with wet hands will help.)
4. In a small bowl, stir together cinnamon and remaining ¼ cup (50 grams) sugar. Sprinkle loaves generously with cinnamon sugar, gently pressing into dough.
5. Bake until pale golden, 24 to 25 minutes. Using parchment as handles, carefully remove from pans, and let cool on wire racks for 15 minutes. Leave oven on.
6. Using a serrated knife, cut loaves crosswise into about ¾-inch slices. Place slices, cut side down, on prepared pans.
7. Bake for 10 minutes. Turn slices, and bake until golden and edges are dry, about 10 minutes more. Let cool completely on pans.
8. In the top of a double boiler, melt white chocolate over simmering water until smooth and glossy. Dip bottom of cooled biscotti in melted white chocolate. Return dipped biscotti to pans. Refrigerate until chocolate is set, about 20 minutes. Store in an airtight container for up to 5 days.

Photo by Laura Kasavan

SALTED CARAMEL SNICKERDOODLES

Makes about 46 cookies

Recipe by Erin Clarkson

This recipe is inspired by one of Erin's favourite cookies—a giant cookie with melty pockets of salted caramel studded throughout. She added a holiday snickerdoodle spin on this, adding crushed caramel into the dough for extra chew, and rolling it in cinnamon sugar for a classic snickerdoodle taste.

Salted Caramel (recipe follows)
1   cup (227 grams) unsalted butter, softened
¾   cup (150 grams) granulated sugar, divided
¼   cup (55 grams) firmly packed dark brown sugar
1   large egg (50 grams)
1   teaspoon (4 grams) vanilla extract
2¾ cups plus 2 teaspoons (350 grams) all-purpose
     flour
½   teaspoon (2.5 grams) baking soda
½   teaspoon (1.5 grams) kosher salt
½   teaspoon (1 gram) ground cinnamon
Flaked sea salt, for finishing

1. Prepare Salted Caramel. Break into large chunks, and weigh out 1 cup (200 grams) caramel. Place into a resealable plastic bag, and break with a rolling pin until it forms small chunks. Set aside.
2. Place remaining Salted Caramel in the work bowl of a food processor; pulse until finely ground. Weigh out ¾ cup (150 grams) ground caramel. (The caramel, once ground, will pull moisture out of the environment very quickly and start to clump, so use the ground caramel fresh out of the food processor.)
3. Preheat oven to 350°F (180°C). Line several baking sheets with parchment paper.
4. In the bowl of a stand mixer fitted with the paddle attachment, beat ¾ cup (150 grams) ground caramel, butter, ½ cup (100 grams) granulated sugar, and brown sugar at high speed until creamy, 2 to 3 minutes, stopping to scrape sides of bowl. With mixer on medium speed, add egg and vanilla, beating until combined.

5. In a medium bowl, sift together flour, baking soda, and salt. With mixer on low speed, gradually add flour mixture to butter mixture, beating just until combined. Stir in 1 cup (200 grams) caramel chunks until evenly distributed.
6. In a small bowl, stir together cinnamon and remaining ¼ cup (50 grams) granulated sugar. Using a 1-tablespoon spring-loaded scoop, scoop dough, and roll into balls. Roll balls in cinnamon sugar mixture. Place 2 inches apart on prepared pans. Freeze for 5 minutes.
7. Bake, one batch at a time, until golden brown and puffed up, 11 to 12 minutes. Let cool completely on pans. Sprinkle with sea salt. Store in an airtight container.

Note: *If you do not want to bake all of these cookies at once, the dough, once rolled in the cinnamon sugar, can be stored in a resealable plastic bag in the freezer. Freeze until solid on a baking sheet before transferring to a bag.*

SALTED CARAMEL
Makes about 2 cups

2   cups (400 grams) granulated sugar
1   teaspoon (3 grams) kosher salt

1. Line a half sheet pan with a nonstick baking mat.
2. In a medium saucepan, heat sugar over medium heat, whisking occasionally, until sugar is dissolved. (Sugar will clump as you heat, but continue to stir, and it will soon smooth out.) Cook until sugar turns amber colored and is just beginning to smoke slightly. Immediately pour onto prepared pan, and sprinkle with salt. Let cool completely.

PRO TIP
Have everything ready to go for the Salted Caramel. There are a few seconds between a toasty caramel and a burnt sugar, so you want to be able to pour out the caramel as soon as it is ready.

Photo by Erin Clarkson

BIG ON
Bars
· · · · ·

Serving up the flavor of all your favorite cookies but without the hassle of shaping and batch-baking, these bars just need to be sliced and they're ready to serve

BUTTERSCOTCH MAGIC BARS

Makes 24 to 30 bars

Rich with butterscotch, coconut, toffee, and pecans, these bars have a little something for every holiday craving.

2 cups (204 grams) old-fashioned oats*
½ cup (48 grams) superfine blanched almond flour*
¼ cup (50 grams) granulated sugar
½ teaspoon kosher salt, divided
6 tablespoons (84 grams) unsalted butter, melted
4 ounces (113 grams) white chocolate, chopped (about ⅔ cup)
1 (14-ounce) can (396 grams) sweetened condensed milk, divided
2 cups (168 grams) sweetened flaked coconut
1 cup (170 grams) butterscotch chips
1 cup (113 grams) chopped toasted pecans
½ cup (85 grams) toffee pieces

1. Preheat oven to 350°F (180°C). Line a 13x9-inch baking pan with parchment paper, letting excess extend over sides of pan. Spray parchment with cooking spray.
2. In the work bowl of a food processor, pulse oats until finely ground, stopping to scrape sides of bowl. Add flour, sugar, and ¼ teaspoon salt; pulse just until combined. Add melted butter; pulse until well combined and mixture holds together when pressed, stopping to scrape sides of bowl. Using a small measuring cup or the bottom of a glass, press mixture into bottom of prepared pan.
3. Bake until top is dry, set, and fragrant, 10 to 12 minutes. Let cool on a wire rack for 15 minutes. Leave oven on.
4. Sprinkle white chocolate onto prepared crust. Reserve ½ cup (150 grams) condensed milk; drizzle half of remaining condensed milk over white chocolate. (Condensed milk does not have to completely cover crust; it will spread as it bakes.) Sprinkle with half of coconut, half of butterscotch chips, half of pecans, and half of toffee pieces. Drizzle with remaining condensed milk. Sprinkle with remaining coconut, remaining butterscotch chips, remaining pecans, and remaining toffee pieces. Pour reserved ½ cup (150 grams) condensed milk evenly over top; sprinkle with remaining ¼ teaspoon salt.
5. Bake until edges are just light golden brown, 24 to 28 minutes. Let cool completely in pan on a wire rack. Using excess parchment as handles, remove from pan, and cut into bars.

We used Bob's Red Mill Gluten Free Old Fashioned Rolled Oats and Bob's Red Mill Super-Fine Blanched Almond Flour.

PECAN STICKY BARS

Makes 16 bars

Recipe by Cheryl Norris

These chewy bars combine the flavors of cinnamon, butter, oats, and pecans with a caramel pecan topping. They're simple yet full of flavor.

¾   cup (94 grams) all-purpose flour
¾   cup (63 grams) quick-cooking oats
½   cup (100 grams) granulated sugar
¼   cup (28 grams) finely chopped toasted pecans
2   teaspoons (10 grams) baking powder
½   teaspoon (1 gram) ground cinnamon
½   teaspoon (1 gram) ground nutmeg
¼   teaspoon kosher salt
½   cup plus 1 tablespoon (127 grams) unsalted butter, melted, plus more for brushing
Pecan Caramel Topping (recipe follows)

1. Preheat oven to 350°F (180°C). Line bottom of an 8-inch square baking pan with parchment paper, letting ends extend over sides of pan. Brush sides of pan with melted butter.
2. In a large bowl, whisk together flour, oats, sugar, pecans, baking powder, cinnamon, nutmeg, and salt until combined. Add melted butter, and stir until no flour streaks remain. Transfer to prepared pan, pressing into bottom of pan.

3. Bake until edges are browned, about 20 minutes, rotating pan halfway through baking. Immediately pour Pecan Caramel Topping on top, spreading with an offset spatula. Let cool completely, 1½ to 2 hours.
4. Using an offset spatula, loosen caramel from sides of pans. Using excess parchment as handles, remove from pan, and cut into bars. Store with wax paper between layers in an airtight container for up to 3 weeks.

Pecan Caramel Topping
Makes 1½ cups

1   cup plus 1 teaspoon (225 grams) firmly packed light brown sugar
½   cup plus 1 tablespoon (127 grams) unsalted butter, room temperature
½   cup (120 grams) heavy whipping cream
2   tablespoons (42 grams) light corn syrup
2   teaspoons (8 grams) vanilla extract
½   teaspoon (1.5 grams) kosher salt
¼   teaspoon ground cinnamon
4   ounces (113 grams) pecans, coarsely chopped

1. In a 4-quart saucepan, heat brown sugar, butter, cream, and corn syrup over medium heat, whisking constantly, until sugar dissolves and butter is melted. Cook, stirring occasionally, until an instant-read thermometer registers 240°F (116°C). Remove from heat, and stir in vanilla, salt, and cinnamon. Stir in pecans. Use immediately.

Photo by Cheryl Norris

RED VELVET-CHEESECAKE SWIRL BROWNIES

Makes 12 brownies

All the classic flavors of red velvet cake, reworked into a brownie! These rich, red-tinted brownies get a lusciously tangy Cheesecake Swirl. With crisp edges, a gooey center, and a cream cheese twist to tie it all together, they're the perfect holiday treat.

12 ounces (340 grams) 60% cacao bittersweet chocolate, chopped
1 cup (227 grams) unsalted butter, cubed
1½ cups (300 grams) granulated sugar
1 cup (220 grams) firmly packed light brown sugar
2 cups (250 grams) all-purpose flour
¼ cup (21 grams) unsweetened cocoa powder, sifted
1½ teaspoons (4.5 grams) kosher salt
6 large eggs (300 grams), room temperature and lightly beaten
1 tablespoon (13 grams) vanilla extract
2 tablespoons (30 grams) red liquid food coloring*
Cheesecake Swirl (recipe follows)

1. Preheat oven to 325°F (170°C). Line a 13x9-inch baking pan with parchment paper, letting excess extend over sides of pan; spray with baking spray with flour.
2. In the top of a double boiler, combine chocolate and butter. Cook over simmering water, stirring occasionally, until melted and smooth. Turn off heat, and whisk in sugars until well combined. (Mixture will not be completely smooth.) Remove from heat, and let cool slightly, 3 to 5 minutes.
3. In a medium bowl, whisk together flour, cocoa, and salt.

4. Slowly add eggs to chocolate mixture, whisking until combined. Whisk in vanilla and food coloring. Fold in flour mixture just until combined. Reserve 1 cup (about 276 grams) batter in a small bowl. Spread remaining batter in prepared pan. Spoon Cheesecake Swirl on top of batter in pan, smoothing flat with an offset spatula. Dollop reserved batter by tablespoonfuls (about 35 grams) on top of Cheesecake Swirl. Using a wooden skewer, swirl layers.
5. Bake until top is shiny, edges are set, center jiggles slightly, and an instant-read thermometer inserted in center registers 165°F (74°C), 40 to 45 minutes. Let cool completely in pan. Refrigerate for at least 1 hour. Using excess parchment as handles, remove from pan, and cut into bars. Refrigerate in an airtight container for up to 6 days. Let come to room temperature before serving.

We used McCormick Red Food Color.

CHEESECAKE SWIRL
Makes about 2½ cups

16 ounces (454 grams) cream cheese, softened
1 cup (200 grams) granulated sugar
¼ cup (31 grams) all-purpose flour
2 large eggs (100 grams), room temperature
1 tablespoon (13 grams) vanilla extract

1. In a medium bowl, whisk cream cheese until smooth. Add sugar and flour, and whisk until combined; scrape sides of bowl. Add eggs, whisking well. Whisk in vanilla. Use immediately.

TIRAMISÙ CHEESECAKE BARS

Makes 9 bars

Recipe by Emma Duckworth

Layers of mascarpone cheesecake filling and Coffee Syrup-soaked ladyfingers sit on top of a traditional cheesecake crust. The digestive biscuit base provides the perfect foundation for this delectable cheesecake bar with a twist.

17 digestive biscuits* (250 grams)
¼   cup (50 grams) granulated sugar
1   teaspoon (2 grams) instant espresso powder
½   cup (113 grams) unsalted butter, melted
Mascarpone Filling (recipe follows)
14 ladyfingers or Savoiardi biscuits (120 grams)
Coffee Syrup (recipe follows)
1   tablespoon (5 grams) unsweetened cocoa powder
Garnish: unsweetened cocoa powder, grated dark
    chocolate, espresso beans

1. Spray a 9-inch square baking dish with cooking spray. Line pan with parchment paper, letting excess extend over sides of pan.
2. In the work bowl of a food processor, place digestive biscuits, sugar, and espresso powder; pulse until fine crumbs form. Add melted butter, and pulse until well combined and mixture resembles wet sand. Using your hands or the back of a spoon, press mixture into bottom of prepared pan. Refrigerate for 30 minutes.
3. Spoon half of Mascarpone Filling (about 540 grams) onto prepared crust, spreading with an offset spatula.
4. Dip a ladyfinger into Coffee Syrup, lightly coating all sides, and place on top of Mascarpone Filling in pan. Repeat with remaining ladyfingers until surface of filling in pan is covered. (You might need to break a few ladyfingers into pieces to fit.) Spoon remaining Mascarpone Filling on top of ladyfingers, and spread with an offset spatula. Cover with plastic wrap, and refrigerate for at least 6 hours or up to overnight.
5. Using excess parchment as handles, remove from pan. Trim edges, if desired. Garnish with cocoa, grated chocolate, and espresso beans, if desired. Using a large sharp knife, cut into bars, wiping knife clean between each cut. Refrigerate in an airtight container for up to 5 days.

We used McVitie's Digestive Biscuits.

MASCARPONE FILLING
Makes 3½ cups

1½ cups (180 grams) confectioners' sugar
1½ cups (360 grams) heavy whipping cream
1⅓ cups (300 grams) cold mascarpone cheese
1⅓ cups (300 grams) cold cream cheese
1   teaspoon (4 grams) fine salt
1   teaspoon (4 grams) vanilla extract

1. In the bowl of a stand mixer fitted with the whisk attachment, beat all ingredients at low speed until combined. Gradually increase mixer speed to high, and beat until thickened and smooth. (Watch closely; it can overwhip quite quickly due to the high fat content from mascarpone.) Use immediately.

COFFEE SYRUP
Makes about 1 cup

¾   cup (180 grams) hot water (105°F/41°C to
    110°F/43°C)
2   tablespoons (10 grams) instant espresso powder
2   tablespoons (30 grams) coffee liqueur* (optional)
1   tablespoon (12 grams) granulated sugar
1   teaspoon (4 grams) vanilla extract

1. In a medium bowl, whisk together ¾ cup (180 grams) hot water, espresso powder, liqueur (if using), sugar, and vanilla. (See Note.)

We used Kahlúa.

Note: *You will not need all of the Coffee Syrup for the bars. Refrigerate in an airtight container for up to 1 week.*

Photo by Emma Duckworth

SPICED CRANBERRY-WHITE CHOCOLATE BLONDIES

Makes 10 blondies

Don't be a square this holiday season. This spruced-up take on the traditional blondie formula features spices, white chocolate, and cranberries. Topped with a velvety White Chocolate Frosting, these bars will be on your to-bake list all year long.

1½ cups (330 grams) firmly packed light brown sugar
¾   cup (170 grams) unsalted butter, melted and cooled
2   large eggs (100 grams), room temperature
1   teaspoon (4 grams) vanilla extract
1½ cups (188 grams) all-purpose flour
1   teaspoon (5 grams) baking powder
1   teaspoon (3 grams) kosher salt
½   teaspoon (1 gram) ground nutmeg
½   teaspoon (1 gram) ground cinnamon
½   teaspoon (1 gram) ground ginger
¼   teaspoon ground cloves
5   ounces (142 grams) white chocolate, roughly chopped
½   cup (78 grams) roughly chopped dried sweetened cranberries
White Chocolate Frosting (recipe follows)
Garnish: assorted holiday sprinkles

1. Preheat oven to 350°F (180°C). Butter a 9-inch square baking pan; line pan with parchment paper, letting excess extend over sides of pan.
2. In a large bowl, whisk together brown sugar and melted butter until well combined; whisk in eggs and vanilla.
3. In a medium bowl, combine flour, baking powder, salt, nutmeg, cinnamon, ginger, and cloves. Fold flour mixture into sugar mixture just until combined. Fold in white chocolate and cranberries. Spoon batter into prepared pan; spread into an even layer using a small offset spatula.

4. Bake until golden brown and a wooden pick inserted in center comes out with just a few moist crumbs, 25 to 30 minutes. Let cool completely in pan on a wire rack.
5. Using excess parchment as handles, remove from pan. Cut in half, creating 2 rectangles. Cut each half into 5 triangles with 3-inch-wide bases.
6. Place White Chocolate Frosting in a large piping bag fitted with an open star piping tip (Wilton 1M); pipe frosting onto cooled blondies, working from tip to base of each triangle. Garnish with sprinkles, if desired.

WHITE CHOCOLATE FROSTING
Makes 2½ cups

⅔   cup (150 grams) unsalted butter, softened
7.5 ounces (215 grams) white chocolate, melted and cooled for 5 minutes
1¼ cups (150 grams) confectioners' sugar
¼   teaspoon vanilla extract
⅛   teaspoon kosher salt
Green gel food coloring*

1. In the bowl of a stand mixer fitted with the paddle attachment, beat butter at medium speed until smooth, 30 seconds to 1 minute. Beat in melted white chocolate. With mixer on low speed, gradually add confectioners' sugar, beating until combined. Add vanilla and salt; increase mixer speed to medium, and beat until light and fluffy, about 2 minutes, stopping to scrape sides of bowl. Stir in enough food coloring until desired color is reached. Use immediately.

We used Wilton Gel Icing Color in Kelly Green and Juniper Green.

CREAMY WHITE RUSSIAN BARS

Makes 32 bars

The elegant White Russian cocktail is the delectable inspiration for these cheesecake bars loaded with coffee liqueur and cream. Velvety black cocoa helps create the tuxedo of dessert bars: always classy, never out of style.

Black Cocoa Shortcrust (recipe follows)
3   (8-ounce) packages (680 grams) cream cheese, room temperature and divided
¼   cup (60 grams) coffee liqueur*
2½ teaspoons (5 grams) dark-roast instant coffee granules
1   cup (200 grams) granulated sugar, divided
2   tablespoons (16 grams) all-purpose flour
3   teaspoons (12 grams) vanilla extract, divided
¼   teaspoon kosher salt
2   large eggs (100 grams), room temperature
¼   cup (60 grams) heavy whipping cream
1   teaspoon (2 grams) black cocoa powder

1. Preheat oven to 350°F (180°C). Spray a 13x9-inch baking pan with cooking spray. Line pan with parchment paper, letting excess extend almost to top of pan.
2. Let Black Cocoa Shortcrust stand at room temperature until slightly softened, 10 to 15 minutes, if necessary. Transfer dough to prepared pan, pressing to cover bottom of pan. Top with a piece of parchment paper, letting excess extend over edges of pan. Add pie weights.
3. Bake until edges are set and crust is fragrant, 15 to 20 minutes. Carefully remove parchment and weights. Let cool in pan on a wire rack for 25 minutes. Leave oven on.
4. In the bowl of a stand mixer fitted with the paddle attachment, beat 2 packages (454 grams) cream cheese at medium speed until smooth and creamy, 1 to 2 minutes, stopping to scrape sides of bowl.
5. In a small bowl, stir together liqueur and instant coffee until granules dissolve. Add liqueur mixture, ¾ cup (150 grams) sugar,

flour, ¾ teaspoon (3 grams) vanilla, and salt to cream cheese; beat until well combined, 1 to 2 minutes, stopping to scrape sides of bowl. Add eggs, one at a time, beating just until combined after each addition. Pour cream cheese mixture onto prepared crust, spreading into an even layer with a small offset spatula. Gently tap sides of pan several times to release any air bubbles, popping any that rise to the surface with a wooden pick.
6. Bake until edges are set, top has a dulled finish, center is almost set, and an instant-read thermometer inserted in center registers 150°F (66°C) to 155°F (68°C), about 20 minutes. Immediately run a knife around pan to loosen bars from parchment; let cool in pan on a wire rack for 1½ to 2 hours.
7. Clean bowl of stand mixer and paddle attachment. Using the paddle attachment, beat remaining 1 package (226 grams) cream cheese at medium speed until smooth and creamy, 1 to 2 minutes, stopping to scrape sides of bowl. Add cream, remaining ¼ cup (50 grams) sugar, and remaining 2¼ teaspoons (9 grams) vanilla; beat until smooth and well combined. Transfer ¼ cup (about 54 grams) cream cheese mixture to a small bowl; stir in black cocoa.
8. Spoon and spread remaining cream cheese mixture onto cooled cheesecake layer in pan. Drop small dollops of black cocoa mixture on top of cream cheese mixture; using a wooden pick, swirl as desired, being careful not to hit cheesecake layer underneath. Refrigerate for at least 1 hour or up to overnight, loosely covering with foil only when completely cool to prevent condensation from forming on top.
9. Using excess parchment as handles, remove from pan. Using a warm, dry knife, cut into bars.

We used Kahlúa.

BLACK COCOA SHORTCRUST
Makes 1 (13x9-inch) crust

3   cups plus 2 tablespoons (391 grams) all-purpose flour
⅔   cup (133 grams) granulated sugar
½   cup (43 grams) black cocoa powder
1   teaspoon (3 grams) kosher salt
1   cup (227 grams) cold unsalted butter, cubed
2   large eggs (100 grams)

1. In the work bowl of a food processor, place flour, sugar, black cocoa, and salt; pulse until combined. Add cold butter, and pulse until butter pieces are no larger than ⅛ to ¼ inch. Add eggs; pulse just until dough comes together.
2. Turn out dough, and shape into a disk. Wrap in plastic wrap, and refrigerate for at least 25 minutes before using.

PEPPERMINT PATTY BROWNIES

Makes 16 brownies

Recipe by Mike Johnson

This Peppermint Patty Brownies recipe is perfect for the chocolate-peppermint lovers in your life. These brownies should be refrigerated but can be enjoyed chilled or at room temperature.

1   cup (200 grams) granulated sugar
½   cup (63 grams) all-purpose flour
⅓   cup (25 grams) unsweetened natural or Dutch process cocoa powder
¼   teaspoon (1.25 grams) baking powder
¼   teaspoon kosher salt
½   cup (113 grams) unsalted butter, melted
2   large eggs (100 grams)
1   teaspoon (4 grams) vanilla extract
Peppermint Filling (recipe follows)
Chocolate Topping (recipe follows)

1. Preheat oven to 350°F (180°C). Spray an 8-inch square baking pan with cooking spray. Line pan with parchment paper, letting excess extend over sides of pan.
2. In a large bowl, whisk together sugar, flour, cocoa, baking powder, and salt.
3. In a medium bowl, whisk together melted butter, eggs, and vanilla until well combined. Add butter mixture to sugar mixture, stirring just until combined. Pour batter into prepared pan, spreading into an even layer.
4. Bake until a wooden pick inserted in center comes out with a few moist crumbs, 30 to 33 minutes. Let cool completely in pan.
5. Top cooled brownie layer with Peppermint Filling; using a damp offset spatula, smooth Peppermint Filling into an even layer. Refrigerate until set, about 30 minutes.

6. Top Peppermint Filling with Chocolate Topping. Slam pan on a kitchen towel-lined counter to release any air bubbles. Refrigerate until topping is set, about 2 hours.
7. Using excess parchment as handles, remove from pan, and cut into bars. Serve chilled or at room temperature. Refrigerate in an airtight container for up to 3 days.

PEPPERMINT FILLING
Makes about 1 cup

2½   cups (300 grams) confectioners' sugar, sifted
1   tablespoon (14 grams) unsalted butter, softened
½   teaspoon (2 grams) peppermint extract
¼   teaspoon (1.5 grams) vanilla bean paste
2 to 4 tablespoons (30 to 60 grams) boiling water

1. In a medium bowl, place confectioners' sugar, butter, peppermint extract, and vanilla bean paste. Add 2 tablespoons (30 grams) boiling water, and stir until combined. (It should resemble a thick paste.) Add up to remaining 2 tablespoons (30 grams) boiling water, 1 teaspoon (5 grams) at a time, if needed. Use immediately.

CHOCOLATE TOPPING
Makes about ¾ cup

3.5   ounces (100 grams) 70% cacao dark chocolate, chopped
¼   cup (57 grams) unsalted butter

1. In the top of a double boiler, combine chocolate and butter. Cook over simmering water, stirring frequently, until melted and smooth. Use immediately.

Photo by Mike Johnson

CRANBERRY MERINGUE BARS

Makes 12 bars

Recipe by Michele Song

Are you looking for a new showstopper to add to your holiday tradition? These festive and vibrant cranberry-orange meringue bars are guaranteed to impress your family and friends. The tart, luscious cranberry curd filling pairs perfectly with the sweet, toasty notes of the Brown Sugar Meringue and the spiced cookie crust.

1¼ cups (145 grams) speculaas cookies
3 tablespoons (42 grams) unsalted butter, melted
1 cup (200 grams) plus 2 tablespoons (24 grams) granulated sugar, divided
½ teaspoon kosher salt, divided
12 ounces (340 grams) fresh or thawed frozen cranberries
¼ cup (60 grams) water
1 large orange (131 grams)
3 tablespoons (24 grams) cornstarch
4 large eggs (200 grams)
2 large egg yolks (37 grams)
¾ cup (180 grams) fresh orange juice
½ cup (113 grams) unsalted butter
Brown Sugar Meringue (recipe follows)

1. Preheat oven to 350°F (180°C). Line an 8-inch square baking pan with parchment paper, letting excess extend over sides of pan.
2. In the work bowl of a food processor, pulse cookies until finely ground. Add melted butter, 2 tablespoons (24 grams) sugar, and ¼ teaspoon salt; pulse until combined and mixture sticks together when rubbed between fingertips. Press into bottom of prepared pan.
3. Bake for 10 minutes. Let cool completely. Reduce oven temperature to 325°F (170°C).
4. In a medium saucepan, combine cranberries and ¼ cup (60 grams) water. Cook over medium-high heat, whisking occasionally, until cranberries start to burst, 7 to 10 minutes. Remove from heat; let cool slightly. Transfer cranberries to the container of a blender, and purée until smooth. Strain mixture, discarding skins. Set aside.
5. In a small bowl, place remaining 1 cup (200 grams) sugar. Zest orange over sugar, and rub together with fingertips to help release oils in zest. Add cornstarch, and stir until well combined.
6. In a metal or glass bowl, whisk together eggs and egg yolks. Gradually add sugar mixture, whisking constantly, until combined.

7. In a large saucepan, cook puréed cranberries, orange juice, butter, and remaining ¼ teaspoon salt over medium-high heat, whisking occasionally. Remove from heat; gradually pour half of hot cranberry mixture into egg mixture, whisking constantly. Return mixture to saucepan. Bring to a boil over medium heat, stirring constantly. Reduce heat to medium-low, and simmer for 2 minutes to ensure cornstarch is cooked through. Strain through a fine-mesh sieve. Pour mixture onto prepared crust.
8. Bake until set but slightly jiggly, 20 to 25 minutes. Let cool to room temperature, about 1 hour. Refrigerate until set, at least 4 hours or up to overnight.
9. Top with Brown Sugar Meringue, and create peaks using a rubber spatula. Using a kitchen torch, toast meringue until top is golden brown. Best served same day or when cold; refrigerate any leftovers in an airtight container. (To make ahead, make the cranberry bars, and refrigerate overnight; make the Brown Sugar Meringue when ready to serve.)

BROWN SUGAR MERINGUE
Makes about 4 cups

¾ cup (165 grams) firmly packed light brown sugar
¼ cup (50 grams) granulated sugar
¼ cup (60 grams) water
4 large egg whites (120 grams), room temperature
½ teaspoon (2 grams) cream of tartar
1 teaspoon (4 grams) vanilla extract

1. In a medium saucepan, combine sugars and ¼ cup (60 grams) water. Using your index finger, gently stir sugars and water together until sugar is wet and mixture resembles wet sand. Wipe any excess sugar from sides of pan using wet hands. (This will prevent sugar from crystallizing.) Cook over medium-high heat until an instant-read thermometer registers 240°F (116°C), 5 to 7 minutes.
2. Meanwhile, in the bowl of a stand mixer fitted with the whisk attachment, beat egg whites and cream of tartar at medium speed until soft peaks form, 1 to 2 minutes.
3. With mixer on medium speed, slowly pour hot sugar syrup into egg white mixture. Increase mixer speed to high, and beat until shiny, smooth, stiff peaks form. Add vanilla, and beat to combine. Use immediately.

Photo by Michele Song

EGGNOG NANAIMO BARS

Makes 24 bars

The classic Canadian dessert gets a bold, boozy revamp thanks to a touch of eggnog and bourbon. The nutmeg in the eggnog helps cut the richness with aromatic spice, and the crunchy walnuts and coconut impart extra chewiness.

⅔   cup (150 grams) unsalted butter
½   cup (43 grams) unsweetened cocoa powder
⅓   cup plus 2 tablespoons (91 grams) granulated sugar
1   teaspoon (3 grams) kosher salt
1   large egg (50 grams)
1   large egg yolk (19 grams)
2⅓ cups (295 grams) shortbread cookie crumbs*
1¼ cups (105 grams) sweetened flaked coconut
½   cup (57 grams) finely chopped toasted walnuts
1   teaspoon (4 grams) vanilla extract
Eggnog Custard Filling (recipe follows)
6   ounces (170 grams) 64% cacao semisweet chocolate, finely chopped
2   tablespoons (28 grams) vegetable oil

1. Spray a 9-inch square baking pan with cooking spray. Line pan with parchment paper, letting excess extend over sides of pan.
2. In the top of a double boiler, combine butter, cocoa, sugar, and salt. Cook over simmering water, stirring frequently, until butter is melted. Whisk in egg and egg yolk until well combined; cook, stirring occasionally, until thickened and an instant-read thermometer registers 160°F (71°C), about 10 minutes. Remove from heat; stir in cookie crumbs, coconut, walnuts, and vanilla. Press mixture into bottom of prepared pan; let cool in pan on a wire rack for 30 minutes.
3. Using a small offset spatula, spread Eggnog Custard Filling onto prepared crust in a smooth, even layer. Refrigerate for 30 minutes.

4. In the clean top of a double boiler, combine chocolate and oil. Cook over simmering water, stirring frequently, until chocolate is melted and mixture is smooth. Working quickly, pour chocolate mixture over chilled filling. Using a small offset spatula and tilting pan as needed, spread chocolate mixture into an even layer; tap pan on a kitchen towel-lined counter several times to smooth chocolate mixture and release any air bubbles. Refrigerate for at least 1 hour or up to overnight.
5. Using excess parchment as handles, remove from pan; using a warm, dry, serrated knife, cut into bars. Serve at room temperature.

*We used Walkers Pure Butter Shortbread Cookies.

EGGNOG CUSTARD FILLING
Makes about 2 cups

¾   cup (170 grams) unsalted butter, softened
2½ tablespoons (24 grams) custard powder*
1   tablespoon (15 grams) bourbon
1   teaspoon (4 grams) vanilla extract
½   teaspoon (1 gram) ground nutmeg
3   cups (360 grams) confectioners' sugar
3½ tablespoons (52.5 grams) prepared eggnog

1. In the bowl of a stand mixer fitted with the paddle attachment, beat butter and custard powder at medium-low speed until creamy, 2 to 3 minutes, stopping to scrape sides of bowl. Beat in bourbon, vanilla, and nutmeg. With mixer on low speed, gradually add confectioners' sugar alternately with eggnog, beating until well combined and stopping to scrape sides of bowl. Increase mixer speed to medium, and beat for 1 minute. Use immediately.

*We used Bird's Custard Powder, available at select grocery stores and amazon.com.

GINGERBREAD COOKIE CHEESECAKE BARS

Makes 12 bars

An indulgent layer of cheesecake filling is sandwiched between chewy, delicately spiced gingerbread dough. It's a simple formula, but when that molasses-rich gingerbread meets that vanilla-scented cheesecake, you'll get flavor fireworks.

1½	cups (340 grams) unsalted butter, softened
1¼	cups (250 grams) granulated sugar
¾	cup (165 grams) firmly packed dark brown sugar
½	cup (170 grams) unsulphured molasses
2	large eggs (100 grams)
4	cups (500 grams) all-purpose flour
2	teaspoons (4 grams) ground cinnamon
2	teaspoons (4 grams) ground ginger
1½	teaspoons (4.5 grams) kosher salt
1	teaspoon (5 grams) baking powder
1	teaspoon (5 grams) baking soda
¼	teaspoon ground nutmeg
⅛	teaspoon ground allspice
⅛	teaspoon ground cloves
3	tablespoons (33 grams) minced candied ginger

Cheesecake Layer (recipe follows)

1. Preheat oven to 350°F (180°C). Line a 13x9-inch baking pan with parchment paper, letting excess extend over sides of pan.
2. In the bowl of a stand mixer fitted with the paddle attachment, beat butter and sugars at medium speed until fluffy, 3 to 4 minutes, stopping to scrape sides of bowl. Add molasses, beating until no streaks remain. Add eggs, one at a time, beating well after each addition.

3. In a large bowl, whisk together flour, cinnamon, ground ginger, salt, baking powder, baking soda, nutmeg, allspice, and cloves. With mixer on low speed, gradually add flour mixture to butter mixture, beating just until combined. Beat in candied ginger.
4. Spread 3¾ cups (about 1,000 grams) dough in prepared pan. Top with Cheesecake Layer. Crumble remaining dough (about 2 cups [563 grams]) on top.
5. Bake until edges are set, center jiggles just slightly, and an instant-read thermometer inserted in center registers 175°F (79°C) to 180°F (82°C), 45 to 55 minutes, covering with foil after 35 minutes of baking to prevent excess browning, if necessary. Let cool completely in pan. Cover and refrigerate for at least 4 hours or up to overnight. Using excess parchment as handles, remove from pan. Trim edges, and cut into bars.

CHEESECAKE LAYER
Makes 3⅓ cups

16	ounces (454 grams) cream cheese, softened
1	cup (200 grams) granulated sugar
1	tablespoon (8 grams) all-purpose flour
2	large eggs (100 grams)
1	tablespoon (13 grams) vanilla extract

1. In the bowl of a stand mixer fitted with the paddle attachment, beat cream cheese at medium speed until smooth. Add sugar and flour, and beat until combined, stopping to scrape sides of bowl. Add eggs, one at a time, beating well after each addition. Beat in vanilla. Use immediately.

BLACK FOREST BROWNIES

Makes 12 brownies

Your favorite German cake, now in a fudgy brownie package. Plump with kirsch-drunk cherries and dark chocolate chips, these decadent bars get pushed over the edge with a tangy Crème Fraîche Glaze.

2⅔ cups (453 grams) 63% cacao dark chocolate chips, divided
1 cup (227 grams) unsalted butter, cubed
1 teaspoon (2 grams) espresso powder
2 cups (400 grams) granulated sugar
4 large eggs (200 grams), lightly beaten
2 tablespoons (30 grams) half-and-half
1 teaspoon (4 grams) vanilla extract
1½ cups (188 grams) all-purpose flour
½ cup (43 grams) Dutch process cocoa powder
1 teaspoon (3 grams) kosher salt
1 cup (250 grams) strained, halved, and packed Drunken Cherries (recipe follows)
Crème Fraîche Glaze (recipe follows)

1. Preheat oven to 350°F (180°C). Butter a 13x9-inch baking pan. Line pan with parchment paper, letting excess extend over sides of pan.
2. In the top of a double boiler, combine 1⅔ cups (283 grams) chocolate chips, butter, and espresso powder. Cook over simmering water, stirring occasionally, until mixture is smooth. Turn off heat, and whisk in sugar. Remove from heat, and let cool slightly.
3. Add half of beaten eggs to chocolate mixture, whisking until combined. Add remaining beaten eggs, and whisk until combined. Whisk in half-and-half and vanilla.
4. In a medium bowl, whisk together flour, cocoa, and salt. Fold flour mixture into chocolate mixture until a few bits of flour remain. Fold in Drunken Cherries and remaining 1 cup (170 grams) chocolate chips. Spread batter in prepared pan.
5. Bake until a wooden pick inserted in center comes out with a few crumbs, 35 to 40 minutes. Let cool completely in pan. Using excess parchment as handles, remove from pan, and cut into squares. Drizzle with Crème Fraîche Glaze.

DRUNKEN CHERRIES
Makes 3 cups

3 cups (420 grams) frozen pitted dark sweet cherries
⅔ cup (133 grams) granulated sugar
⅔ cup (160 grams) cherry brandy

1. Place cherries in a medium bowl.
2. In a small saucepan, heat sugar and brandy over low heat, stirring constantly, until sugar is dissolved. Pour mixture over cherries. Cover and refrigerate overnight.

CRÈME FRAÎCHE GLAZE
Makes 1 cup

1 cup (120 grams) confectioners' sugar
½ cup (120 grams) crème fraîche
2 teaspoons (10 grams) whole milk
1 teaspoon (5 grams) cherry brandy

1. In a small bowl, whisk together all ingredients until smooth. Use immediately.

MULLED SPICE BROWNIES

Makes 16 brownies

These fudgy stir-together brownies get rich, sophisticated notes from a blend of mulling spices and port-soaked orange peel.

1¾	cups (350 grams) granulated sugar
1¼	cups (284 grams) unsalted butter, melted
⅔	cup (147 grams) firmly packed light brown sugar
1	teaspoon (4 grams) vanilla extract
5	large eggs (250 grams), room temperature
1	cup (85 grams) unsweetened natural cocoa powder, sifted
¾	cup (94 grams) all-purpose flour
3¾	teaspoons (7.5 grams) Mulled Spice Mix (recipe follows)
1	teaspoon (3 grams) kosher salt
¾	teaspoon (3.75 grams) baking powder
1½	teaspoons (5 grams) finely chopped port-soaked orange peel (reserved from Spiced Port Syrup [recipe follows])

Ganache Frosting (recipe follows)
Spiced Port Syrup (recipe follows)
Garnish: Mulled Spice Mix (recipe follows)

1. Preheat oven to 350°F (180°C). Spray a 9-inch square baking pan with cooking spray; line pan with parchment paper, letting excess extend over sides of pan.
2. In a large bowl, whisk together granulated sugar, melted butter, brown sugar, and vanilla until well combined. Add eggs, one at a time, beating until well combined after each addition.
3. In a large bowl, whisk together cocoa, flour, Mulled Spice Mix, salt, and baking powder. Gradually stir cocoa mixture into sugar mixture until combined. Fold in chopped orange peel, breaking up any clumps if needed. Spoon batter into prepared pan, smoothing top.
4. Bake until a wooden pick inserted in center comes out with just a few moist crumbs, 45 to 50 minutes. Let cool completely in pan on a wire rack.
5. Spread Ganache Frosting onto cooled brownies, using a small offset spatula or the back of a spoon to create swirls. (For deeper swirls, refrigerate brownies for about 15 minutes to slightly firm up frosting before swirling.) Using excess parchment as handles, remove from pan. Cut into bars. Drizzle with Spiced Port Syrup just before serving. Garnish with Mulled Spice Mix, if desired.

MULLED SPICE MIX
Makes 7½ teaspoons

2	teaspoons (4 grams) ground cinnamon
2	teaspoons (4 grams) ground ginger
1	teaspoon (2 grams) ground nutmeg
1	teaspoon (2 grams) ground cloves
1	teaspoon (2 grams) ground allspice
½	teaspoon (1 gram) ground black pepper

1. In a small bowl, stir together all ingredients until well combined.

GANACHE FROSTING
Makes about 1¾ cups

4	ounces (115 grams) unsweetened chocolate baking bars, chopped
¼	cup (57 grams) unsalted butter, cubed and softened
1	teaspoon (5 grams) ruby port wine
⅔	cup (160 grams) evaporated milk
½	cup (100 grams) granulated sugar
⅓	cup (73 grams) firmly packed light brown sugar
¼	teaspoon kosher salt

1. In the container of a blender, place chocolate, butter, and port.
2. In a medium saucepan, combine evaporated milk, sugars, and salt. Cook over medium heat, stirring constantly, until sugars and salt are dissolved. Add to blender. Let stand for 5 minutes.
3. Process until thick and smooth, about 15 seconds. Using a spatula, stir mixture to check consistency. If needed, blend in additional 15-second intervals to thicken more.

SPICED PORT SYRUP
Makes about ⅓ cup

½	medium navel orange (about 100 grams)
1	cup (224 grams) ruby port wine
⅓	cup (67 grams) granulated sugar
1	(2½- to 3-inch) cinnamon stick
8	whole black peppercorns
⅛	teaspoon ground nutmeg
⅛	teaspoon ground allspice
⅛	teaspoon ground cloves

1. Using a Y-peeler, remove orange peel in long strips. Using a small paring knife, carefully remove any white pith from peel. Reserve remaining orange for another use.

2. In a 10-inch stainless steel skillet, stir together orange peel, port, and all remaining ingredients. Bring to a boil over medium-high heat. Reduce heat to medium, and cook, stirring occasionally, until thickened and reduced to ⅓ cup, 12 to 15 minutes.

3. Strain mixture through a fine-mesh sieve into a medium bowl. Finely chop 1½ teaspoons (5 grams) cooked orange peel; reserve for Mulled Spice Brownies. Discard remaining solids. Let syrup cool completely before using.

MILLIONAIRE BARS

Makes 25 bars

It doesn't get much richer than Millionaire Bars. Also called millionaire's shortbread, this treat traditionally consists of a shortbread base topped with a layer of gooey caramel filling and chocolate. For a sophisticated holiday spin, these bars feature a homemade Chestnut Praline Paste in the caramel. A final sprinkling of cacao nibs and fleur de sel over the velvety ganache creates an ultra-crunchy topping to offset the sweetness.

2   cups (250 grams) all-purpose flour
⅓   cup (67 grams) granulated sugar
¼   cup (32 grams) cornstarch
1   teaspoon (3 grams) kosher salt
1¼   cups (284 grams) cold unsalted butter, cubed
1   vanilla bean, split lengthwise, seeds scraped and reserved
Chestnut Praline Caramel Filling (recipe follows)
Dark Chocolate Ganache (recipe follows)
Garnish: cacao nibs, fleur de sel

1. Preheat oven to 350°F (180°C). Line a 10-inch square baking dish with parchment paper, letting excess extend over sides of pan.
2. In the bowl of a stand mixer fitted with the paddle attachment, beat flour, sugar, cornstarch, and salt at low speed for 1 minute. Add cold butter and vanilla bean seeds; beat until a ball starts to form, 2 to 3 minutes. Press dough into bottom of prepared pan.
3. Bake until edges are golden brown, about 30 minutes. Let cool completely in pan.
4. Pour warm Chestnut Praline Caramel Filling over prepared crust. Let cool at room temperature for 1 hour. Wrap pan in plastic wrap, and refrigerate overnight.
5. Pour warm Dark Chocolate Ganache over Chestnut Praline Caramel Filling, spreading in an even layer with an offset spatula, if necessary. Let set for 5 minutes. Sprinkle with cacao nibs and fleur de sel, if desired. Refrigerate until firm, about 1 hour.
6. Using excess parchment as handles, remove from pan, and cut into bars. Store in an airtight container at room temperature for up to 3 days or in refrigerator for up to 2 weeks.

CHESTNUT PRALINE CARAMEL FILLING
Makes 3 cups

1   cup (240 grams) heavy whipping cream
¾   cup (255 grams) light corn syrup
½   cup (100 grams) granulated sugar
½   cup (110 grams) firmly packed light brown sugar
½   cup (113 grams) unsalted butter
¼   cup (75 grams) Chestnut Praline Paste (recipe follows)
½   teaspoon (1.5 grams) kosher salt

1. In a 5-quart enamel-coated Dutch oven or large stainless steel saucepan, bring cream, corn syrup, sugars, and butter to a boil over medium heat, stirring frequently. Cook, without stirring, until a candy thermometer registers 248°F (120°C), about 20 minutes. Remove from heat; add Chestnut Praline Paste and salt, stirring to combine. Use immediately.

CHESTNUT PRALINE PASTE
Makes ½ cup

½   cup (80 grams) roasted peeled chestnuts*
¼   cup (60 grams) water
1   tablespoon (12 grams) granulated sugar
¼   teaspoon (1 gram) vanilla extract

1. In a medium saucepan, bring all ingredients to a boil over medium heat. Reduce heat to low; cover and simmer until chestnuts are softened, about 30 minutes.
2. Transfer to the container of a blender; pulse until smooth. (Alternatively, an immersion blender can be used.) Use immediately, or refrigerate in an airtight container for up to 1 week.

We used Gefen Organic Whole Roasted & Peeled Chestnuts.

DARK CHOCOLATE GANACHE
Makes 1½ cups

11   ounces (315 grams) 70% cacao dark chocolate, chopped
¼   cup plus 3 tablespoons (105 grams) heavy whipping cream

1. In the top of a double boiler, combine chocolate and cream. Cook over simmering water, whisking constantly, until melted and smooth. Use immediately.

Stellar Sandwich COOKIES

· · · · ·

Two cookies come together to create sandwich cookies filled with
notes of bright fruit, rich chocolate, and warm holiday spices

RED VELVET SANDWICH COOKIES

Makes about 20 sandwich cookies

Tender red velvet cookies surround a tangy cream cheese filling. A final roll in peppermint candies sends this sweet sandwich cookie straight to the happy holiday zone.

½   cup (113 grams) plus 2 tablespoons (28 grams) unsalted butter, softened and divided
1½ cups (300 grams) granulated sugar, divided
1   large egg (50 grams)
1½ teaspoons (6 grams) vanilla extract, divided
1½ cups (188 grams) all-purpose flour
1   tablespoon (5 grams) unsweetened cocoa powder
½   teaspoon (2.5 grams) baking soda
¼   teaspoon kosher salt
Red gel food coloring*
4   ounces (113 grams) cream cheese, softened
2   cups (240 grams) confectioners' sugar
Garnish: crushed peppermint candies

1. In the bowl of a stand mixer fitted with the paddle attachment, beat ½ cup (113 grams) butter and 1 cup (200 grams) granulated sugar at medium speed until fluffy, 3 to 4 minutes, stopping to scrape sides of bowl. Add egg and 1 teaspoon (4 grams) vanilla, beating until combined.
2. In a medium bowl, stir together flour, cocoa, baking soda, and salt. With mixer on low speed, gradually add flour mixture to butter mixture, beating until combined. Beat in food coloring until dough reaches desired color. Cover with plastic wrap, and refrigerate for 1 hour.
3. Preheat oven to 350°F (180°C). Line baking sheets with parchment paper.
4. Roll dough into 1½-inch balls. Roll balls in remaining ½ cup (100 grams) sugar. Place 2 inches apart on prepared pans; flatten slightly with a spatula.
5. Bake until just set, 7 to 9 minutes. Let cool on pans for 5 minutes. Remove from pans, and let cool completely on wire racks.
6. In a large bowl, beat cream cheese and remaining 2 tablespoons (28 grams) butter with a mixer at medium speed until combined. Gradually add confectioners' sugar, beating until smooth. Add remaining ½ teaspoon (2 grams) vanilla, beating until combined.
7. Spread cream cheese mixture onto flat side of half of cookies. Place remaining cookies, flat side down, on top of filling. Roll edges of cookies in crushed peppermint candies, if desired. Cover and refrigerate for up to 2 days.

We used McCormick Red Food Color.

CHEWY OATMEAL COOKIES WITH SPICED RUM CARAMEL BUTTERCREAM

Makes 30 sandwich cookies

Recipe by Lori Sepp

A rum and caramel twist on crème-filled oatmeal cookies, these are great sandwich cookies to have on hand. A blend of nostalgia and the indulgence of the season, this homemade version of the classic is perfect for the holidays.

3 cups (240 grams) old-fashioned oats
1 cup (227 grams) unsalted butter, softened
1 cup (220 grams) firmly packed dark brown sugar
½ cup (100 grams) granulated sugar
2 large eggs (100 grams)
1 tablespoon (21 grams) unsulphured molasses
2 teaspoons (8 grams) vanilla extract
2 cups (250 grams) all-purpose flour
4 teaspoons (20 grams) baking powder
1 tablespoon (6 grams) ground cinnamon
2 teaspoons (4 grams) ground nutmeg
1 teaspoon (3 grams) kosher salt
½ teaspoon (2.5 grams) baking soda
½ teaspoon (1 gram) ground ginger
Spiced Rum Caramel Buttercream (recipe follows)

1. Preheat oven to 350°F (180°C). Line baking sheets with parchment paper.
2. In the work bowl of a food processor, pulse oats 5 times (1-second pulses). (This gives oats varying consistencies; don't overprocess.)
3. In the bowl of a stand mixer fitted with the paddle attachment, beat butter and sugars at medium speed until light and fluffy, about 3 minutes, stopping to scrape sides of bowl. Add eggs, and beat at low speed until combined; scrape sides of bowl. Beat in molasses and vanilla until combined.
4. In a medium bowl, whisk together flour, baking powder, cinnamon, nutmeg, salt, baking soda, and ginger. With mixer on low speed, gradually add flour mixture, beating until combined. Add oats, beating until well combined.
5. Using a 1-tablespoon spring-loaded scoop, scoop dough (about 15 grams each), and place 2 inches apart on prepared pans.
6. Bake until golden brown, 8 to 10 minutes. Let cool on pans for 10 minutes. Remove from pans, and let cool completely on wire racks.

7. Place Spiced Rum Caramel Buttercream in a pastry bag fitted with a large open star piping tip (Wilton 1M). Pipe buttercream in a circular motion onto flat sides of half of cookies, leaving a ¼-inch border around edges. Place remaining cookies, flat sides down, on top of buttercream, and gently press together. Store in an airtight container for up to 3 days, or refrigerate in an airtight container for up to 5 days.

PRO TIPS
Make the Spiced Rum Caramel and cookie dough ahead— freezing the balls of dough—to allow for easy assembly on baking days. Add 1 to 2 minutes to the bake time for frozen cookie dough.

A 4- to 5-inch round cutter can be used to form still-warm cookies into a more circular shape, if desired. Place cutter around 1 cookie; gently move cutter in a circular counterclockwise motion while making contact with edges of cookie until desired shape is reached. Repeat as needed.

SPICED RUM CARAMEL BUTTERCREAM
Makes 2½ cups

1 cup (200 grams) granulated sugar
4 large egg whites (120 grams)
¼ teaspoon cream of tartar
1 cup (227 grams) cold unsalted butter, cut into small cubes
1 teaspoon (4 grams) vanilla extract
Spiced Rum Caramel (recipe follows)
¼ teaspoon grated fresh nutmeg (optional)

1. In the heatproof bowl of a stand mixer, whisk together sugar, egg whites, and cream of tartar by hand until combined. Place bowl over a saucepan of simmering water (see Notes), and cook, whisking constantly, until sugar dissolves and an instant-read thermometer registers 158°F (70°C), about 5 minutes.
2. Carefully return bowl to stand mixer. Using the whisk attachment (see Notes), beat at high speed until bowl is still fairly warm to the touch but not too hot, 2 to 3 minutes. Reduce mixer speed to low, and add butter, 1 cube at a time, beating for about 5 seconds after each addition. Add vanilla, and increase mixer speed to medium, beating until well combined. (Mixture may look curdled, but keep mixing and it

will come together.) Beat until stiff peaks form; scrape sides of bowl. With mixer on low speed, gradually add Spiced Rum Caramel, beating until smooth and well combined.

3. Switch to the paddle attachment. Beat at low speed for about 2 minutes, stopping to scrape sides of bowl. Add nutmeg (if using), and beat until combined. Refrigerate in an airtight container for up to 5 days, or freeze in an airtight container for up to 1 month. Let come to room temperature and rewhip before using.

Notes: *Ensure the bottom of the mixer bowl does not touch the water.*

Make sure that the whisk attachment is completely clean and free of any oil, as any fat will deflate the egg whites, breaking the meringue.

SPICED RUM CARAMEL
Makes about ¾ cup

¼   cup (57 grams) unsalted butter
¾   cup (165 grams) firmly packed light brown sugar
1½   teaspoons (11 grams) light corn syrup
¼   cup (60 grams) heavy whipping cream
1½   tablespoons (23 grams) spiced rum*
½   teaspoon (2 grams) vanilla extract

1. In a medium saucepan, melt butter over medium heat. Add brown sugar and corn syrup. Stir once, and cook for about 2 minutes. Stir in cream, and bring to a boil; cook, stirring occasionally, for about 2 minutes. Stir in rum and vanilla. (Be careful, as mixture will splatter.) Cook until an instant-read thermometer registers 230°F (110°C), 8 to 9 minutes. Pour into a heatproof glass jar, and let cool. Refrigerate for up to 2 weeks. (Caramel will thicken.)

*We used Austrian Stroh 80 Rum, and it gives a very distinct flavor (think butter rum-flavored Life Savers) that you won't have with other brands.

Note: *If Spiced Rum Caramel is made ahead of time, rewarm in a small saucepan until just melted, or microwave on high in 15-second intervals, stirring between each, until melted and smooth. You want it to be smooth and pourable but not hot or warm.*

CHOCOLATE LINZER COOKIES

Makes about 20 sandwich cookies

These gorgeous cocoa-rich Linzer cookies receive a sweet boost from a tangy Cream Cheese Frosting. The cookies get a final snowy dusting of confectioners' sugar for a wintry holiday finish.

½   cup (113 grams) unsalted butter, softened
⅓   cup plus 1 tablespoon (87 grams) firmly packed light brown sugar*
⅓   cup (67 grams) granulated sugar*
1   large egg (50 grams), room temperature
½   teaspoon (3 grams) vanilla bean paste
1½   cups (188 grams) all-purpose flour
⅓   cup (25 grams) sifted Dutch process cocoa powder
1   teaspoon (2 grams) instant espresso powder
½   teaspoon (1.5 grams) kosher salt
¼   teaspoon (1.25 grams) baking powder
Garnish: confectioners' sugar

1. In the bowl of a stand mixer fitted with the paddle attachment, beat butter, brown sugar, and granulated sugar at medium-low speed just until combined; increase mixer speed to medium, and beat until fluffy, 2 to 3 minutes, stopping to scrape sides of bowl. Beat in egg and vanilla bean paste until combined.
2. In a medium bowl, whisk together flour, cocoa, espresso powder, salt, and baking powder. With mixer on low speed, gradually add flour mixture to butter mixture, beating just until combined. Turn out dough onto a sheet of parchment paper; top with another sheet of parchment paper, and roll dough to ⅛-inch thickness. Transfer dough and parchment to a baking sheet; refrigerate for 40 minutes.
3. Preheat oven to 350°F (180°C). Line 4 baking sheets with parchment paper.
4. Remove top sheet of parchment paper. Using a 2¼-inch fluted round cutter dipped in flour, cut dough. Using 1¼- to 1½-inch holiday cutters, cut centers from half of dough circles; use a wooden pick to help remove dough from centers, if necessary.

Reroll scraps between sheets of parchment paper as needed, and cut dough. (For cleanest edges, rerolled dough can be refrigerated for 20 minutes or frozen for 10 minutes before cutting.) Gently place ¾ to 1 inch apart on prepared pans. Freeze for 10 minutes.
5. Bake, one batch at a time, until edges are set, tops bounce back slightly when touched, and cookies are fragrant, 9 to 13 minutes. Let cool on pan for 1 minute. Remove from pan, and let cool completely on wire racks.
6. Spoon Cream Cheese Frosting into a pastry bag fitted with a ¼-inch round piping tip (Ateco #802). Pipe about 1¾ teaspoons (7 grams) frosting onto flat side of whole cookies, and smooth with a small offset spatula. Place remaining cookies, flat side down, on top of frosting. Garnish with confectioners' sugar before serving, if desired.

*We used C&H® Golden Brown Sugar and C&H® Granulated Sugar.

CREAM CHEESE FROSTING
Makes about 1½ cups

4   ounces (113 grams) cream cheese, softened
¼   cup (57 grams) unsalted butter, softened
1   teaspoon (6 grams) vanilla bean paste
½   teaspoon (1.5 grams) kosher salt
2½   cups (300 grams) confectioners' sugar, sifted

1. In the bowl of a stand mixer fitted with the paddle attachment, beat cream cheese and butter at medium speed until smooth and well combined, 1 to 2 minutes, stopping to scrape sides of bowl. Beat in vanilla bean paste and salt. With mixer on low speed, gradually add confectioners' sugar, beating just until combined. Increase mixer speed to medium; beat until fluffy, 1 to 2 minutes, stopping to scrape sides of bowl. Use immediately.

EARL GREY SANDWICH COOKIES

Makes 15 sandwich cookies

Filled with a festively green-tinted buttercream, these Christmas tree sandwich cookies have a tender, melt-in-your-mouth texture. Punctuated by a hint of Earl Grey tea and the vanilla- and citrus-scented buttercream, these delicious cookies will become your new favorite recipe!

1   cup (227 grams) unsalted butter*, softened
⅔   cup (133 grams) granulated sugar
1   teaspoon (6 grams) vanilla bean paste
¾   teaspoon (2.25 grams) kosher salt
2⅓   cups (292 grams) all-purpose flour
1   tablespoon (6 grams) finely ground
     Earl Grey tea
2   tablespoons (12 grams) sanding sugar
Vanilla Orange Buttercream (recipe follows)

1. In the bowl of a stand mixer fitted with the paddle attachment, beat butter, granulated sugar, vanilla bean paste, and salt at medium speed until creamy, 2 to 3 minutes, stopping to scrape sides of bowl. With mixer on low speed, gradually add flour and tea, beating until dough begins to clump together. Turn out dough onto a lightly floured surface, and shape into a disk. Wrap in plastic wrap, and refrigerate until chilled, about 1 hour.
2. Preheat oven to 350°F (180°C). Line baking sheets with parchment paper.
3. On a lightly floured surface, roll dough to ⅛-inch thickness. Using a 3½-inch Christmas tree-shaped cutter, cut dough, rerolling scraps, and place 1 inch apart on prepared pans. Sprinkle with sanding sugar. Freeze until firm, about 10 minutes.

4. Bake until edges are lightly golden brown, 10 to 12 minutes. Let cool on pans for 5 minutes. Remove from pans, and let cool completely on wire racks.
5. Spoon Vanilla Orange Buttercream into a pastry bag fitted with a large French star piping tip (Ateco #862). Pipe about 2 tablespoons (about 26 grams) buttercream onto flat side of half of cookies. Place remaining cookies, flat side down, on top of buttercream. Serve immediately.

We used Kerrygold Unsalted Butter.

VANILLA ORANGE BUTTERCREAM
Makes about 1¾ cups

¾   cup (170 grams) unsalted butter, softened
⅛   teaspoon kosher salt
2   teaspoons (6 grams) tightly packed orange
     zest
1   teaspoon (6 grams) vanilla bean paste
2   cups (240 grams) confectioners' sugar
1   tablespoon (15 grams) heavy whipping cream,
     room temperature
Green gel food coloring

1. In the bowl of a stand mixer fitted with the paddle attachment, beat butter and salt at medium speed until smooth, 2 to 3 minutes. Beat in orange zest and vanilla bean paste. With mixer on low speed, gradually add confectioners' sugar, beating until combined. Add cream; increase mixer speed to medium, and beat until light and airy, 1 to 2 minutes. Beat in food coloring until desired shade is reached. Use immediately.

HOLIDAY GLITTER
SANDWICH COOKIES

Makes about 12 sandwich cookies

Glittering with a beautiful blend of blue and white sparkling sugars and aromatic vanilla sugar, these sandwich cookies are sure to bring holiday twinkle to your cookie swap.

1¾ cups (397 grams) unsalted butter, softened and divided
2½ cups (300 grams) confectioners' sugar, divided
2   teaspoons (12 grams) vanilla bean paste*, divided
2¼ cups (281 grams) all-purpose flour
¾   teaspoon (1.5 grams) kosher salt, divided
¼   cup (50 grams) white sparkling sugar
2   tablespoons (24 grams) vanilla sugar*, divided
¼   cup (50 grams) blue sparkling sugar
2   tablespoons (42 grams) honey
1   tablespoon (15 grams) cold heavy whipping cream

1. Preheat oven to 400°F (200°C). Line baking sheets with parchment paper.
2. In the bowl of a stand mixer fitted with the paddle attachment, beat 1 cup (227 grams) butter and ½ cup (60 grams) confectioners' sugar at low speed; slowly increase mixer speed to medium, beating until light and creamy, 3 to 4 minutes, stopping to scrape sides of bowl. Beat in 1 teaspoon (6 grams) vanilla bean paste.
3. In a medium bowl, whisk together flour and ½ teaspoon (1.5 grams) salt. With mixer on low speed, gradually add flour mixture to butter mixture, beating until a dough forms. Using a 1½-tablespoon spring-loaded scoop, scoop dough (about 24 grams each), and roll into balls.

4. In a small bowl, stir together white sparkling sugar and 1 tablespoon (12 grams) vanilla sugar. In another small bowl, stir together blue sparkling sugar and remaining 1 tablespoon (12 grams) vanilla sugar. Roll half of dough balls in each sugar mixture, and place 3 inches apart on prepared pans; leave rounded, or gently press into 2-inch disks.
5. Bake, one batch at a time, until edges are lightly golden, 8 to 10 minutes, rotating pan halfway through baking. Let cool on pan for 3 minutes. Remove from pan, and let cool completely on wire racks.
6. Clean bowl of stand mixer and paddle attachment. Using the paddle attachment, beat remaining ¾ cup (170 grams) butter and remaining ¼ teaspoon salt at medium speed until smooth, 2 to 3 minutes. Beat in honey and remaining 1 teaspoon (6 grams) vanilla bean paste. With mixer on low speed, gradually add remaining 2 cups (240 grams) confectioners' sugar, beating until combined. Add cold cream; increase mixer speed to medium-high, and beat until light and fluffy, 1 to 2 minutes.
7. Spoon buttercream into a pastry bag fitted with a large round piping tip (Wilton 1A). Pipe buttercream onto flat side of half of cookies. Place remaining cookies, flat side down, on top of buttercream. Serve immediately.

We used Heilala Pure Vanilla Bean Paste and Heilala Vanilla Sugar.

HOT COCOA CREAM PIES

Makes 12 to 15 sandwich cookies

Recipe by Josh Lehenbauer

Pillowy Marshmallow Buttercream pressed between two soft and chewy milk chocolate cookies makes for warm and cozy "hot cocoa" hugs with every bite.

8   ounces (226 grams) 30% cacao milk chocolate, chopped
½   cup (113 grams) cold unsalted butter
¾   cup (150 grams) granulated sugar
¾   cup (170 grams) firmly packed light brown sugar
2   large eggs (100 grams)
1   teaspoon (4 grams) vanilla extract
1¼   cups (156 grams) all-purpose flour
3   tablespoons (15 grams) Dutch process cocoa powder
1   teaspoon (5 grams) baking powder
½   teaspoon (1.5 grams) kosher salt
Marshmallow Buttercream (recipe follows)

1. In the top of a double boiler, combine chocolate and cold butter. Cook over simmering water, stirring occasionally, until melted and smooth. Remove from heat, and let cool for 15 minutes.
2. In the bowl of a stand mixer fitted with the whisk attachment, beat sugars and eggs at medium-high speed for 4 minutes, stopping to scrape sides of bowl halfway through mixing and after mixing. With mixer on low speed, slowly add chocolate mixture, beating until well combined, about 1 minute. Beat in vanilla.
3. In a medium bowl, whisk together flour, cocoa, baking powder, and salt. Sift flour mixture over sugar mixture, and gently fold with a silicone spatula until combined and no streaks of flour remain. Let dough stand, uncovered, for 30 minutes to hydrate. (This allows some of the moisture to redistribute, giving you a more scoopable dough, deeper flavor, and even bake).

4. Preheat oven to 350°F (180°C). Line several baking sheets with parchment paper.
5. Using a 1½-tablespoon spring-loaded scoop, scoop dough, and place 3 to 4 inches apart on prepared pans.
6. Bake, one batch at a time, until edges are set, centers are still soft, and tops look crackly, 9 to 13 minutes. Let cool on pan for 10 minutes. (Cookies will deflate and become even more crackly on top as they cool). Remove from pan, and let cool completely on wire racks.
7. Place Marshmallow Buttercream in a pastry bag fitted with a wide round piping tip (Wilton No. 12 or 2A). Pipe buttercream in a spiral motion onto flat sides of half of cookies. Place remaining cookies, flat sides down, on top of buttercream. Best enjoyed same day. Store in an airtight container for up to 2 days, or refrigerate in an airtight container for up to 5 days. If refrigerating, let stand at room temperature for 30 minutes to 1 hour before serving to let buttercream soften.

MARSHMALLOW BUTTERCREAM
Makes 4 cups

1   cup (227 grams) unsalted butter, softened
4   cups (480 grams) confectioners' sugar, sifted
7   ounces (198 grams) marshmallow crème

1. In the bowl of a stand mixer fitted with the paddle attachment, beat butter at medium-high speed until fluffy, about 2 minutes. Scrape sides of bowl. With mixer on low speed, add confectioners' sugar, ½ cup (60 grams) at a time, beating until combined after each addition (1 to 2 minutes total). Increase mixer speed to medium-high, and beat for 2 minutes. Using a spatula, gently fold in marshmallow crème until combined. Refrigerate in an airtight container until ready to use.

Photo by Josh Lehenbauer

LINZER COOKIES

Makes about 24 sandwich cookies

Nothing could be more festive on the holiday table than a tray of these buttery, confectioners' sugar-dusted, jam- and buttercream-filled Linzer Cookies. The nuttiness of the hazelnut flour in the cookies is balanced beautifully by the Nutmeg Buttercream and the slightly tart blackberry preserves.

1 cup (227 grams) unsalted butter, softened
1½ cups (180 grams) confectioners' sugar, plus more for dusting
1 large egg (50 grams), room temperature
½ teaspoon (2 grams) vanilla extract
2½ cups (313 grams) all-purpose flour
1 cup (96 grams) hazelnut flour
½ teaspoon (1.5 grams) kosher salt
½ teaspoon (1 gram) ground nutmeg
Nutmeg Buttercream (recipe follows)
½ cup (160 grams) blackberry preserves

1. In the bowl of a stand mixer fitted with the paddle attachment, beat butter and confectioners' sugar at medium speed until light and fluffy, 2 to 3 minutes, stopping to scrape sides of bowl. Beat in egg and vanilla until well combined, stopping to scrape sides of bowl.

2. In a medium bowl, whisk together flours, salt, and nutmeg. With mixer on low speed, gradually add flour mixture to butter mixture, beating just until combined and stopping to scrape sides of bowl. Turn out onto a lightly floured surface, and divide dough in half (about 423 grams each). Shape each half into a disk, and wrap in plastic wrap. Refrigerate until firm, about 2 hours.

3. Preheat oven to 350°F (180°C). Line baking sheets with parchment paper.

4. On a lightly floured surface, roll half of dough to ¼-inch thickness. (Keep remaining dough refrigerated until ready to use.) Using a 2½-inch snowflake cutter, cut dough, and place 2 inches apart on prepared pans. Using a 1⅛-inch snowflake cutter, cut centers from half of cookies. Reroll scraps, and cut dough; place 2 inches apart on prepared pans.

5. Bake, one batch at a time, until edges are lightly golden, 10 to 12 minutes. (Let remaining cutout dough stand at room temperature until ready to bake.) Let cool on pan for 5 minutes. Remove from pan, and let cool completely on wire racks. Repeat with remaining dough.

6. Dust cooled cookies with cutouts with confectioners' sugar. Place Nutmeg Buttercream in a pastry bag fitted with a large round piping tip (Ateco #805). Pipe dollops of buttercream at base of each point on flat side of solid cookies. Spoon a scant 1 teaspoon (6 grams) of preserves into center of all solid cookies. Place cookies with cutouts, flat side down, on top of preserves and buttercream. Refrigerate in an airtight container for up to 5 days.

NUTMEG BUTTERCREAM
Makes about 2 cups

⅔ cup (150 grams) unsalted butter, softened
¼ teaspoon kosher salt
2¼ cups (270 grams) confectioners' sugar
2 tablespoons (30 grams) whole milk, room temperature
2 teaspoons (4 grams) ground nutmeg
½ teaspoon (2 grams) vanilla extract

1. In the bowl of a stand mixer fitted with the paddle attachment, beat butter and salt at medium speed until creamy, about 1 minute, stopping to scrape sides of bowl. With mixer on low speed, gradually add confectioners' sugar alternately with milk, beginning and ending with confectioners' sugar, beating just until combined after each addition. Beat in nutmeg and vanilla. Increase mixer speed to medium, and beat until light and fluffy, about 2 minutes, stopping to scrape sides of bowl. Use immediately.

PUMPKIN SPICE WHOOPIE PIES

Makes 12 whoopie pies

The pumpkin spice latte, the most viral fall beverage, inspired these epic sandwiches. Packed with pumpkin spice and airy Mascarpone Filling, these sandwich cookies are the perfect parallel to the latte's creamy and spicy joys.

1   cup (227 grams) unsalted butter, softened
2   cups (440 grams) firmly packed dark brown sugar
1½ cups (366 grams) canned pumpkin
2   teaspoons (8 grams) vanilla extract
2   large eggs (100 grams)
3   cups (375 grams) all-purpose flour
2   teaspoons (4 grams) pumpkin pie spice
1   teaspoon (5 grams) baking soda
½   teaspoon (2.5 grams) baking powder
½   teaspoon (1.5 grams) kosher salt
Mascarpone Filling (recipe follows)

1. Preheat oven to 350°F (180°C). Line baking sheets with parchment paper.
2. In the bowl of a stand mixer fitted with the paddle attachment, beat butter and brown sugar at medium speed until fluffy, 2 to 3 minutes, stopping to scrape sides of bowl. Beat in pumpkin and vanilla. Add eggs, one at a time, beating well after each addition.
3. In a medium bowl, whisk together flour, pumpkin pie spice, baking soda, baking powder, and salt. With mixer on low speed, gradually add flour mixture to butter mixture, beating until combined. Using a scant ¼-cup spring-loaded scoop, scoop batter, and drop 2 inches apart on prepared pans. Using damp fingers, pat batter to flatten tops, creating 2½-inch rounds.

4. Bake until a wooden pick inserted in center comes out clean, 13 to 15 minutes. Let cool on pans for 5 minutes. Remove from pans, and let cool completely on wire racks.
5. Place Mascarpone Filling in a pastry bag fitted with a large round tip (Wilton No. 12). Pipe Mascarpone Filling onto flat side of half of cookies. Place remaining cookies, flat side down, on top of filling. Refrigerate in an airtight container for up to 3 days.

MASCARPONE FILLING
Makes 3½ cups

1   cup (227 grams) unsalted butter, softened
4   cups (480 grams) confectioners' sugar
2   tablespoons (30 grams) heavy whipping cream
1   teaspoon (2 grams) pumpkin pie spice
¼   teaspoon kosher salt
8   ounces (226 grams) mascarpone cheese, room temperature

1. In the bowl of a stand mixer fitted with the paddle attachment, beat butter at medium speed until smooth, about 2 minutes. Add confectioners' sugar, 1 cup (120 grams) at a time, beating well after each addition. Beat in cream, pumpkin pie spice, and salt. Using a spatula, carefully fold in mascarpone. (Do not overmix, or mixture will break.) Use immediately.

CHOCOLATE HALVAH SANDWICH COOKIES WITH CARDAMOM BUTTERCREAM

Makes about 16 sandwich cookies

Recipe by Amisha Gurbani

Halvah has a nutty flavor and combines really well with chocolate—a match made in heaven. Add cardamom to the mix and you get luxurious cookies, especially with the chocolate coating and gold specks. These make for beautiful, festive cookies that are perfect for entertaining!

½   cup (113 grams) unsalted butter, softened
½   cup (100 grams) granulated sugar
1   teaspoon (4 grams) vanilla extract
1¼ cups (156 grams) all-purpose flour
⅓   cup (32 grams) almond flour
¼   cup (21 grams) dark cocoa powder, plus more for rolling
1   teaspoon (6 grams) salt
½   cup (65 grams) shredded halvah
1½ cups (255 grams) chocolate chips
1½ tablespoons (21 grams) coconut oil
Small food-safe paintbrush
Edible gold paint*
Cardamom Buttercream (recipe follows)

1. In the bowl of a stand mixer fitted with the paddle attachment, beat butter and sugar at high speed until combined, about 1 minute, stopping to scrape sides of bowl with a rubber spatula. Add vanilla, and beat at low speed until combined, about 15 seconds.
2. In a medium bowl, sift together flours, cocoa, and salt. With mixer on low speed, add flour mixture to butter mixture, gradually increasing mixer speed to medium until the mixture starts coming together, about 2 minutes. Add halvah, and beat until well combined. (Dough should be dark brown without any specks of halvah showing. It will look a bit crumbly, but don't worry—it will come together in the refrigerator when it sets.) Shape dough into a disk, and wrap tightly in plastic wrap. Refrigerate for 1 hour.
3. Preheat oven to 350°F (180°C). Line 2 baking sheets with parchment paper.
4. Dust a sheet of parchment paper with cocoa. Turn out dough onto parchment, and dust with cocoa. Top with another sheet of parchment paper, and roll dough to ¼-inch thickness. Remove top layer of parchment; using a 2-inch square cutter, cut dough,

rerolling scraps. Using a small offset spatula, gently remove cookies, and place on prepared pans. Freeze for 10 minutes.
5. Bake for 12 to 13 minutes. Let cool on pans for 5 minutes. Remove from pans, and let cool completely on a wire rack, about 1 hour.
6. In a small microwave-safe bowl, combine chocolate and oil; heat on high in 30-second intervals, stirring between each, until chocolate is melted and mixture is smooth (about 1½ minutes total).
7. Line 2 baking sheets with parchment paper. Dip cookies halfway into chocolate mixture, shaking off excess. Place on prepared pans, and freeze until chocolate is set, about 10 minutes.
8. Cover the undipped half of 1 cookie with a piece of parchment paper. Dip brush in edible gold paint, and flick paint onto chocolate-covered portion of cookie. Freeze for 2 minutes. Repeat process with all remaining cookies.
9. Place Cardamom Buttercream in a pastry bag fitted with a ⅓-inch round tip (Ateco #804), and pipe buttercream onto flat side of half of cookies. Place remaining cookies, flat side down, on top of buttercream. Refrigerate in an airtight container for up to 1 week.

We used AmeriColor Amerimist Airbrush Color in Gold Sheen, available at amazon.com. You can also combine dry edible gold dust with a couple drops of any alcohol, like rum or vodka, mix, and use that mixture as paint. We like Super Gold Luster Dust, available at amazon.com.

CARDAMOM BUTTERCREAM
Makes about 1⅓ cups

½   cup (113 grams) unsalted butter, softened
1   teaspoon (4 grams) vanilla extract
½   teaspoon (3 grams) salt
½   teaspoon (1 gram) ground cardamom
2   cups (240 grams) confectioners' sugar

1. In the bowl of a stand mixer fitted with the paddle attachment, beat butter, vanilla, salt, and cardamom until combined, about 30 seconds. Scrape sides of bowl. Add confectioners' sugar, and beat at low speed for about 30 seconds. Gradually increase mixer speed to high, and beat until well combined, about 1 minute. Use immediately.

Photo by Amisha Gurbani

MINCEMEAT RUM CHOCOLATE SANDWICH COOKIES

Makes 15 cookies

Recipe by Edd Kimber

This sandwich cookie hearkens back to a British classic, the mince pie. Originally made with meat, they're individual pies filled with a syrupy spiced fruit filling. These cookies follow the same pattern, served alongside a rum-infused buttercream.

¾ cup plus 2 tablespoons (198 grams) unsalted butter, softened
½ cup plus 2 tablespoons (124 grams) granulated sugar
½ cup plus 1 tablespoon (124 grams) firmly packed light brown sugar
1 teaspoon (4 grams) vanilla extract
2 cups plus 2 tablespoons (266 grams) all-purpose flour
½ cup (43 grams) black cocoa powder
½ teaspoon (2.5 grams) baking soda
½ teaspoon (1.5 grams) kosher salt
Rum Buttercream (recipe follows)
Quick Mincemeat Filling (recipe follows)
Garnish: confectioners' sugar

1. In the bowl of a stand mixer fitted with the paddle attachment, beat butter, granulated sugar, and brown sugar at medium speed until fluffy, 2 to 3 minutes, stopping to scrape sides of bowl. Beat in vanilla.
2. In a medium bowl, whisk together flour, black cocoa, baking soda, and salt. With mixer on low speed, gradually add flour mixture to butter mixture, beating just until dough starts to come together. (If you overmix the dough, your cookies will end up chewy rather than crisp.) Turn out dough onto a work surface, and bring together into a uniform dough. Divide dough in half, and shape each half into a disk. Wrap in plastic wrap, and refrigerate for at least 1 hour.
3. Preheat oven to 350°F (180°C). Line 2 half sheet pans with parchment paper.
4. On a lightly floured surface, roll half of dough to ⅛-inch thickness. Using a 2¾-inch fluted round cutter, cut dough, reserving scraps. Place cookies on prepared pans. Using a 1-inch star-shaped cutter, cut centers from half of cookies. Repeat with remaining dough. Gather all scraps, and briefly knead back into a uniform dough. Refrigerate until firm before repeating procedure once. (Don't use the second round of scraps because working

the dough further will make tough cookies.) Refrigerate for 20 minutes.
5. Bake until firm, about 9 minutes. Let cool on pans for 10 minutes. Remove from pans, and let cool completely on wire racks.
6. Place Rum Buttercream in a pastry bag fitted with a small round piping tip. Pipe a ring of Rum Buttercream on flat side of all solid cookies. Fill centers with Quick Mincemeat Filling. Dust cookies with cutouts with confectioners' sugar, if desired. Place cookies with cutouts, flat side down, on top of filling. Store in an airtight container for up to 3 days.

RUM BUTTERCREAM
Makes 1½ cups

½ cup (113 grams) unsalted butter, softened
2 cups (240 grams) confectioners' sugar
2 tablespoons (30 grams) spiced rum
1 teaspoon (4 grams) vanilla extract
⅛ teaspoon kosher salt

1. In the bowl of a stand mixer fitted with the paddle attachment, beat butter at medium speed until smooth and creamy. Add confectioners' sugar, and beat until fluffy, about 5 minutes. Add rum, vanilla, and salt, and beat until combined, about 1 minute. Use immediately.

QUICK MINCEMEAT FILLING
Makes 1 cup

Zest and juice of 1 orange (131 grams)
½ cup (64 grams) sultanas
½ cup (64 grams) raisins
¼ cup (55 grams) firmly packed light brown sugar
1 teaspoon (2 grams) mixed spice*
2 tablespoons (30 grams) spiced rum

1. In a small saucepan, combine orange zest and juice, sultanas, raisins, brown sugar, and mixed spice. Cook over medium-high heat until sugar is dissolved and liquid has reduced and become syrupy. Remove from heat; stir in rum. Cover with plastic wrap, and refrigerate until ready to use. When fully cooled, mixture should be thick like caramel. If too loose, it needs to cook slightly longer.

*Mixed spice, available on amazon.com, is the most traditional British spice mix used in most classic Christmas fruit dessert recipes. You can substitute with pumpkin pie spice, available at American grocery stores, or make your own mixed spice. Stir together 1 tablespoon (6 grams) ground allspice, 1 tablespoon (6 grams) ground cinnamon,

1 tablespoon (6 grams) ground nutmeg, 2 teaspoons (4 grams) ground ginger, ½ teaspoon (1 gram) ground cloves, and ½ teaspoon (1 gram) ground coriander.

Photo by Edd Kimber

CRÈME FRAÎCHE
SANDWICH COOKIES

Makes about 18 sandwich cookies

Recipe by Laura Kasavan

Sandwiched with sweet Vanilla Frosting and rolled in holiday sprinkles, these melt-in-your-mouth crème fraîche cookies will be the star of your holiday cookie platter! You'll love each buttery bite.

1½   cups (340 grams) unsalted butter, softened
¾   cup (180 grams) crème fraîche
1½   teaspoons (6 grams) vanilla extract
¼   teaspoon kosher salt
1   cup (120 grams) confectioners' sugar
3   cups (375 grams) all-purpose flour
1   tablespoon (8 grams) cornstarch
Vanilla Frosting (recipe follows)
¼   cup (45 grams) holiday sprinkles*

1. Line baking sheets with parchment paper.
2. In the bowl of a stand mixer fitted with the paddle attachment, beat butter and crème fraîche at medium speed until combined, 1 to 2 minutes. Beat in vanilla and salt. With mixer on low speed, gradually add confectioners' sugar, beating until combined.
3. In a medium bowl, whisk together flour and cornstarch. Gradually add flour mixture to butter mixture, beating until a soft dough forms. Divide dough in half. Transfer half of dough to a large pastry bag fitted with a large closed star tip (Wilton No. 2D). Pipe 2½-inch spirals 2 inches apart on prepared pans. Repeat with remaining dough. Refrigerate for 30 minutes.

4. Preheat oven to 350°F (180°C).
5. Bake until lightly golden, 14 to 16 minutes, rotating pans halfway through baking . Let cool on pans for 10 minutes. Remove from pans, and let cool completely on wire racks.
6. Pipe or spoon 1 to 2 tablespoons Vanilla Frosting onto flat side of half of cookies. Place remaining cookies, flat side down, on top of frosting, gently pressing together until frosting reaches edges of cookies. Roll cookies in sprinkles. Place cookies in a single layer on a baking sheet, and refrigerate for 20 minutes before serving.

We used Wilton Holiday Nonpareils.

VANILLA FROSTING
Makes about 3 cups

1   cup (227 grams) unsalted butter, softened
¼   teaspoon kosher salt
2   teaspoons (8 grams) vanilla extract
½   teaspoon (2 grams) almond extract
3   cups (360 grams) confectioners' sugar
1   tablespoon (15 grams) milk

1. In the bowl of a stand mixer fitted with the paddle attachment, beat butter and salt at medium speed until smooth, 2 to 3 minutes. Beat in extracts. With mixer on low speed, gradually add confectioners' sugar, beating until combined. Add milk, and beat at medium speed until smooth, 1 to 2 minutes. Use immediately.

Photo by Laura Kasavan

GINGER BOMBS

Makes 22 cookies

Recipe by Rebecca Firth

These Ginger Buttercream-stuffed molasses cookies encompass the best of the holiday season (minus the greenery). There are heaps of ginger in these, but don't let the quantities scare you off—it's just the right amount.

1   cup (227 grams) unsalted butter, softened
1   cup (220 grams) firmly packed dark brown sugar
2   large eggs (100 grams), room temperature
1   large egg yolk (19 grams), room temperature
⅓   cup (113 grams) unsulphured molasses
1½ tablespoons (11 grams) grated fresh ginger
1   tablespoon (13 grams) vanilla extract
2   cups (264 grams) bread flour
1   cup (130 grams) all-purpose flour
1½ tablespoons (9 grams) ground ginger
2   teaspoons (10 grams) baking soda
2   teaspoons (4 grams) ground cinnamon
1   teaspoon (3 grams) sea salt
1   teaspoon (2 grams) ground cloves
Ginger Buttercream (recipe follows)

1. In the bowl of a stand mixer fitted with the paddle attachment, beat butter and brown sugar at medium speed until creamy, 2 to 3 minutes, stopping to scrape sides of bowl. Add eggs and egg yolk, one at a time, beating well after each addition. Add molasses, grated ginger, and vanilla, and beat for 1 minute.
2. In a medium bowl, whisk together flours, ground ginger, baking soda, cinnamon, sea salt, and cloves. With mixer on low speed, gradually add flour mixture to butter mixture, beating just until combined, about 1 minute. Using a spatula, scrape sides and bottom of bowl to ensure everything is incorporated. Shape dough into a disk, and wrap tightly in plastic wrap. Refrigerate until firm, about 1 hour.
3. Preheat oven to 350°F (180°C). Line several baking sheets with parchment paper.
4. Roll dough into 1-tablespoon (14-gram) balls, and place 2 inches apart on prepared pans. If dough is a little sticky, use 2 spoons or a cookie scoop to help.
5. Bake for 9 to 10 minutes. Let cool on pans for 5 minutes. Remove from pans, and let cool completely on wire racks. Smear Ginger Buttercream onto flat side of half of cookies. Place remaining cookies, flat side down, on top of buttercream. Store in an airtight container for up to 3 days.

GINGER BUTTERCREAM
Makes 2 cups

¼   cup (57 grams) unsalted butter, softened
2   ounces (55 grams) cream cheese, softened
2   cups (240 grams) confectioners' sugar
3   tablespoons (33 grams) finely minced candied ginger
1   tablespoon (15 grams) whole milk

1. In the bowl of a stand mixer fitted with the paddle attachment, beat butter, cream cheese, and confectioners' sugar at low speed until smooth and creamy, about 2 minutes. Add candied ginger and milk, and beat until milk is completely absorbed and small bits of candied ginger are visible throughout, about 1 minute. Use immediately.

Photo by Rebecca Firth

GERMAN CHOCOLATE SANDWICH COOKIES

Makes 20 sandwich cookies

Recipe by Elisabeth Farris

No mixer necessary for these chewy double-chocolate cookies filled with the most delicious Coconut Pecan Filling that melts in your mouth. Coconut lovers will fall in love all over again!

2½   cups (425 grams) 60% cacao dark chocolate chips, divided
½   cup (113 grams) unsalted butter, softened
1¾   cups (219 grams) all-purpose flour
¼   cup (21 grams) unsweetened cocoa powder
1   teaspoon (5 grams) baking powder
1   teaspoon (5 grams) baking soda
½   teaspoon (1.5 grams) kosher salt
¾   cup (150 grams) granulated sugar
¾   cup (165 grams) firmly packed light brown sugar
3   large eggs (150 grams)
2   teaspoons (8 grams) vanilla extract
Coconut Pecan Filling (recipe follows)

1. In the top of a double boiler, combine 1½ cups (255 grams) chocolate chips and butter. Cook over simmering water, stirring frequently, until chocolate is melted and mixture is smooth. (Alternatively, combine chocolate chips and butter in a large microwave-safe bowl. Heat on high in 30-second intervals, stirring between each, until chocolate is melted and mixture is smooth.) Remove from heat; set aside.
2. In a medium bowl, whisk together flour, cocoa, baking powder, baking soda, and salt. Set aside.
3. Add sugars, eggs, and vanilla to chocolate mixture, and whisk to combine. Add flour mixture to chocolate mixture, stirring just until combined. Fold in remaining 1 cup (170 grams) chocolate chips. Cover and refrigerate for at least 1 hour or for up to 3 days.
4. Preheat oven to 350°F (180°C). Line 2 large baking sheets with parchment paper.

5. Using a 2-tablespoon spring-loaded scoop, scoop dough, and shape into smooth, round balls (30 grams each). Place 2 inches apart on prepared pans.
6. Bake until slightly cracked, 8 to 10 minutes. Let cool on pans for 5 minutes. Remove from pans, and let cool completely on wire racks. Spoon 1 to 2 tablespoons Coconut Pecan Filling onto flat side of half of cookies. Place remaining cookies, flat side down, on top of filling. Store in an airtight container for up to 3 days.

Note: *If you do not want to bake all of these cookies at once, the dough can be stored in a resealable plastic bag in the freezer. Freeze the scooped dough until solid on a baking sheet before transferring to a bag.*

COCONUT PECAN FILLING
Makes about 2 cups

1   cup (220 grams) firmly packed light brown sugar
1   cup (240 grams) evaporated milk
½   cup (113 grams) unsalted butter, softened
3   large egg yolks (56 grams)
1   cup (113 grams) chopped toasted pecans
1   cup (60 grams) sweetened flaked coconut
1   teaspoon (4 grams) vanilla extract
⅛   teaspoon kosher salt

1. In a medium saucepan, bring brown sugar, evaporated milk, butter, and egg yolks to a low boil over medium heat, whisking occasionally; cook, stirring constantly, until thickened, about 5 minutes. Remove from heat; stir in pecans, coconut, vanilla, and salt. Let cool completely.

Note: *This filling can be made a day ahead and refrigerated until ready to use. Let come to room temperature before assembling cookies.*

Photo by Elisabeth Farris

HAZELNUT BUTTER COOKIES

Makes 20 cookies

Step aside, Nutter Butter cookies. This hazelnut revamp of a classic sandwich cookie comes equipped with our homemade Hazelnut Butter, your new condiment obsession and the perfect homemade holiday gift. A dip in dark chocolate and a roll in even more hazelnuts sends this cookie right over the nutty edge.

1   cup (227 grams) unsalted butter, softened
⅓   cup (87 grams) Hazelnut Butter (recipe follows)
½   cup (110 grams) firmly packed dark brown sugar
1   large egg (50 grams)
1½   teaspoons (9 grams) vanilla bean paste
1⅔   cups (200 grams) all-purpose flour
1   teaspoon (5 grams) baking soda
¾   teaspoon (3.75 grams) baking powder
¼   teaspoon kosher salt
1¼   cups (100 grams) old-fashioned oats
¼   cup (28 grams) chopped dry-roasted unsalted hazelnuts
       Hazelnut Buttercream (recipe follows)
1   (10-ounce) package (283.5 grams) dark chocolate melting wafers
       Garnish: finely chopped roasted hazelnuts

1. In the bowl of a stand mixer fitted with the paddle attachment, beat butter and Hazelnut Butter at medium speed until smooth, about 3 minutes. Add brown sugar, and beat until creamy, 2 to 3 minutes, stopping to scrape sides of bowl. Add egg and vanilla bean paste, and beat at low speed just until combined, about 30 seconds.
2. In a medium bowl, whisk together flour, baking soda, baking powder, and salt. Gradually add flour mixture to butter mixture, beating just until combined. Add oats and hazelnuts, beating just until combined. Shape dough into a disk, and wrap in plastic wrap. Refrigerate until firm, about 2 hours.
3. Preheat oven to 325°F (170°C). Line 2 baking sheets with parchment paper.
4. Between 2 sheets of parchment paper, roll dough to ¼-inch thickness. Transfer dough between parchment to freezer. Freeze until set, about 20 minutes.
5. Using a 2¼-inch round cutter, cut dough, and place 2 inches apart on prepared pans.
6. Bake until golden brown, about 12 minutes, rotating pans halfway through baking. Let cool on pans for 5 minutes. Remove from pans, and let cool completely on wire racks.

(While first round of cookies is baking, reroll any scraps between parchment again, freeze until set, and cut out cookies. Reroll scraps a third time if needed. Keep cut cookies in freezer until ready to bake.)
7. Place Hazelnut Buttercream in a piping bag fitted with an Ateco #855 closed star tip. Pipe Hazelnut Buttercream onto flat side of half of cookies in a spiral starting at center. Place remaining cookies, flat side down, on top of filling. Refrigerate for 15 minutes.
8. In a microwave-safe bowl, heat chocolate melting wafers on high in 30-second intervals, stirring between each, until melted and smooth. Let cool slightly, 3 to 5 minutes. Line a baking sheet with parchment paper. Place chopped hazelnuts on a plate. Dip half of each cookie in melted chocolate, and roll in hazelnuts, if desired. Place on prepared pan. Let stand until chocolate is set, 8 to 10 minutes. Store in an airtight container at room temperature if unfilled, or in refrigerator if filled, for up to 3 days.

HAZELNUT BUTTER
Makes ⅔ cup

1¼   cups (178 grams) dry-roasted unsalted hazelnuts
1½   tablespoons (18 grams) granulated sugar
½   teaspoon (1 gram) ground cinnamon
¼   teaspoon kosher salt

1. In the work bowl of a food processor, process hazelnuts until smooth, about 3 minutes. Add sugar, cinnamon, and salt; process until combined, about 30 seconds. Refrigerate in an airtight container for up to 3 weeks.

HAZELNUT BUTTERCREAM
Makes 3½ cups

¾   cup (170 grams) unsalted butter, softened
⅓   cup (87 grams) Hazelnut Butter (recipe precedes)
4½   cups (540 grams) confectioners' sugar
¼   cup (60 grams) heavy whipping cream
¼   teaspoon kosher salt

1. In the bowl of a stand mixer fitted with the paddle attachment, beat butter and Hazelnut Butter at medium speed until smooth, 2 to 3 minutes. With mixer on low speed, gradually add confectioners' sugar alternately with cream, beating until combined. Add salt, and beat until fluffy, about 3 minutes. Use immediately.

Cookies
THAT SNAP

. . . . .

With a bit of bite, a whole lot of flavor, and a crisp finish,
these crunchy cookies are a treat for all the senses

CHOCOLATE GINGERBREAD COOKIES

Makes about 30 cookies

Recipe by Annalise Sandberg

You can't go wrong adding chocolate to this favorite. Traditional gingerbread cookies with cocoa powder are even more tempting than the classic.

10 tablespoons (140 grams) unsalted butter, softened
¾ cup (165 grams) firmly packed light brown sugar
½ cup (170 grams) unsulphured molasses
1 large egg (50 grams)
1 large egg yolk (19 grams)
1 teaspoon (4 grams) vanilla extract
3 cups (375 grams) all-purpose flour
½ cup (43 grams) unsweetened cocoa powder
2 teaspoons (4 grams) ground ginger
2 teaspoons (4 grams) ground cinnamon
1 teaspoon (5 grams) baking soda
½ teaspoon (1.5 grams) kosher salt
½ teaspoon (1 gram) ground allspice
½ teaspoon (1 gram) ground cloves
Vanilla Icing (recipe follows)
Garnish: silver nonpareils

1. In the bowl of a stand mixer fitted with the paddle attachment, beat butter and brown sugar at medium-high speed until pale and fluffy, 3 to 4 minutes, stopping to scrape sides of bowl. Add molasses, and beat until combined. Add egg and egg yolk, one at a time, beating well after each addition. Beat in vanilla.
2. In a medium bowl, whisk together flour, cocoa, ginger, cinnamon, baking soda, salt, allspice, and cloves. Add flour mixture to butter mixture, and beat at low speed just until combined.
3. Scoop dough onto a sheet of plastic wrap; using plastic wrap, shape dough into a large disk. Wrap tightly, and refrigerate for at least 2 hours or up to 3 days.

4. Preheat oven to 350°F (180°C). Line 3 baking sheets with parchment paper.
5. On a heavily floured surface, roll dough to about ¼-inch thickness. Using a 4-inch gingerbread person cutter or other desired cutter, cut dough, and place 2 inches apart on prepared pans. (Roll and cut dough in batches to keep it cold and firm.)
6. Bake, one batch at a time, until puffed and cookies appear dry, 8 to 10 minutes. Let cool on pan for 5 minutes. Remove from pan, and let cool completely on wire racks.
7. Using Vanilla Icing, decorate cooled cookies as desired. Garnish with sprinkles, if desired. Let stand until icing is set, about 1 hour. Store in an airtight container for up to 5 days.

PRO TIP
A small squeeze bottle is the easiest way to decorate these cookies, but you can also use a pastry bag fitted with a small round piping tip or even a resealable plastic bag with a small corner cut out of it.

VANILLA ICING
Makes 1 cup

1 cup (120 grams) confectioners' sugar
2 to 3 tablespoons (30 to 45 grams) whole milk
1 teaspoon (7 grams) light corn syrup
½ teaspoon (2 grams) vanilla extract

1. In a small bowl, whisk together confectioners' sugar, 2 tablespoons (30 grams) milk, corn syrup, and vanilla until smooth; add up to remaining 1 tablespoon (15 grams) milk if needed to achieve desired consistency, and whisk until smooth. Store in an airtight container for up to 1 week. Whisk before using.

Photo by Annalise Sandberg

DUTCH KRUIDENOTEN

Makes about 38 cookies

Recipe by Lori Sepp

Ask anyone living in the Netherlands what cookies embody the holiday season and the first response will always be kruidenoten. These tiny, addictive, spicy, and crunchy treats can be found lining store shelves in the months of November and December, dwindling after the celebration of Sinterklaas on December 5. This holiday season, you can bring the taste of the Netherlands to your own kitchen with this simple yet highly addictive take on these classic little cookies. They're great for cookie exchanges and shipping, and they are guaranteed to become a favorite.

⅓   cup (76 grams) unsalted butter, softened
⅓   cup (73 grams) firmly packed dark brown sugar
1   cup (125 grams) all-purpose flour
¼   cup (24 grams) blanched almond flour
½   teaspoon (2.5 grams) baking powder
½   teaspoon (1.5 grams) kosher salt
2   teaspoons (4 grams) Spice Mix (recipe follows)
1   tablespoon (5 grams) packed orange zest (1 to 2 medium to large oranges)
1   teaspoon (4 grams) vanilla extract
4 to 5 teaspoons (20 to 25 grams) whole milk

1. In the bowl of a stand mixer fitted with the paddle attachment, beat butter at medium speed for 2 minutes; scrape sides of bowl. Add brown sugar, and beat at high speed until creamy, about 2 minutes; scrape sides of bowl.
2. In a medium bowl, whisk together flours, baking powder, and salt until combined. With mixer on low speed, gradually add flour mixture and Spice Mix to butter mixture, beating until combined. (Mixture will be crumbly.) Beat in orange zest and vanilla. Add milk, 1 teaspoon (5 grams) at a time, beating until combined after each addition and a cohesive dough forms. (See PRO TIPS.) Cover and refrigerate for at least 30 minutes or up to overnight.

3. Preheat oven to 325°F (170°C). Line baking sheets with parchment paper.
4. Scoop dough by ½ teaspoonfuls (about 8 grams each), and roll into balls. Place about 1 inch apart on prepared pans.
5. Bake until slightly soft when touched and bottoms are slightly browned, 14 to 16 minutes. (They shouldn't collapse.) Let cool completely on pans. Store in an airtight container for up to 2 weeks.

SPICE MIX
Makes ¼ cup plus 2¾ teaspoons

Dutch bakeries are known for creating their own personal spice mixes for both kruidennoten and also speculaas cookies. In the Netherlands, premade spice mix is readily available in supermarkets (koek en speculaas kruiden), but nothing is as tasty as creating your own, customized to your palette. If you prefer a slight kick to your mix, be sure to include the peppers, but if not, feel free to leave them out.

2   tablespoons (12 grams) ground cinnamon
1   tablespoon (6 grams) grated fresh nutmeg
1   tablespoon (6 grams) ground ginger
1   teaspoon (2 grams) ground allspice
½   teaspoon (1 gram) ground cardamom
½   teaspoon (1 gram) ground anise
¼   teaspoon ground cloves
¼   teaspoon ground red pepper (optional)
¼   teaspoon ground black pepper (optional)

1. In a small bowl, stir together cinnamon, nutmeg, ginger, allspice, cardamom, anise, cloves, red pepper (if using), and black pepper (if using). Store in an airtight container.

PRO TIPS

Taste the dough after mixing. If the flavor isn't as strong as you would like, add 1 teaspoon (2 grams) Spice Mix, and beat at low speed until combined. Do not overmix.

These cookies are delicious and addictive as is, but if you really want to take them to the next level, dip them in a simple white chocolate coating. In a small microwave-safe bowl, heat ¾ cup (128 grams) chopped white chocolate and ¼ teaspoon (1.25 grams) neutral oil (such as grapeseed or canola) on high in 30-second intervals, stirring between each, until white chocolate is melted and mixture is smooth. Let cool slightly. Using a fork, dip your cooled cookies in the coating, tapping the side of the bowl to release excess chocolate. Place on a wire rack, and let stand until coating is set. For a festive look, sprinkle with colorful sprinkles after dipping in the white chocolate coating.

MUSCOVADO TOFFEE CRUNCH COOKIES

Makes about 34 cookies

Recipe by Lauren Newsome

These toffee-filled muscovado cookies are the epitome of pure decadence. Muscovado, with its caramel notes and hints of molasses, gives these chewy treats an intensely rich flavor. The addition of buttery homemade toffee pairs perfectly. It not only amplifies that intense caramel flavor but also melts while baking, giving these cookies a wonderful crunch with each bite.

1   cup (227 grams) unsalted butter, softened
1½   cups (330 grams) firmly packed light muscovado sugar
½   cup (100 grams) granulated sugar
2   large eggs (100 grams)
1   tablespoon (13 grams) vanilla extract
3   cups (375 grams) all-purpose flour
1   teaspoon (5 grams) baking soda
1   teaspoon (5 grams) baking powder
1   teaspoon (3 grams) cornstarch
¾   teaspoon (2.25 grams) kosher salt
Toffee Pieces (recipe follows), divided
Garnish: flaked sea salt

1. In the bowl of a stand mixer fitted with the paddle attachment, beat butter and sugars at medium speed until light and fluffy, 2 to 3 minutes, stopping to scrape sides of bowl. Add eggs, one at a time, beating well after each addition. Beat in vanilla.
2. In a medium bowl, whisk together flour, baking soda, baking powder, cornstarch, and kosher salt. With mixer on low speed, gradually add flour mixture to butter mixture, beating just until combined; scrape sides and bottom of bowl to make sure all flour is incorporated. Stir in 1 cup (175 grams) Toffee Pieces. Cover and refrigerate for at least 1 hour.
3. Preheat oven to 350°F (180°C). Line 3 baking sheets with parchment paper.
4. Using a 1½-tablespoon spring-loaded scoop, scoop dough (about 30 grams each), and place 2 inches apart on prepared pans. Gently press remaining Toffee Pieces into tops of dough scoops. Refrigerate until ready to bake.
5. Bake, one batch at a time, until edges are light brown and set and centers appear slightly underbaked, 10 to 12 minutes. Let cool on pan for 10 minutes. Garnish

with sea salt, if desired. Remove from pan, and let cool completely on wire racks. Store in an airtight container for up to 3 days.

Notes: *Because the Toffee Pieces melt while the cookies are baking, these cookies will slightly spread and lose their shape. Shaping them with a cutter as soon as they come out of the oven will ensure they have a perfect round shape. Place a cutter larger than the cookies around 1 hot cookie; gently move cutter in a counterclockwise circular motion while making contact with edges of cookie until desired shape is reached. Repeat as needed.*

These cookies are very soft once they come out of the oven. It is imperative they cool for the allotted time before moving them to a wire rack to cool or they will break apart.

TOFFEE PIECES
Makes 1½ cups

½   cup (113 grams) unsalted butter
1   cup (200 grams) granulated sugar
1   teaspoon (4 grams) vanilla extract
½   teaspoon (1.5 grams) kosher salt

1. Line a rimmed baking sheet with parchment paper.
2. In a medium heavy-bottomed saucepan, melt butter over medium heat. Add sugar, vanilla, and salt, and cook, whisking constantly, until combined, about 1 minute. Using a damp pastry brush, brush off any sugar that crystallizes on sides of pan. Bring to a boil, stirring constantly with a wooden spoon; cook, stirring constantly, until mixture starts to smoke and brown and looks like melted peanut butter, about 7 minutes. Turn off heat, and stir for 1 minute.
3. Remove mixture from heat, and carefully pour onto prepared pan, letting mixture spread. Let cool and harden for 20 minutes.
4. Place toffee sheet on a cutting board or in a resealable plastic bag. Using a rolling pin or mallet, crack toffee into small pieces. Store in an airtight container for up to 5 days.

Note: *While making the homemade toffee, be sure to stay by the stove and keep stirring. The sugar mixture will burn very quickly if left unattended.*

Photo by Lauren Newsome

ORANGE, CINNAMON, AND CARDAMOM SABLÉS

Makes 24 cookies

Recipe by Cheryl Norris

These cookies are buttery and crisp, and the cinnamon and cardamom are perfect with the orange zest and orange glaze. The taste and texture make them perfect with tea, and they're so easy to make that they're the perfect holiday cookie to send to friends.

Sablés:
½ cup (113 grams) unsalted butter, room temperature
1 cup (120 grams) confectioners' sugar, sifted
1 teaspoon (1 gram) orange zest
½ teaspoon (1 gram) ground cinnamon
¼ teaspoon kosher salt
¼ teaspoon ground cardamom
1 large egg (50 grams), room temperature and lightly beaten
1¾ cups plus 1½ tablespoons (231 grams) all-purpose flour

Glaze:
1½ cups (180 grams) confectioners' sugar, sifted
½ teaspoon orange zest
3 tablespoons (45 grams) fresh orange juice
1 tablespoon (15 grams) fresh lemon juice
⅛ teaspoon kosher salt

1. For sablés: In the bowl of a stand mixer, place butter. Sift confectioners' sugar over butter. Add orange zest, cinnamon, salt, and cardamom. Using the paddle attachment, beat at medium speed until combined, about 2 minutes; scrape sides and bottom of bowl. Add egg, and beat until combined. (Mixture will look a little soupy.) Sift flour over butter mixture, and beat at low speed until combined; scrape sides and bottom of bowl.

2. Turn out dough onto a heavily floured surface. Lightly flour top of dough, and shape into a 1-inch-thick square. Wrap in plastic wrap or wax paper, and refrigerate for at least 2 hours or up to overnight.
3. Preheat oven to 325°F (170°C). Line 2 baking sheets with parchment paper.
4. Let dough stand at room temperature for 5 minutes. On a heavily floured surface, roll dough to ¼-inch thickness. Using desired 2-inch cutter (see Notes), cut dough, rerolling scraps as necessary, and place 1 inch apart on prepared pans. (Dough should still be cool to the touch so it can be baked right away. If the dough has become warm or really soft, refrigerate for 20 minutes.) (See Notes.)
5. Bake until slightly firm and bottoms are lightly browned, 10 to 12 minutes. Let cool on pans for 2 minutes. Remove from pans, and place on a wire rack.
6. Meanwhile, for glaze: In a medium bowl, stir together confectioners' sugar, orange zest and juice, lemon juice, and salt until fluid. (If you want a thinner consistency, add orange juice or water, 1 teaspoon [5 grams] at a time, until desired consistency is reached.)
7. Dip tops of warm cookies in glaze until coated, shaking off excess. Return cookies to wire rack. Let stand until glaze is set, about 30 minutes. Store in an airtight container for up to 2 weeks.

Notes: *If cutting cookies larger than 2 or 2½ inches, you may need to add 1 to 2 minutes to the bake time.*

Cutout dough can be frozen for up to 1 month before baking and then baked directly from the freezer. You may need to add 2 to 3 minutes to the bake time.

Photo by Cheryl Norris

PUMPKIN BISCOTTI WITH MAPLE GLAZE

Makes 24 biscotti

Recipe by Emma Duckworth

Biscotti has the illusion of being tricky. This recipe dispels that myth with a one-bowl, no-mixer-required pumpkin-flavored biscotti recipe. Packed full of spices, drizzled with a maple syrup glaze, and garnished with pecans, these biscotti have all the heartwarming qualities you need during the winter months. Dunk in espresso, gift to friends, or keep all to yourself.

2⅓ cups (292 grams) all-purpose flour
⅔ cup (147 grams) firmly packed light brown sugar
2 teaspoons (4 grams) ground cinnamon
1½ teaspoons (3 grams) ground ginger
1 teaspoon (4 grams) fine salt
½ teaspoon (2.5 grams) baking powder
½ teaspoon (1 gram) ground cloves
½ teaspoon (1 gram) ground nutmeg
½ cup (122 grams) canned pumpkin
¼ cup (57 grams) unsalted butter, melted and cooled
3 large eggs (150 grams), room temperature and divided
1 teaspoon (4 grams) vanilla extract
1 teaspoon (5 grams) whole milk
Maple Glaze (recipe follows)
Garnish: chopped toasted pecans

1. Preheat oven to 350°F (180°C). Line a large baking sheet with parchment paper.
2. In a large bowl, whisk together flour, brown sugar, cinnamon, ginger, salt, baking powder, cloves, and nutmeg until combined. Make a well in center; add pumpkin, melted butter, 2 eggs (100 grams), and vanilla. Using a wooden spoon, starting from center, gently stir just until combined. Using a wooden spoon or your hands, gently knead dough a couple of times until it comes together. (Dough will feel a little sticky. If desired, refrigerate for 30 to 45 minutes to make it easier to handle when shaping.)

3. Turn out dough onto a lightly floured surface. Using lightly floured hands, divide dough in half (about 355 grams each), and roll each half into a log. Place logs on prepared pan, and shape each into a 12-inch log (about 2 inches thick). (Leave space between logs, as dough will spread while baking.) Using moistened hands, flatten tops and smooth dough.
4. In a small bowl, whisk together remaining 1 egg (50 grams) and milk. Brush egg wash onto logs.
5. Bake until firm and golden, 20 to 30 minutes. Let cool on pan for 10 minutes. Reduce oven temperature to 275°F (135°C).
6. Place 1 dough log on a cutting board. Using a serrated knife, cut log diagonally into ¾-inch-thick slices. Return slices, cut side down, to pan. Repeat with remaining dough log.
7. Bake until dry and crisp, 15 to 20 minutes, turning halfway through baking. Let cool completely on pan. (See Note.)
8. Drizzle Maple Glaze onto cooled biscotti. Garnish with pecans, if desired. Let stand until glaze is set. Store in an airtight container for up to 2 weeks.

Note: *Once cooled, there will still be a little give in the biscotti. If you want very dry, hard biscotti, add another 10 or so minutes to the bake time in step 7.*

MAPLE GLAZE
Makes about ½ cup

1 cup (120 grams) confectioners' sugar, plus more if needed
3 to 4 tablespoons (63 to 84 grams) maple syrup

1. In a medium bowl, sift confectioners' sugar. Add 3 tablespoons (63 grams) maple syrup, whisking until combined; add up to remaining 1 tablespoon (21 grams) maple syrup, 1 teaspoon (7 grams) at a time, if glaze is too thick. If glaze is too thin, add confectioners' sugar, whisking until combined and desired consistency is reached.

Photo by Emma Duckworth

HUNDREDS AND THOUSANDS BISCUITS

Makes about 32 cookies

Recipe by Erin Clarkson

These cookies are a combination of Erin Clarkson's two favorite childhood biscuits (what they call cookies in New Zealand)—her great-grandmother's shortbread recipe and hundreds and thousands biscuits, which are vanilla cookies with pink icing and sprinkles.

¾ cup plus 3 tablespoons (212 grams) unsalted butter, softened
⅔ cup (80 grams) confectioners' sugar, sifted
1 teaspoon (6 grams) vanilla bean paste
½ teaspoon (1.5 grams) kosher salt
2½ cups plus 1 tablespoon (321 grams) all-purpose flour
Royal Icing (recipe follows)
Nonpareils

1. In the bowl of a stand mixer fitted with the paddle attachment, beat butter, confectioners' sugar, vanilla bean paste, and salt at low speed; gradually increase mixer speed to high, beating until light and fluffy, 3 to 4 minutes, and stopping to scrape sides of bowl. Add flour, and beat at low speed just until combined.
2. Turn out dough onto a piece of plastic wrap, and press out into a rough rectangle. Wrap tightly in plastic wrap, and refrigerate for at least 2 hours or overnight.
3. Let dough stand at room temperature for 10 to 15 minutes.
4. Cut 4 (18x13-inch) sheets of parchment paper.
5. Divide dough in half, and place each half between 2 prepared parchment sheets. Using a rolling pin, gently flatten dough. Roll each half into an 18x13-inch rectangle (about ¼ inch thick). (Remove top parchment and smooth down again if you are getting wrinkles.) Transfer dough rectangles, still between parchment, to baking sheets, and freeze for 15 to 20 minutes.
6. Preheat oven to 325°F (170°C). Line 3 to 4 baking sheets with parchment paper.
7. Using a 2½-inch fluted round cutter, cut dough, and place 1 inch apart on prepared pans. Reroll scraps, and freeze for 5 to 10 minutes; cut dough. (If dough starts to soften, freeze for about 5 minutes to firm up.) Freeze for 10 minutes.

8. Bake, one batch at a time, until set and starting to turn golden, 12 to 13 minutes. Let cool on pans for 15 minutes. Remove from pans, and let cool completely on wire racks. Store in an airtight container until ready to ice.
9. Dip each cookie in Royal Icing. Let stand for 2 minutes; sprinkle with nonpareils. Let stand until icing is set, at least 1 hour. Store in an airtight container for up to 2 days.

Notes: *Store dough you are not working with in the freezer until ready.*

You will have a little Royal Icing left over—you need enough to be able to comfortably dip the cookies in it to get a good coating. Cover Royal Icing with a piece of plastic wrap, pressing wrap directly onto surface of icing, and refrigerate in an airtight container.

The sprinkles will start to bleed after 1 day, so just keep this in mind when you are preparing cookies.

ROYAL ICING
Makes 1⅓ cups

2 teaspoons (10 grams) water
Pink gel food coloring (optional)
3⅓ cups (400 grams) confectioners' sugar, sifted
2 large pasteurized egg whites* (60 grams), room temperature

1. In a medium bowl, whisk together 2 teaspoons (10 grams) water and food coloring (if using). Add confectioners' sugar and egg whites, and stir until well combined. Use immediately, or cover with a piece of plastic wrap, pressing wrap directly onto surface of icing, and refrigerate until ready to use.

*Pasteurized egg whites have been gently heated to kill harmful bacteria without cooking the actual egg, reducing the risk of salmonella.

Note: *Dissolving the food coloring in the water before you mix in the other ingredients helps the color disperse evenly.*

Photo by Erin Clarkson

PEPPERMINT MOCHA RED VELVET MARBLE COOKIES

Makes about 54 cookies

Red velvet gets a magically marbled look in these slice-and-bake cookies. Two doughs—one creamy peppermint and one crimson mocha—get folded and swirled together before being rolled in festive nonpareils.

1   cup (227 grams) unsalted butter, softened
1¼   cups (250 grams) granulated sugar
2   large eggs (100 grams), room temperature and divided
3   cups (375 grams) all-purpose flour
¾   teaspoon (2.25 grams) kosher salt
½   teaspoon (2.5 grams) baking powder
½   teaspoon (2 grams) peppermint extract
4   teaspoons (8 grams) dark-roast instant coffee granules
1   teaspoon (5 grams) water
1   tablespoon (5 grams) unsweetened cocoa powder
Red gel food coloring*
½   cup (100 grams) holiday nonpareils*

1. In the bowl of a stand mixer fitted with the paddle attachment, beat butter and sugar at medium-low speed just until combined. Increase mixer speed to medium, and beat until fluffy, 2 to 3 minutes, stopping to scrape sides of bowl. Beat in 1 egg (50 grams) until well combined.
2. In a large bowl, whisk together flour, salt, and baking powder. With mixer on low speed, gradually add flour mixture to butter mixture, beating just until combined. Transfer half of dough (about 447 grams) to a medium bowl; gently knead in peppermint extract. Cover and set aside.
3. In a small bowl, stir together instant coffee and 1 teaspoon (5 grams) water until granules dissolve. Add coffee mixture and cocoa to dough in stand mixer bowl; beat at low speed until combined. Add food coloring until desired color is reached, kneading together by hand as needed.

4. Divide each dough into 10 portions (about 44 grams each). Layer pieces, in a random, alternating fashion, into 1 large dough log. Cut log in half, and shape each half into a 7-inch log (about 2 inches thick). Wrap each log in plastic wrap; while holding ends of plastic wrap, roll log over work surface, creating a more rounded shape. Refrigerate until firm, about 2 hours. (See Note.)
5. Preheat oven to 350°F (180°C).
6. In a large rimmed baking dish or plate, place nonpareils.
7. In a small bowl, whisk remaining 1 egg (50 grams). Working with 1 dough log at a time, unwrap log, and brush outside with egg; roll in nonpareils.
8. Working in batches, cut each log crosswise into ¼-inch-thick slices; round edges, if necessary, and roll in nonpareils, if desired. Place, cut side down, 1 to 1¼ inches apart on prepared pans, flattening slightly with your hand so dough rounds are flush with pan. (If dough rounds crack when flattening, simply press and smooth back together.)
9. Bake until set and bottoms are lightly golden, about 10 minutes. Let cool on pans for 2 minutes. Remove from pans, and let cool completely on wire racks.

We used Wilton Color Right Performance Food Coloring and Wilton Holiday Nonpareils.

Note: *Let dough that has been refrigerated for longer time spans stand at room temperature until slightly softened and easier to slice, 15 to 30 minutes.*

CHOCOLATE-PEANUT BUTTER-PISTACHIO BISCOTTI

Makes about 36 biscotti

For bakers looking to send loved ones homemade comfort, crisp biscotti is a shipping dream, with a long shelf life and a rigid shape that can handle the long, bumpy road ahead. This chocolate-peanut butter combo is made all the more decadent by the addition of yuletide-green pistachios.

6   ounces (170 grams) 64% cacao semisweet chocolate*, finely chopped and divided
½   cup (113 grams) unsalted butter, softened
1   cup (200 grams) granulated sugar
¼   cup (55 grams) firmly packed light brown sugar
2   large eggs (100 grams), room temperature
2   teaspoons (8 grams) vanilla extract
1¾ cups (219 grams) all-purpose flour
¾   cup (70 grams) Dutch process cocoa powder, sifted
1   teaspoon (5 grams) baking powder
1   teaspoon (1 gram) instant espresso powder*
¾   teaspoon (2.25 grams) kosher salt
½   cup (82 grams) peanut butter chips
½   cup (66 grams) roasted pistachios, roughly chopped

1. Preheat oven to 325°F (170°C). Line a rimmed baking sheet with parchment paper.
2. In the top of a double boiler, place 4 ounces (113 grams) chocolate. Cook over simmering water, stirring frequently, until melted and smooth. Remove from heat; set aside.
3. In the bowl of a stand mixer fitted with the paddle attachment, beat butter and sugars at medium speed until fluffy, 2 to 3 minutes, stopping to scrape sides of bowl. Add eggs and vanilla; beat until well combined, stopping to scrape sides of bowl. Add melted chocolate, beating until well combined.
4. In a medium bowl, whisk together flour, cocoa, baking powder, espresso powder, and salt. With mixer on low speed, gradually add flour mixture to butter mixture, beating just until combined and stopping to scrape sides of bowl. Fold in peanut butter chips, pistachios, and remaining 2 ounces (57 grams) chocolate.
5. Turn out dough onto a lightly floured surface, and divide in half. Shape each half into a 9x3-inch loaf, and place 2 to 2½ inches apart on prepared pan.
6. Bake until set and loaves spring back when touched, 35 to 40 minutes. Let cool on pan on a wire rack for 15 minutes. Reduce oven temperature to 300°F (150°C).
7. Line 2 rimmed baking sheets with parchment paper.
8. Place 1 cooled loaf on a cutting board. Using a serrated knife, cut crosswise into ½-inch-thick slices. Gently place, cut side down, ½ to ¾ inch apart on prepared pans. Repeat with remaining loaf.
9. Bake, one batch at a time, until cut sides feel toasted and mostly dry, about 25 minutes, turning slices halfway through baking. Let cool on pan for 2 minutes. Carefully remove from pan, and let cool completely on wire racks. (Biscotti will continue to crisp as they cool.) Store in an airtight container for up to 2 weeks.

*We used Guittard 64% Cacao Semisweet Chocolate Baking Bars and Williams Sonoma Espresso Powder.

TOASTED ALMOND SABLÉS

Makes about 22 cookies

European-style butter makes these sparkling sablés the ultimate buttery, melt-in-your-mouth cookies. Here, it imparts a creaminess that complements the flavor of toasted almonds exquisitely.

⅓   cup (38 grams) sliced almonds
2   cups (250 grams) all-purpose flour
¾   cup plus 2 tablespoons (198 grams) unsalted butter*, softened
⅓   cup (40 grams) confectioners' sugar
1¼ cups (250 grams) granulated sugar, divided
1   teaspoon (3 grams) kosher salt
1   vanilla bean, split lengthwise, seeds scraped and reserved
1   large egg yolk (19 grams)

1. Preheat oven to 325°F (170°C).
2. On a rimmed baking sheet, spread almonds in an even layer.
3. Bake until fragrant and toasted, about 10 minutes. Let cool completely.
4. In the work bowl of a food processor, process toasted almonds until finely ground. (Be sure not to overprocess the almonds, or you'll end up with almond butter.) Transfer to a medium bowl; add flour, whisking until combined.
5. In the bowl of a stand mixer fitted with the paddle attachment, beat butter at medium-low speed until smooth, about 1 minute. Add confectioners' sugar, ¼ cup (50 grams) granulated sugar, and salt, and beat until smooth, about 1 minute. Add reserved vanilla bean seeds and egg yolk, and beat until combined, about 1 minute. Add flour mixture to butter mixture in two additions, beating just until combined. Turn out dough onto a work surface, and gently knead 3 to 4 times.
6. Place dough between 2 large sheets of parchment paper, and roll to ½-inch thickness. Transfer dough between parchment to refrigerator. Refrigerate until set, at least 2 hours.
7. Preheat oven to 325°F (170°C). Line 2 baking sheets with parchment paper.
8. Using a 2-inch round cutter dipped in flour, cut dough, and place at least 1 inch apart on prepared pans. Reroll scraps between parchment, if necessary. Freeze until set before cutting dough, about 5 minutes.
9. Bake in batches until bottom edges turn golden, 15 to 16 minutes. Let cool on pans for 1 minute.
10. On a plate, place remaining 1 cup (200 grams) granulated sugar. Using a spatula, place cookies, a few at a time, in sugar. Cover tops and sides with sugar. Using spatula, lift cookies, and place on wire racks to let cool completely.

*We used Président® Butter.

SLICE-AND-BAKE HOLIDAY CONFETTI COOKIES

Makes about 50 cookies

Slice-and-bake cookies are easy to make and easier to ship. Packed with holiday nonpareils and glistening with sparkling sugar, this recipe makes enough to fill several care packages.

1   cup (227 grams) unsalted butter, softened
⅔   cup (133 grams) granulated sugar
2   teaspoons (8 grams) vanilla extract
½   teaspoon (2 grams) almond extract
2   cups (250 grams) all-purpose flour
½   teaspoon (1.5 grams) kosher salt
⅓   cup (70 grams) holiday nonpareils
½   cup (112 grams) white sparkling sugar, plus more for sprinkling
1   large egg (50 grams), lightly beaten

1. In the bowl of a stand mixer fitted with the paddle attachment, beat butter and granulated sugar at medium speed until creamy, 2 to 3 minutes, stopping to scrape sides of bowl. Beat in extracts.

2. In a medium bowl, whisk together flour and salt. With mixer on low speed, gradually add flour mixture to butter mixture, beating until combined. Fold in nonpareils. (Dough will be rather soft at this point.) Divide dough in half. Shape each half into a 7-inch log (about 2 inches thick). Wrap each log in plastic wrap; holding ends of plastic wrap, roll log over work surface, creating a more rounded shape. Refrigerate until firm, about 2 hours. (See Note.)

3. Preheat oven to 325°F (170°C). Line 2 to 3 rimmed baking sheets with parchment paper.

4. In a large rimmed baking dish or plate, place sparkling sugar.

5. Working with one dough log at a time, unwrap log, and brush outside with egg; roll in sparkling sugar. Working in batches and using a serrated knife, cut logs crosswise into ¼-inch-thick rounds, and place 1 to 1¼ inches apart on prepared pans; flatten rounds slightly so they lay flat on baking sheet. (If dough rounds crack when flattening, simply press and smooth back together.) Sprinkle tops with sparkling sugar.

6. Bake, one batch at a time, until edges are lightly golden, about 15 minutes. Let cool on pan for 5 minutes. Using a large offset or flat metal spatula, remove from pan, and let cool completely on wire racks. Store in an airtight container for up to 1 week.

Note: *Let dough that has been refrigerated for longer time spans stand at room temperature until slightly softened and easier to slice, 15 to 30 minutes.*

ORANGE ZEST SHORTBREAD WITH CRANBERRY-CHAMPAGNE BUTTERCREAM

Makes about 20 sandwich cookies

Recipe by Amisha Gurbani

A riff on the cranberry mimosa, these sparkly, elegant cookies will go very quickly at your next brunch party.

1   cup (227 grams) unsalted butter, softened
⅔   cup (133 grams) granulated sugar
1   tablespoon (3 grams) orange zest
1   tablespoon (13 grams) vanilla extract
2   cups (250 grams) all-purpose flour
⅔   cup (64 grams) almond flour
1   teaspoon (6 grams) salt
1   teaspoon (2 grams) ground star anise
¾   cup (90 grams) confectioners' sugar
2   tablespoons (30 grams) cranberry juice
Edible silver sprinkles
Cranberry-Champagne Buttercream
    (recipe follows)

1. In the bowl of a stand mixer fitted with the paddle attachment, beat butter, granulated sugar, and orange zest at medium speed until creamy, about 2 minutes, stopping to scrape sides of bowl. Add vanilla, beating until combined.
2. In a medium bowl, combine flours, salt, and star anise. With mixer on medium-low speed, add flour mixture to butter mixture, beating just until combined. Divide dough in half, and shape each half into a disk (about 1 inch thick). Wrap tightly in plastic wrap, and refrigerate for at least 1 hour.
3. Preheat oven to 350°F (180°C). Line several baking sheets with parchment paper.
4. On a lightly floured surface, roll dough to ¼-inch thickness. Using a 2-inch fluted round cutter, cut dough, and place on prepared pans.
5. Bake until light golden brown, 12 to 15 minutes. Remove from pans, and let cool on wire racks for 30 minutes.
6. In a small bowl, stir together confectioners' sugar and cranberry juice with a small rubber spatula until well combined. Drizzle on top of half of cookies. Top with sprinkles.

7. Place Cranberry-Champagne Buttercream in a pastry bag fitted with a ⅓-inch round piping tip (Ateco #804). Pipe buttercream onto flat side of undecorated cookies. Place decorated cookies, flat side down, on top of buttercream. Refrigerate in an airtight container for up to 1 week.

CRANBERRY-CHAMPAGNE BUTTERCREAM
Makes about 1½ cups

½   cup (113 grams) unsalted butter, softened
1   teaspoon (4 grams) vanilla extract
½   teaspoon (3 grams) salt
2½ cups (300 grams) confectioners' sugar
2   tablespoons (30 grams) Champagne
1   tablespoon (20 grams) Cranberry Jam* (recipe follows)

1. In the bowl of a stand mixer fitted with the paddle attachment, beat butter, vanilla, and salt at medium speed until combined, about 30 seconds, stopping to scrape sides of bowl. Add confectioners' sugar, Champagne, and Cranberry Jam, and beat at low speed for 30 seconds. Gradually increase mixer speed to high, beating until fully combined, about 1 minute.

*You can also use any tart red store-bought jam.

CRANBERRY JAM
Makes about ⅓ cup

1   cup (170 grams) fresh or frozen cranberries
½   cup (100 grams) granulated sugar
¼   cup (60 grams) water
¼   cup (60 grams) fresh orange juice

1. In a medium saucepan, bring cranberries, sugar, ¼ cup (60 grams) water, and orange juice to a boil over medium-high heat. Cook for about 5 minutes. Using a potato masher, crush cranberries to release pulp. Cook until thickened, about 5 minutes. Using a fine-mesh sieve, strain mixture, discarding solids. Pour jam into a small bottle; refrigerate, and let cool completely before using.

Photo by Amisha Gurbani

ICED LEMON GINGER THINS

Makes about 80 cookies

Recipe by Allie Roomberg

Delightfully thin and crisp, these wafers pack a zingy punch of bright lemon flavor, plus a hint of tongue-tingling warmth from seasonal ginger.

¾   cup (170 grams) unsalted butter, softened
1   cup (200 grams) granulated sugar
1   large egg (50 grams)
1   large egg yolk (19 grams)
1   tablespoon (3 grams) lemon zest (about 1 lemon)
2   tablespoons (30 grams) fresh lemon juice (about ½ lemon)
1   teaspoon (4 grams) lemon extract
2½ cups (313 grams) all-purpose flour
½   cup (64 grams) cornstarch
1½ teaspoons (3 grams) ground ginger
¼   teaspoon (1.25 grams) baking soda
¼   teaspoon kosher salt
Lemon Ginger Icing (recipe follows)

1. Line baking sheets with parchment paper.
2. In the bowl of a stand mixer fitted with the paddle attachment, beat butter and sugar at medium-low speed until smooth and fluffy, 3 to 4 minutes, stopping to scrape sides of bowl. Add egg and egg yolk, beating until combined. Beat in lemon zest and juice and lemon extract; scrape sides and bottom of bowl with a silicone spatula. Add flour, cornstarch, ginger, baking soda, and salt, and beat at low speed until dough comes together and begins to pull away from sides of bowl.
3. Working with a handful of dough at a time, between 2 sheets of parchment paper, roll dough to ¹⁄₁₆-inch thickness. Using a 2½-inch fluted round cutter, cut dough. Place ½ inch apart on prepared pans. Refrigerate for 40 minutes.
4. Preheat oven to 375°F (190°C).
5. Bake until set and edges are barely beginning to turn golden, 10 to 12 minutes. Let cool completely.
6. Spread a thin layer of Lemon Ginger Icing on top of cooled cookies. Store in an airtight container for up to 1 week.

LEMON GINGER ICING
Makes about 1 cup

1½ cups (180 grams) confectioners' sugar
1½ teaspoons (1.5 grams) lemon zest (about ½ lemon)
3   tablespoons (45 grams) fresh lemon juice (about 1 lemon)
½   teaspoon (1 gram) ground ginger

1. In a small bowl, stir together all ingredients until smooth.

Photo by Allie Roomberg

recipe index

· · · · ·

index

CREDITS

· · · · ·

Editorial
Editor-in-Chief Brian Hart Hoffman
VP/Culinary & Custom Content
Brooke Michael Bell
Group Creative Director
Deanna Rippy Gardner
Art Director Liz Kight
Managing Editor Kyle Grace Mills
Baking and Pastry Editor
Tricia Manzanero Stuedeman
Assistant Editor Olivia Kavanagh
Senior Copy Editor Rhonda Lother
Copy Editor Meg Lundberg

Cover
Photography by
Stephanie Welbourne Steele
Food Styling by
Katie Moon Dickerson
Styling by Courtni Bodiford

Bake from Scratch **Photographers**
Jim Bathie, Steve Rizzo,
Stephanie Welbourne Steele

Test Kitchen Director
Laura Crandall

Bake from Scratch **Food Stylists/
Recipe Developers**
Becca Cummins,
Katie Moon Dickerson,
Kathleen Kanen, Megan Lankford,
Vanessa Rocchio, Izzie Turner

Test Kitchen Assistant/Prep Cook
Aaron Conrad

Bake from Scratch **Stylists**
Courtni Bodiford, Sidney Bragiel,
Lucy Finney, Mary Beth Jones,
Lily Simpson

Contributing Photographer
Johanna Chadwick

**Contributing Food Stylists/Recipe
Developers**
Emily Hutchinson, Spencer Lawson,
Lori Sepp

**Contributing Food Stylists/Recipe
Developers & Photographers**
Sarah Brunella, Connie Chong,
Erin Clarkson, Jenn Davis,
Marcella DiLonardo, Elisabeth Farris,
Rebecca Firth, Kimberlee Ho,
Tessa Huff, Mike Johnson,
Laura Kasavan, Sarah Kieffer,
Edd Kimber, Josh Lehenbauer,
Lauren Newsome, Cheryl Norris,
Annalise Sandberg, Michele Song,
Joshua Weissman, Becky Sue
Wilberding

Resources:
Photo on page 22 by Kimberlee Ho.
Photo on page 83
by Becky Sue Wilberding.
Photo on page 168
by Emma Duckworth.
Photo on page 196 by Laura Kasavan.